Emerging Technologies and Museums

EMERGING TECHNOLOGIES AND MUSEUMS

Mediating Difficult Heritage

Edited by
Theopisti Stylianou-Lambert, Alexandra Bounia
and Antigone Heraclidou

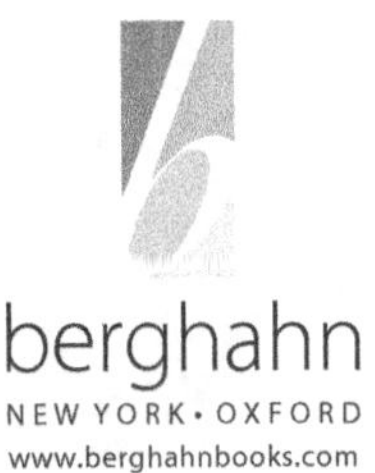

berghahn
NEW YORK · OXFORD
www.berghahnbooks.com

First published in 2022 by
Berghahn Books
www.berghahnbooks.com

Library of Congress Cataloging-in-Publication Data

Names: Stylianou-Lambert, Theopisti, editor. | Bounia, Alexandra, editor. | Heraclidou,
Antigone, editor.
Title: Emerging technologies and museums : mediating difficult heritage / edited by
Theopisti Stylianou-Lambert, Alexandra Bounia and Antigone Heraclidou.
Description: New York : Berghahn Books, 2022. | Includes bibliographical references.
Identifiers: LCCN 2021040526 (print) | LCCN 2021040527 (ebook) |
ISBN 9781800733749 (hardback) | ISBN 9781800733756 (ebook)
Subjects: LCSH: Museums—Educational aspects. | Museum exhibits—Technological
innovations. | Museum techniques—Technological innovations. | Historical
museums—Interpretive programs—Moral and ethical aspects. | Historical museums—
Interpretive programs—Psychological aspects.
Classification: LCC AM7 .E43 2022 (print) | LCC AM7 (ebook) | DDC 069.07—dc23
LC record available at https://lccn.loc.gov/2021040526
LC ebook record available at https://lccn.loc.gov/2021040527

British Library Cataloguing in Publication Data

A catalogue record for this book is available from the British Library

EU GPSR Authorized Representative

LOGOS EUROPE, 9 rue Nicolas Poussin, 17000, LA ROCHELLE, France
Email: Contact@logoseurope.eu

ISBN 978-1-80073-374-9 hardback
ISBN 978-1-80758-033-9 paperback
ISBN 978-1-80758-957-8 epub
ISBN 978-1-80073-375-6 web pdf

https://doi.org/10.3167/9781800733749

CONTENTS

Part III. Creating a Sense of Presence, Immersion and Embodiment

Introduction

Emerging Technologies, Museums and Difficult Heritage

Theopisti Stylianou-Lambert, Alexandra Bounia
and Antigone Heraclidou

Emerging technologies such as virtual reality, augmented reality, holograms, haptics, gamification and more have, for some years now, become a significant part of museums, galleries and cultural sites worldwide. While the integration of emerging technologies in museum spaces – their effect, appeal, shortcomings or implications – remains a topic of debate among museum professionals, technology has already become a standard that visitors expect (Shehade and Stylianou-Lambert 2019). Technology in museums has already been shown to present content in a more interactive and engaging manner, provide an entry point to visitors who do not usually engage with museums and introduce items and experiences that would not otherwise be possible to introduce. This edited volume explores the potential of a specific function of emerging technologies: that of mediating difficult heritage. It examines theoretical approaches and case studies that demonstrate how emerging technologies can display, reveal and negotiate difficult, dissonant, negative or undesirable heritage. The focus is on how emerging technologies in museums can reveal unheard or silenced stories, challenge preconceptions, encourage emotional and empathetic responses, create a sense of presence, immersion or embodiment, and ultimately provide unique experiences. This introduction investigates the relationship between museums and difficult heritage, as well as the role that emerging technologies can play in contributing to narratives of difficult heritage. It also presents the chapters that follow.

Difficult Heritage and Museums as Mediators

Museums are considered to be trustworthy institutions that accumulate, preserve, interpret and exhibit objects, knowledge and stories. However, when dealing with difficult heritage, these basic museum functions can be complicated and contested. The concept of difficult heritage – even though it was not always titled as such – has been a topic of discussion over the last thirty-five years or so in various fields such as history, anthropology, archaeology, geography and tourism (Silverman 2011). However, it was the 1990s that saw a

> paradigm shift towards a socially engaged, politically aware study of the past that regards heritage as contested, recognizes the role of power in the construction of history, focuses on the production of identity, emphasizes representation and performance, and preferably analyses formerly colonial states and societies and their subaltern populations. (Silverman 2011: 5)

This paradigm shift forced museums to acknowledge that heritage is by its nature constructed by people, groups and nations who are constantly engaged in power struggles. With this came the realisation that museums *themselves* play a substantial role in heritage construction. What followed is a conscious – at least in theory – repositioning of the role of museums as active social actors that are willing to negotiate issues of social justice, human rights, global equality and planetary wellbeing, in addition to their traditional roles of educating, studying and entertaining (see the new definition of museums proposed by the International Council of Museums [ICOM], ICOM 2019). Actual museum practices can range from merely acknowledging injustice and power imbalances to creating museums that actively engage in activism and explicitly address issues of inequalities, injustices and environmental challenges (Janes and Sandell 2019). The more socially engaged and politically aware museum professionals are, the more conscious they become of their responsibility to deal with contested but urgent issues. Indeed, more and more exhibitions about difficult heritage are being produced each year, more relevant books and articles are being published, and more museum-related conferences are choosing to dedicate sessions to difficult heritage.

Over the years, researchers and theoreticians have used different terms to describe more or less the same thing, 'namely the challenge of what to do with the material remains of an historical period, site, or event that is today generally perceived as problematic for one reason or another' (Samuels 2015: 113). Some of the terms that have been used are: dissonant heritage (Tunbridge and Ashworth 1996), negative heritage (Meskell 2002), undesirable heritage (Macdonald 2006), difficult heritage (Macdonald 2009), ambivalent heritage (Breglia 2006; Chadha 2006) and contested heritage (Silverman 2011). For the purpose of this volume, we chose to use the term 'difficult heritage', which was first introduced by Sharon Macdonald as 'a past that is recognized as meaningful in the present but that is also contested and awkward for public reconciliation with a positive, self-affirming contemporary identity' (2009: 1). The reason for choosing this term over others is because it places an emphasis on the *process* of dealing with the past in the present time. That is, the difficulty lies not in the object, site or event per se but with the 'practice of heritage-making' (Samuels 2015: 114) – the processes of interpreting and presenting 'loaded' objects and sites, stories of underrepresented minorities, sensitive issues or traumatic events. The emphasis is also on *today*. As Gross and Terra (2018: 55) mention: 'What makes difficult history difficult is not how it confirms or complicates a particular student's prior historical understanding but the degree to which it challenges or undermines the dominant societal narratives'. The authors might be referring to difficult history, but their argument can easily apply to difficult heritage: the difficulty lies in the fact that parts of our heritage challenge dominant societal narratives today. This might not have been true in the past or might not present a challenge in the future.

Difficult heritage has for some years now puzzled museums. The International Council of Museums (ICOM) recognises that there is still difficulty in addressing issues such as who has the right to decide what is remembered (and what is forgotten) and how to do so (Altayli and Viau Courville 2018). The past is not always virtuous, and museums are called to narrate traumatic events that might still have an effect on people, such as histories of genocide, slavery, war, disease, racism and sexism. These histories of oppression, violence and trauma are defined by Rose (2016) as 'difficult history'.

But history and heritage are not synonymous. It is important to untangle the tension between 'difficult history' and 'difficult heritage', two terms that are sometimes used interchangeably. While history and heritage are both connected with the past and can be constantly reinterpreted, they are also different. History is our attempt to reconstruct and understand the events, lives and experiences of those who came before us. But whose histories will be preserved, heard and discussed depends on choices made in the present. History often aims to communicate a shared understanding of the past and has been extensively used to create national stories and provide narratives that bring people together, often by excluding those that are not considered welcome or important for these stories (Gross and Terra 2018). On the other hand, heritage is what has survived from the past – tangible or intangible. Objects, buildings, customs and beliefs survive the passage of time and are branded as heritage only when people value them enough to pass them on to future generations. After all, heritage is something that is inherited, passed down from previous generations, and usually has positive connotations. But as MacNamara (2019) aptly points out, the monuments we have inherited from our past were never intended to be neutral. Positive and glorified stories aside, what happens with objects, buildings and customs associated with shame, violence, abuse and overall unethical behaviour? How about collections and sites that are not part of a positive narrative of a shared past? Are these collected and interpreted in a way that will shed light to these behaviours, or will they be silenced, erased or even destroyed? There are, in fact, many examples of heritage that have been appropriated, misused, obliterated or excluded to serve the needs of the present (Silverman 2011).

Museums are, by their nature, implicated in all these power struggles and imbalances. Their collections, archives and practices are shaped by these struggles: they are the venues where history is made public, they are the places that hold the evidence that history will use in order to create narratives about the past. Museums select not only which stories will be presented but also which evidence will survive as building material for future stories. Museum collections (at their core, a selection process) and their documentation are often considered 'neutral' and 'academic', but they can also support silences, half-truths or even misrepresentations.

As a result, museums are at the heart of both 'difficult history' *and* 'difficult heritage'. They provide the evidence necessary for history to offer understandings of the past. They are the places where the history of contentious or shameful pasts – that may challenge and undermine social narratives – are presented (or not). They choose to collect and safeguard tangible and intangible heritage that enables the interpretation and communication of difficult history (or not). They can offer voice to silenced and misrepresented groups by opening up their collections' management and curatorial strategies, and by bringing to the surface missing or underrepresented voices (or not). However, regardless of their choices, museums are places where people across generations can get involved in a robust engagement with the past, revise their historical understandings, and co-create a shared, inclusive, constantly developing knowledge of the past. Affect and empathy, as well as immersion and embodiment, can facilitate this engagement. As we will see in the chapters that follow, immersive and interactive technologies have the potential to help museums address these challenges.

However, interpreting and narrating difficult histories is, well, difficult and unavoidably involves certain risks. As several groups and people with often conflicting points of view are involved, ethical, emotional and political issues tend to arise. There is a very real risk of alienating audiences and hurting their sensibilities (Rose 2016). Furthermore, if stories of minorities or victims are not treated ethically and with sensitivity, there is a risk of revictimisation. As Pabst (2018: 86) argues: 'Working with sensitive, contested histories involves weighing many considerations and balancing many different needs'. However, the risks are well worth the effort as engaging with difficult heritage comes with important potential benefits: creating forums and advocating for social justice, remembering marginalised communities and revealing silenced voices, advocating for human rights, cultivating critical thinking, warning against future violence, and supporting reconciliation, community engagement and healing (Rose 2016). All roles that 'new' and 'aware' museums are willing to adopt.

Balancing diverse needs in a considerate and professional way and communicating with different parties is often the role of mediators. We argue that museums can use emerging technologies to help them take on exactly such a role – i.e. as go-betweens – that would allow visitors to engage with difficult heritage and histories 'without reinforcing ethnic, religious, and cultural divisions on the one hand, or undermining social cohesion on the other' (Gross and Terra 2018: 56). Emerging technologies have certain characteristics that make them well suited to represent difficult heritage: they can bring to the surface missing or underrepresented voices, elicit affective and empathetic responses, and cultivate a sense of presence, immersion and embodiment.

Emerging Technologies as Mediation Tools

Parry (2007) sees the museum as a medium that contains multiple other media (glass cases, text panels, interactives, etc.). He also argues that

> a medium can send its own messages, the medium is part of the message, and that, moreover, the reciprocity between medium and content is compounded in the use of modern media (such as digital media) where the act of communication is so instantaneous. (Parry 2007: 11)

This is especially true when it comes to emerging technologies. As there are usually no glass cases with objects and texts, the technology becomes part of the message; it is simultaneously the medium and the content, and it is difficult to separate one from the other.

A growing body of literature is focused on the investigation of the possibilities of different technologies and their advantages for museums (see, for example, Freeman et al. 2016; Loumos et al. 2018; Shah and Ghazali 2018; Stogner 2011). The research, however, tends to focus on the technical considerations of projects (Cameron and Kenderdine 2010) or how these technologies have changed audience engagement, whereas the actual evaluation of the effects of these technologies or their possible implications and limitations remains an understudied area (Kidd 2014; Shehade and Stylianou-Lambert 2019). For example, some of the themes discussed in the literature include: changes in audience accessibility through social or other digital media, new tools to visualise heritage and art, education through technological tools, new methods for managing collections, and new forms of curatorship and co-creation or communication. This volume aims to move away from the discussion of technical tools, collection management systems, education, communication or exhibition design, and how technologies have changed them. Instead, the work aims to contribute to the existing discussion by going one step further, i.e. by focusing on a very specific category of heritage and the transformational role emerging technologies might play in how museums present and discuss narratives that are often traumatic, difficult to present, sensitive or controversial.

By emerging technologies, we refer to contemporary advances and innovations in technology that can be used in museums, such as virtual reality, augmented reality, mixed reality, holograms, artificial intelligence, smart systems, etc. Several examples from museums around the world provide insights on how these technologies operate and add value to exhibits by enhancing visitors' experience (Pop and Borza 2016; Ross et al. 2005). For instance, some of the more interesting attempts include: *Mona Lisa: Beyond the Glass* (the first virtual reality experience offered by the Louvre Museum); *Dalí Lives* (a video installation featuring an interactive deepfake recreation of Salvador Dalí at the Dalí Museum in St Petersburg, Florida, see Kidd and Rees in this book), 'Walking among Dinosaurs' (an AR installation at the Smithsonian Museum of Natural History); the MR 'Kennin-Ji Temple' exhibition (Kyoto National Museum); the digital 'Lifeline Table' (Churchill War Rooms in England); 'Dimensions in History' (at the Illinois Holocaust Museum and Education Center, which presents stories of the Holocaust through holograms of its survivors; see Stylianou in this book), and many more.

Emerging technologies are usually associated with new technologies that are still under development and are expected to change the status quo. The advances in technology are so fast that the list of what is considered an emerging technology changes year upon year. According to Kidd (2014), all media were new at some point, and newness is always being reinvented and redefined. For this reason, our emphasis is not on specific technologies or their 'newness' but on new potentials that they bring to the foreground.

We focus on emerging technologies instead of more traditional museum media (such as audio guides, videos and touchscreen interactives), because the former are still developing and museum professionals should ideally be aware of their advantages and limitations so they can influence their future development and uses in museums. But most importantly, emerging technologies have certain characteristics that can be valuable when dealing with difficult heritage: they can be more affective, immersive and 'clever' than traditional museum media. According to Stogner (2011: 117): 'Twenty-first century media technologies have excellent potential to create immersive storytelling for cultural exhibitions by heightening sensory engagement and by forging deeper cognitive and emotional contextual connections with artifacts and objects'. This emphasis on immersive storytelling, sensory engagement and cognitive and emotional contextual connections can be found again and again across the case studies discussed in this volume.

This volume asks how immersive technologies can become mediation tools for museums dealing with difficult heritage. How can museums, with the help of technology, bring to surface omitted narratives and stories of underprivileged groups of people (such as minorities, women, and LGBTQI+), allow for the reinterpretation of their collections and thus support the creation of histories that were not previously available? How can museums narrate stories that allow for multiperspectivity, inclusiveness, tolerance and social cohesion? How and to what extent does the use of technology in museums facilitate an understanding of issues around difficult history and allow for self-reflection and problematisation of the way we understand the self and the other? How can we use emerging technologies not only to provide cognitive experiences but also to elicit emotional and empathetic responses? How can we use technology to create a sense of presence, immersion and embodiment that enables an understanding of the past that is both evolving and robust?

Introduction of Chapters

The chapters that follow explore a number of subjects that fall under the broad category of difficult heritage due to their sensitive or contested character. They include, but are not limited to, erased African American heritage (chapter 1), LGBTQI+ rights (chapter 2), women's hidden histories (chapter 3), war and genocide (chapter 4), the Holocaust (chapter 5), child sexual abuse (chapter 6), climate change and global warming (chapter 7), built difficult heritage such as prisons (chapter 8), marginalised experiences centred on the body (chapter 9) and deepfakes as a form of difficult heritage (chapter 10). The chapters examine how museums can use the latest technology to more effectively treat these awkward, contested and rarely discussed subjects and stories. The technologies discussed range from GIS systems (chapter 1), interactive and immersive installations (chapters 2, 8 and 9), artificial intelligence and deepfakes (chapters 3 and 10) and holograms (chapters 6 and 8) to virtual or augmented reality (chapters 4, 5 and 9).

Some chapters focus on the theory and approaches used to treat issues of difficult history in museums and make reference to certain examples. Others go deep with case studies that demonstrate the ways emerging technologies are already being used in museums to deal with issues of difficult heritage. It is worth mentioning that the authors come from different countries, backgrounds and fields of study. Among them are academics in the fields of digital humanities, film and cyberspace, museum studies, art theory and history and cultural technology; artists, media artists, architects and museum professionals; and researchers in the fields of history, informatics and cultural technology. While diverse methods, means and approaches are put under scrutiny, the chapters consistently focus on the connection between museums, difficult heritage and emerging technologies. The volume does not attempt to cover all geographical locations or be comprehensive in its scope – it is simply impossible to do this in just one volume. However, we made a special effort to include a variety of case studies from different parts of the world, including from Australia, China, Iraq, Italy, Sweden, Switzerland, the United Kingdom and the United States of America.

The book is divided into three parts, and each part addresses a potential path for emerging technologies to deal with difficult heritage: bringing to the surface omitted narratives, eliciting emotional and empathetic responses, and creating a sense of presence, immersion and embodiment. Significant overlap as well as commonalities between the categories proved to be unavoidable, as indicated by several parallel threads across the chapters.

Revealing Missing or Underrepresented Narratives

As mentioned in the beginning of this chapter, the tangible and intangible heritage that museums care for is the result of complex histories and various socio-political factors. Thus, not all groups are represented equally or accurately. As Rose (2016: 25) argues:

> The histories of the victors often overshadow the histories of the oppressed, the marginalized, and the underclasses by burying the subjugated stories further away into memory. The artifacts and the archives are not saved or appreciated, and they become scarcer over time as historical actors and their descendants discard objects and memories of tragedies, allowing younger generations to forget the stories these items hold.

Minorities and marginalised groups are often underrepresented or misrepresented in galleries, libraries, archives and museums (GLAM institutions). The heritage of these groups either has not historically been considered worth collecting and documenting or has actually been destroyed, thus rendering it invisible. However, in recent years, the myth of 'archival impartiality' has been progressively dismantled (Findlay 2016: 155); various initiatives have been undertaken to bring people together, to manage information and its sources, in order to challenge discrimination, to enrich and empower heritage institutions to reinterpret their collections, to diversify them and ultimately allow for the creation of more complicated and inclusive stories (Flinn 2011). Flinn also describes this process as 'archival activism', referring to the practices of both established GLAM institutions as well as community-led, independent, archival and museum projects, or hybrids of the two (Flinn 2011; Iacovino 2015). Similarly, the practice of organising exhibitions that aim to mitigate the marginalisation or exclusion of certain groups from grant narratives can be called 'curatorial activism'. Maura Reilly (2018, 2017: n.p.) used the term 'curatorial activism' to refer to a practice of organising art exhibitions 'that commits itself to counter-hegemonic initiatives that give voice to those who have been historically silenced or omitted altogether'.

The idea of going 'outside the institution' to document marginalised or silenced stories is not new; it has been around since the 1970s. However, it is only within the last decade or so that participative initiatives for archiving and presenting previously marginalised histories have become mainstream (McKinney 2020). The role of technology has been instrumental in empowering these new participative forms of engagement with history making. Complex multimedia practices have been used by different communities to collect, circulate and make available information and resources that matter to them, or to document them in a manner that (finally) does justice to the community's past (Iacovino 2015).

However, as Findlay (2016: 158) argues, archival activists, whether they are members of communities or of institutions, need to go further; they need to embrace decentralised models of thinking and operating, as well as the technologies that will allow for such new models to be created. Managing information is critical and information matters for marginalised groups and for their representation in heritage institutions and, eventually, in history. Technological systems that allow for different models of managing information can lead to the creation of new communities and unveil information hidden in older forms of documentation. New structures of metadata are key for such transformational changes.

The chapters in the first part of this book focus on these issues and discuss how, with the help of ideas originating in archival and curatorial activism, as well as community engagement, emerging technologies can be used to challenge traditional models of recording and presenting histories, bring to the fore hidden information and stories and, ultimately, give voice to underrepresented groups.

In chapter 1, Edward González-Tennant discusses a case of heritage that was completely destroyed. The 1923 Rosewood Massacre involved a series of increasingly violent events, culminating in the displacement of the town's mostly African American community and the destruction of all Black-owned structures. The author elaborates on how the town was virtually reconstructed with the help of archaeological excavations, remote sensing, documentary videos and geographic information systems (GIS). With the help of technology, the destroyed heritage of a disadvantaged community was reconstructed and once again brought to the surface to point towards racial injustice. The primary goal uniting this work is the production of public knowledge by rendering research transparent and being honest in engaging with locals, descendants and the public alike.

Similarly, Sharon Webb in chapter 2 explores the work carried out to preserve and make available a part of underrepresented LGBTQI+ history. The chapter describes community engagement work to archive the 'Queer in Brighton' collection, a mainly oral history archive, with long-term digital preservation in mind. It also explores the development of 'Queer Codebreakers' – an interactive installation that uses a low-tech solution to make accessible and visible queer heritage and histories. In particular, it focuses on queer archiving and community curation in museum spaces as forms of archival and curatorial activism and discusses the need to involve communities in archiving and curation processes.

In chapter 3, Anna Foka, Jenny Attermark and Fredrik Wahlberg go beyond claims of digital technology as a means for democratisation of knowledge and focus on archival online repositories of women's history, concentrating on a Swedish case study: the collection of industry leader Carl Sahlin (1861–1943) at the Swedish National Museum of Science and Technology. The chapter contributes a detailed methodology for collection enrichment, including the possibilities and pitfalls of using emerging technologies, specifically AI, for classification and enrichment so as to open up new critical questions about historical women.

Eliciting Affective and Empathetic Responses

Museums are often in the difficult position of narrating traumatic events. However, more often than not, difficult heritage resists straightforward and linear narration because of a lack of historical distance or common agreement about what happened in the past. Other times, when historical distance is there, narration through text and images might help cognitive understanding (i.e. the Holocaust did happen and millions of people died) but not emotional understanding (i.e. how did it feel to be persecuted because of your ethnicity). As Witcomb (2010: 46) explains:

> In reaching out to the senses, in seeking affective responses, multimedia installations in museums may well be more politically effective in achieving alternation in the mind of the citizen than the more traditional use of the objects in didactic displays intent on *reforming* the minds of the citizen.

Indeed, emotional understanding is key in achieving change in the opinions and perceptions of visitors, and empathy plays an important role in this process. Empathy is a twentieth-century term with multiple definitions. Reniers et al. (2011: 85) argue that empathy has two components: 'a comprehension of other people's experience (cognitive empathy) as well as the ability to vicariously experience the emotional experience of others (affective empathy)'. In general, empathy allows us to 'connect to ourselves and with others while awakening us to our connectedness as parts of a greater whole' (Gokcigdem 2016: xix). Empathetic responses to difficult heritage are important because they can influence our worldview; perceptions of the past, present and future; and, perhaps most importantly, our actions. According to Ivcevic and Botín (2019: n.p.): 'Research shows that empathy facilitates forgiveness and relationship quality, it motivates altruistic behavior even when helping involves a cost to oneself, prevents aggression (e.g. bullying), and facilitates creativity and innovation'. But empathy can only be learned by lived experiences.

Alison Landsberg (2003: 148; 2004: 150) introduced the idea of 'prosthetic memory' to discuss 'personal memories' that are created not through individual knowledge as such but as the result of experiential encounters with technologies that often engage people with national and/or collective traumas. She argues that these mediated-through-technology memories can be instrumental in generating empathy, which in her view is crucial for the formation of feelings of solidarity, mutual understanding and, eventually, ethical behaviour. Furthermore, virtual environments can support 'true emotional responses' (Mühlberger et al. 2007: 340) and encourage a visitor to behave 'as an actor rather than an observer' (Tavinor 2005: 20).

Hassapopoulou (2018) argues that prosthetic memory overlaps with 'technomemory' to produce 'hybrid memories'. Despite the fact that she takes a negative stance against VR, arguing that it can reinforce hegemonic cultural narratives instead of promoting counterhegemonic ones, she agrees that 'the fusion of technological tools with the biological functions of information accumulation, recollection and socio-cultural associations' is indeed very powerful and can lead to people undertaking 'collective social responsibility' (2018: 383). Along similar lines, empirical studies of exhibitions created in virtual environments suggest that empathy can affect learning and support ideas like reconciliation (Muller 2020).

Empathy is most often created when the focus is not on the grand story but on individual stories, i.e. how the traumatic event has influenced specific individuals. According to Pabst (2018: 91): 'Several studies of museum exhibitions featuring personal narratives confirm the assumption that hearing another human being talk about feelings attached to specific events leads to stronger reactions than information given without an emotionally affected speaker.' Furthermore, focusing on individuals and collaborating with people who lived through the traumatic events avoids revictimisation and gives voice to the victims. As De Wildt (2018) notes, exhibiting individual stories in a museum means building a relationship with people, but it also means negotiating the way their stories can or should be presented. Therefore, emerging technologies have the potential to become an access point towards immersing into the uniquely personal experiences of individuals, thus empowering them to share their stories and allowing them to receive acknowledgement of past injustices while contributing to the formulation of prosthetic memories which might lead to solidarity, ethical behaviour and reconciliation.

The three chapters in this second section present projects that use emerging technologies to encourage an affective and empathetic reading of the subject at hand. To start with, in chapter 4, Rozhen Kamal Mohammed-Amin examines how augmented reality and virtual reality technologies have entered museums and are changing their reality. She argues that VR and AR technologies mediate novel and multisensory experiences and interactions with heritage for deeper cognitive and affective engagements. The chapter elaborates on the confluence of VR and difficult heritage by discussing the motivation, development and informal evaluation of the *Nobody's Listening* VR exhibition, which aims to memorialise and engage with the Yazidi minority genocide in Iraq. A multidisciplinary team felt the need for a new way to advocate for the Yazidis and amplify their unheard voices. VR technology was thus used for perspective taking.

In chapter 5, Elena Stylianou discusses holography and its history, drawing from examples relevant to how holography is currently used in museums, with a particular emphasis on *Dimensions in Testimony*. The specific interactive installation captures and preserves the testimonies of Holocaust survivors and allows visitors to interact with these survivors' holograms without the use of headsets. Through *Dimensions in Testimony*, the chapter argues that holograms can open up the narrative space of the museum to include personal accounts and offer alternative tools for storytelling that extend curatorial practices relevant to representing difficult and traumatic histories through the politics of affect and testimony.

On the other side of the globe, personal, traumatic accounts of the past have also preoccupied Lilly Hibberd. In October 2018, as part of the national apology following the Australian Royal Commission into Institutional Responses to Child Sexual Abuse, a pledge was made to create a national museum to memorialise its findings. In chapter 6, Hibberd questions what sort of models exist for such a museum, while speculating on the role of experimental technologies in the context of lived trauma, based on insights gathered from the collaborative production of *Parragirls Past, Present*, an immersive-media film coproduced in 2017 with adult survivors of the former Australian child welfare institution, Parramatta Girls Home.

In chapter 7, Colin Sterling questions the value of the approach followed by high-profile exhibitions to communicate the profound challenges of climate change through immersive forms of display and interpretation, in terms of understanding the complexities and injustices of global warming, framed here through the lens of contested heritage. Drawing on three case studies from contemporary arts practice, the chapter explores the different ways in which 'experiencing' climate change and the Anthropocene might prompt meaningful climate action. A concluding discussion argues that museums need to be seen as part of a broader cultural ecosystem, rather than simply spaces of experience, in order to understand their role in confronting climate breakdown.

Creating a Sense of Presence, Immersion and Embodiment

This last section is about the potential of technology to create a sense of presence, immersion and embodiment; to go beyond what physical objects and interpretation can offer, to become a mediation tool that can immerse visitors into an embodied presence.

Perhaps as a reaction to postmodernity and the dominance of 'meaning' and 'interpretation', the concept of 'presence' has been rediscovered and redeveloped in the fields of history and humanities (Kleinberg 2013). Hans Ulrich Gumbrecht (2004) explains that the Western world today adopts a 'meaning culture', in which knowledge is produced by a subject who is observing, rather than participating, in the world. He believes that our 'meaning culture' cannot possibly cover the full complexity of our existence and argues for the development of concepts in the humanities that go beyond the layer of meaning in order to relate to the world in more complex, bodily and space-related ways. For this reason, he argues for a shift from a 'meaning culture' to a 'presence culture'. The main dimension of a 'presence culture' is that of space and more particularly the relationship between human bodies and the world around them.

Emerging, and especially immersive, technologies have the potential to provide experiences that are not exclusively related to meaning, cognitive knowledge and interpretation but can also create a sense of presence, immersion and embodiment. However, when talking about technological applications, the terms presence, immersion and embodiment have slightly different meanings than what the philosopher Gumbrecht refers to. These terms have varied definitions that are nevertheless so interconnected they are often used interchangeably. Having in mind that there are no commonly accepted definitions for immersion, presence and embodiment, we will attempt to briefly clarify these terms. 'Immersion' can be defined as the 'feeling of being present inside an artificial environment, despite physical presence in the real world' (Górski et al. 2017: 396) and is commonly used to describe experiences such as those of VR, AR and MR. The more immersive an experience is, the more easily users can dive into an artificial world and lose awareness of the fact that they are not in the 'real' world. Full immersion can be described as the opposite of looking through a window, or a screen for that matter; a point of view that renders the viewer as an observer. Instead, full immersion places the visitor/user firmly at the centre and 'inside' an experience.

While immersion refers to an objective point of view that a system delivers, 'presence' refers to a reaction to the immersion (Slater 2003). Presence is related to the feeling of 'being there', either in a physical or digital environment. Furthermore, immersive systems try to mobilise the viewer/user by stimulating the body's senses, and this is related to our sense of embodiment. According to Sarah Kenderdine (2016: 29): 'Embodiment is multisensory and results from effects of visual, auditory, tactile, olfactory, and gustatory cues. Embodiment is entanglement through, and with, context and environment. Embodiment is immersive, resulting in emergent response to being in the world'.

Immersion, presence and embodiment of course also connect with empathy (see previous section). Immersive experiences offered by emerging technologies could encourage empathetic responses as well as critique, in the sense that, through immersion, one better realises one's own standpoint as opposed to those of others, a capacity needed when dealing with issues of difficult history. What the chapters in this section argue is that emerging technologies can immerse visitors in, and transport them to, other worlds, thus offering deeper, embodied and more introspective experiences. Furthermore, immersive and embodied experiences free the visitors from external disruptions, allowing them to engage more mindfully and fully with the museum (Stogner 2011).

Francesca Lanz and Elena Montanari, in chapter 8, focus on the challenges and opportunities posed by difficult built heritage. Technology is used to immerse visitors in the previous uses of built heritage. Difficult built heritage consists of architectural assemblages in which diverse and nested levels of awkwardness converge, resulting in a complex intertwinement of contentious meanings, painful stories and physical traces. In this chapter, through the comparison of two emblematic examples – the Horsens Fængselsmuseet and the Museo di Storia della Psichiatria in Reggio Emilia – that sit at the opposite extremes in the integration of digital tools in their exhibition design, the authors outline the challenges and opportunities posed by the reuse of 'difficult built heritage' as a museum, exploring the possible contributions – and drawbacks – of the use of digital technologies in such a musealisation process and in defining visitors' experiences.

As immersive and engaged interfaces and design in museums have begun to augment sensorial encounters with both tangible heritage and living traditions, recent theory has focused on the renegotiation of contested forms of material and immaterial heritage production. Examining a series of examples of recent immersive works collaboratively created for museum exhibitions, Lily Hibberd and Sarah Kenderdine analyse in chapter 9 both the challenges and the possibilities of an emergent domain of digitally embodied historiography – specific to marginalised experiences centred on the body – as a touchstone for future approaches to difficult, intangible and ephemeral forms of heritage within the museum.

Finally, museums and galleries are beginning to investigate how they might make use of deepfake technologies. An example that is investigated in chapter 10 by Jenny Kidd and Arran Rees is *Dalí Lives*, a video installation featuring an interactive deepfake recreation of Salvador Dalí, which was installed in 2019 at the Dalí Museum in St Petersburg, Florida. This installation makes Dalí 'present' again. Kidd explores the technical and ethical dimensions of such a practice, reflecting on the potential for positive, negative and more ambivalent uses within arts and cultural contexts. Drawing on recent examples, it considers deepfakes as a form of difficult heritage, connecting them with ongoing debates about fakery and authenticity, as well as considering issues related to their collection and preservation. This chapter explores deepfake technologies, not merely as tools for interpretation but as material expression in their own right.

Conclusion

The main argument of this book is that emerging technologies not only provide alternative or 'new' media to discuss difficult history and present difficult heritage in museums, but they can also help the transition of museums into ethical spaces of affect, empathy, and embodied presence. They can empower archival activism and, in effect, facilitate new ways of thinking about the role and purpose of museums. They could also offer tools for new curatorial approaches and promote curatorial activism in the sense that they can involve people from different backgrounds, include marginalised or unheard voices in the curatorial process and effectively ignite discussion around difficult matters. And such discussions seem more relevant now than ever, as movements that fight against white supremacy (Black Lives Matter) and sexual violence (#MeToo), challenge racist and imperialist values and legacies, and advocate in favour of decolonising art and education, have become stronger and more vocal. But, most importantly, emerging technologies can be used to establish ethical relationships. As Andrea Witcomb argues (2020: 486): 'The opportunity to use digital representations to encourage more ethical relations between human and non-human relations is particularly applicable in contexts where difficult histories provide the terrain of engagement'.

As the chapters in this volume clearly argue, emerging technologies can be used to bring to the fore hidden stories, make silenced voices heard, encourage more empathetic responses, provide access, represent the oppressed, support the creation of new relationships with the past, present and future, and immerse the user/visitor into new kinds of experiences. However, all contributions support that technology is a powerful tool, but not a panacea; awareness of the political context and multiple actors must be at play, and hard work and constant vigilance are necessary to prevent reinforcing, rather than questioning, hegemonic narratives, or the creation of new exclusions and a different set of silent stories. New technologies are merely tools with a lot of potential. Museums have the responsibility of exploring these potentials when it comes to dealing with difficult heritage in an ethical and responsible manner.

Acknowledgements

This edited volume was initiated by the Museum Lab of CYENS Centre of Excellence. CYENS has received funding from the European Union's Horizon

2020 research and innovation programme under grant agreement No 739578 and the Government of the Republic of Cyprus through the Deputy Ministry of Research, Innovation and Digital Policy.

Theopisti Stylianou-Lambert is Professor in the Department of Multimedia and Graphic Arts at the Cyprus University of Technology and the co-leader of the *ITICA/Museum Lab* research group at CYENS Centre of Excellence. Her research and artistic practice focus on museums, photography and emerging technologies. She co-authored *The Political Museum* (Routledge, 2016) and co-edited *Museums and Technologies of Presence* (Routledge, 2023), *Museums and Visitor Photography* (MuseumsEtc, 2016), *Museums and Photography: Displaying Death* (Routledge, 2017), and *Photography and Cyprus: Time, Place, Identity* (Routledge, 2014). Her artistic work has been showcased in numerous exhibitions internationally. She earned her PhD in museum studies from the University of Leicester (UK) and her MA in visual arts/museum education from the University of Texas at Austin (USA). Theopisti is also the recipient of several scholarships and awards, including a Smithsonian Fellowship in Museum Practice (USA), a Fulbright Fellowship (USA) and an Arts and Humanities Research Council Award (UK).

Alexandra Bounia is Professor of Museology at the University of the Aegean in Greece. Her research interests focus on the history, theory and management of collections, museum ethics, museum and cultural heritage sustainability, the role of museums in dealing with difficult and political issues, as well as digital heritage and museums. She has published in Greek and international journals and participates in national and international research projects. Among her most recent publications are: *The Political Museum: Power, Conflict and Identity in Cyprus* (co-authored with Theopisti Stylianou-Lambert) (2016, Routledge); *Emerging Technologies and Cultural Heritage* (co-edited with Despina Catapoti) (2021, Alexandria Publications, Athens, in Greek). In 2025 the edited volume entitled *The Ethics of Collecting Trauma: the role of museums in collecting and displaying contemporary crises* was published by Routledge (co-edited with Andrea Witcomb). She has served as the Chair of ICOM Greece (2016-2018), and the Secretary of the Board for ICOM-COMCOL (ICOM Committee on Contemporary Collecting) (2019-2022).

Antigone Heraclidou is a Postdoc Fellow at the Centre for Geopolitics, Peace and Security at the UiT The Arctic University of Norway. She holds an MSc in international history from the London School of Economics and a PhD in modern history from the Institute of Commonwealth Studies, University of London. She is the author of *Imperial Control in Cyprus: Education and Political Manipulation in the British Empire* (2017), and co-editor of *Cyprus: From Colonialism* *to the Present: Visions and Realities; Essays in honour of Professor Robert Holland* (2018), and "Political Actors in the Mediterranean, 1918–1964: Cyprus and Malta Compared," special issue of the *Journal of Mediterranean Studies*, 23(1) (2014). She has also published her work in international journals and was the co-organizer of three international academic conferences in London. She has taught history modules at the University of Cyprus, the Open University of Cyprus and the European University of Cyprus. She worked closely with several museums in Nicosia. Her research interests include Cyprus's colonial history, decolonisation and cultural heritage.

References

Altayli, Afsin, and Mathieu Viau-Courville. 2018. 'Editorial', *Museum International* 70(3–4): 3–8.

Breglia, Lisa. 2006. *Monumental Ambivalence: The Politics of Heritage*. Austin: University of Texas Press.

Cameron, Fiona, and Sarah Kenderdine (eds). 2010. *Theorizing Digital Cultural Heritage: A Critical Discourse*. Cambridge, MA: MIT Press.

Chadha, Ashish. 2006. 'Ambivalent Heritage: Between Affect and Ideology in a Colonial Cemetery', *Journal of Material Culture* 11(3): 339–63.

De Wildt, Annemarie. 2018. 'The City Museum as an Empathic Space', *Museum International* 70(3–4): 72–83.

Findlay, Cassie. 2016. 'Archival Activism', *Archives and Manuscripts* 44(3): 155–59.

Flinn, Andrew. 2011. 'Archival Activism: Independent and Community-Led Archives, Radical Public History and the Heritage Professions', *InterActions* 7(2): n.p. Retrieved 4 October 2020 from https://escholarship.org/uc/item/9pt2490xhttps://escholarship.org/uc/item/9pt2490x.

Freeman, Alexander, Samantha Adams Becker, Michele Cummins, E. McKelroy, C. Giesinger and B. Yuhnke. 2016. *NMC Horizon Report: 2016 Museum Edition*. Austin, TX: The New Media Consortium.

Gokcigdem, Elif (ed.). 2016. *Fostering Empathy through Museums*. Lanham, MD: Rowman & Littlefield.

Górski, Filip, et al. 2017. 'Effective Design of Educational Virtual Reality Applications for Medicine Using Knowledge-Engineering Techniques', *EURASIA Journal of Mathematics Science and Technology Education* 13(2): 395–416.

Gross, Magdalena H., and Luke Terra. 2018. 'What Makes Difficult History Difficult?' *Phi Delta Kappan* 99(8): 51–56.

Gumbrecht, Hans Ulrich. 2004. *Production of Presence: What Meaning Cannot Convey*. Stanford, CA: Stanford University Press.

Hassapopoulou, Marina. 2018. 'Playing with History: Collective Memory, National Trauma and Dark Tourism in Virtual Reality Docugames', *New Review of Film and Television Studies* 16(4): 365–92.

Iacovino, Livia. 2015. 'Shaping and Re-shaping Cultural Identity and Memory: Maximizing Human Rights through a Participative Archive', *Archives and Manuscripts* 43(1): 29–41.

ICOM. 2019. 'Creating a New Museum Definition – The Backbone of ICOM'. 2019. ICOM website. Retrieved 30 August 2020 from https://icom.museum/en/resources/standards-guidelines/museum-definition/.

Ivcevic, Zorana, and Fundación Botín, Fundación. 2019. 'Introduction', in Elif M. Gokcigdem (ed.), *Designing for Empathy: Perspectives on the Museum Experience*. American Alliance of Museums. Lanham, MD: Rowman & Littlefield, pp. 1–17.

Janes, R. Robert, and Richard Sandell (eds.). 2019. *Museum Activism*. New York: Routledge.

Kenderdine, Sarah. 2016. 'Embodiment, Entanglement, and Immersion in Digital Cultural Heritage', in Susan Schreibman, Ray Siemens, and John Unsworth (eds.), *A New Companion to Digital Humanities*. Malden, Oxford: John Wiley & Sons, pp. 22–41.

Kidd, Jenny. 2014. *Museums in the New Mediascape*. New York: Routledge.

Kleinberg, Ethan. 2013. 'Prologue', in Ranjan Ghosh and Ethan Kleinberg (eds.), *Presence: Philosophy, History, and Cultural Theory for the Twenty-First Century*. New York: Cornell University Press, pp. 1–7.

Landsberg, Alison. 2003. 'Prosthetic Memory: The Ethics and Politics of Memory in an Age of Mass Culture', in Paul Grainge (ed.), *Memory and Popular Film*. Manchester: Manchester University Press, pp. 144–61.

———. 2004. *Prosthetic Memory: The Transformation of American Remembrance in the Age of Mass Culture*. New York: Columbia University Press.

Loumos, Georgios, Antonios Kargas and Dimitris Varoutas. 2018. 'Augmented and Virtual Reality Technologies in Cultural Sector: Exploring Their Usefulness and the Perceived Ease of Use', *Journal of Media Critiques* 4(14): 307–22.

Macdonald, Sharon. 2006. 'Undesirable Heritage: Fascist Material Culture and Historical Consciousness in Nuremberg', *International Journal of Heritage Studies* 12(1): 9–28.

———. 2009. *Difficult Heritage: Negotiating the Nazi Past in Nuremberg and Beyond*. New York: Routledge.

MacNamara, Julie. 2019. 'Spectacular Defiance', in Robert R. Janes and Richard Sandell (eds.), *Museum Activism*. New York: Routledge, pp. 104–14.

McKinney, Cait. 2020. *Information Activism: A Queer History of Lesbian Media Technologies*. Durham, NC: Duke University Press.

Meskell, Lynn. 2002. 'Negative Heritage and Past Mastering in Archaeology', *Anthropological Quarterly* 75(3): 557–74.

Mühlberger, Andreas, H. Heinrich Bülthoff, Georg Wiedemann and Paulet Pauli. 2007. 'Virtual Reality for the Psycho-physiological Assessment of Phobic Fear: Responses during Virtual Tunnel Driving', *Psychological Assessment* 19: 340–46.

Muller, Adam. 2020. 'Immersive Engagement: Designing and Testing a Virtual Indian Residential School Exhibition', in Hannah Lewi, Walli Smith, Dirk von Lehn, and Steven Cooke (eds.), *The Routledge International Handbook of New Digital Practices in Galleries, Libraries, Archives, Museums and Heritage Sites*. New York: Routledge, pp. 296–304.

Pabst, Kathrin. 2018. 'Considerations to Make, Needs to Balance: Two Moral Challenges Museum Employees Face When Working with Contested, Sensitive Histories', *Museum International* 70(3–4): 84–97.

Parry, Ross. 2007. *Recording the Museum: Digital Heritage and the Technologies of Change*. New York: Routledge.

Pop, L. Izabela, and Anca Borza. 2016. 'Technological Innovations in Museums as a Source of Competitive Advantage'. In *Proceedings of the 2nd International Scientific Conference SAMRO 2016* 1: 398–405.

Reilly, Maura. 2017. 'What Is Curatorial Activism?' Artnews, 7 November 2017. Retrieved 1 October 2020 from https://www.artnews.com/art-news/news/what-is-curatorial-activism-9271/.

———. 2018. *Curatorial Activism: Towards an Ethics of Curating*. London: Thames & Hudson Ltd.

Reniers, Renate, et al. 2011. 'The QCAE: A Questionnaire of Cognitive and Affective Empathy', *Journal of Personality Assessment* 93(1): 84–95.

Rose, Julia. 2016. *Interpreting Difficult History at Museums and Historical Sites*. Lanham, MD: Rowman & Littlefield.

Ross, Seamus, et al. 2005. 'Core Technologies for the Cultural and Scientific Heritage Sector', *DigiCULT Technology Watch Report 3*. Retrieved 1 October 2020 from https://www.digicult.info/downloads/TWR3-lowres.pdf.

Samuels, Joshua. 2015. 'Difficult Heritage: Coming to "Terms" with Italy's Fascist Past', in Kathryn Lafrenz Samuels, Kathryn and Trinidad Rico (eds.), *Heritage Keywords: Rhetoric and Redescription in Cultural Heritage*. Boulder: University Press of Colorado.

Shah, Nurul Fathihin Mohd Noor, and Masitah Ghazali. 2018. 'A Systematic Review on Digital Technology for Enhancing User Experience in Museums', in Natrah Abdullah, Wan Adilah Wan Adnan and Marcus Foth (eds.), *International Conference on User Science and Engineering*. Singapore: Springer, pp. 35–46.

Shehade, Maria, and Theopisti Stylianou-Lambert. 2019. 'The Future of Technology in Museums', in Kerstin Smeds (ed.), *The Future of Tradition in Museology: Materials for a Discussion*. Paris: ICOM, pp. 153–58.

———. 2020. 'Virtual Reality in Museums: Exploring the Experiences of Museum Professionals', *Applied Sciences* 10(11): 4031.

Silverman, Helaine (ed.). 2011. *Contested Cultural Heritage: Religion, Nationalism, Erasure, and Exclusion in a Global World*. New York: Springer-Verlag.

Slater, Mel. 2003. 'A Note on Presence Terminology', *Presence Connect* 3(3): 1–5. Retrieved 10 October 2020 from http://www0.cs.ucl.ac.uk/research/vr/Projects/Presencia/Consortium-Publications/ucl_cs_papers/presence-terminology.htm.

Stogner, Maggie Burnette. 2011. 'The Immersive Cultural Museum Experience – Creating Context and Story with New Media Technology', *The International Journal of the Inclusive Museum* 3(3): 117–30.

Tavinor, Grant. 2005. 'Videogames and Interactive Fiction', *Philosophy and Literature* 29(1): 24–40.

Tunbridge, John E., and Gregory J. Ashworth. 1996. *Dissonant Heritage: The Management of the Past as a Resource in Conflict*. Chichester: John Wiley & Sons.

Witcomb, Andrea. 2010. 'The Materiality of Virtual Technologies: A New Approach to Thinking about the Impact of Multimedia in Museums', in Fiona Cameron and Sarah Kenderdine (eds), *Theorizing Digital Cultural Heritage: A Critical Discourse*. Cambridge, Massachusetts: The MIT Press, pp. 35–48.

———. 2020. 'Afterword', in Hannah Lewi, Walli Smith, Dirk von Lehn, and Steven Cooke (eds), *The Routledge International Handbook of New Digital Practices in Galleries, Libraries, Archives, Museums and Heritage Sites*, London and New York: Routledge, pp. 484–87.

Revealing Missing or Underrepresented Narratives

Chapter 1

THE ROSEWOOD HERITAGE & VR PROJECT

Engaging Difficult Histories with Digital Technologies

Edward González-Tennant

Introduction

Researching difficult heritage faces numerous challenges. This work is increasingly politicised, and historical evidence is increasingly dismissed in daily conversations. Investigating the legacy of racism and structural violence is particularly difficult in the United States, where calls of 'fake news' serve to dismiss historical events that are unpleasant, overtly racist, or both. These sentiments are not new. Some view researching difficult histories as opening old wounds. Supporters of this view claim the past should be left alone, that recent progress renders any lingering problems as increasingly powerless holdovers, a residual ideology (Williams 1977) destined to vanish through various self-correcting behaviours. Other critics of difficult history work are uncomfortable with suffering and trauma. Typically, this group is composed of members whose lives are predicated upon systemic inequities disenfranchising entire communities based on race, nationality, class, sexuality or religion. Adherents to this view simply refuse to acknowledge and engage with their own privilege. Perhaps most troubling, however, are the responses from those who claim certain events never occurred, such as Holocaust deniers. These opinions form the foundation of deeply prejudiced worldviews, which are largely the result of two factors. The first is a lack of information literacy regarding historical evidence. The second is a political commitment to silencing disenfranchised voices. The first results from an inability or reluctance to engage in rational thinking, while the second is an emotional reaction. Digital technologies offer historical researchers powerful tools for addressing both.

For the purposes of this chapter, digital technologies refer to any approach, method or technique made possible with computer code. These include geographic information systems (GIS), 3D technologies (e.g. virtual reality, video games) and digital recordings of audio or video – in other words, new media (Manovich 2001) in all its varied forms as relating to the documentation and interpretation of the past (González-Tennant and González-Tennant 2016). These tools provide new methods for collecting, organising and sharing historical evidence. Digital technologies allow scholars to render transparent the enormous work required for historical research. Revealing how we use data to craft interpretations is key for supporting information literacy in our students, other researchers and the public. These efforts are strengthened when situated alongside disenfranchised voices, a common commitment found in associated methodologies like digital storytelling (Lambert 2009). The ability of digital technologies to share various aspects of the research process – such as which datasets are used for which interpretations – helps to address the challenges previously discussed and thereby engage the more extreme forms of historical erasure promoted by deniers of such events. These methods and their ability to share documents alongside disenfranchised voices provide both emotional and rational tools for confronting historical legacies of racism and structural violence. Providing these tools has become a common political commitment among scholars of difficult history (Nieves 2009; Rose 2016).

Conducting research on difficult heritage associated with African American experiences has taken on new meaning in recent years as the Black Lives Matter and similar movements remind us that events like the 1923 Rosewood Massacre echo across time and space. Theorising the multidimensionality of violence reveals how events like the 1923 Rosewood Massacre directly connect to modern events. My own research (González-Tennant 2018) explores this by examining how interpersonal, structural and symbolic violence changed through time in the United States. Interpersonal violence refers to face-to-face physical harm. Historical examples include race riots and lynching. Structural violence focuses on the ways social structures disenfranchise minority communities. Historical and modern examples include redlining (the practice by real estate agents and bank officials of demarcating neighbourhoods as off-limits to minority buyers), gerrymandering, and various forms of segregation. Symbolic violence refers to violence in one's own mind. Historically, cinema and the infusing of eugenics-based perspectives in state health regimes are central examples.

Changing rates of these three forms of violence are clearly visible to those undertaking these sorts of research. Prior to the twentieth century, interpersonal violence represented the major way racial elites in the United States halted minority participation. Over time, structural and symbolic forms supplanted those. The state – through means like unfair incarceration rates and the disproportionate use of the death penalty – became the main instrument of interpersonal violence, supported by growing structural and symbolic systems that restricted minority access to education, economic advancement and political representation. As such, conducting this sort of research is important to revealing these deeply interconnected *historical* roots to modern social inequality. Finding ways of translating this information in public knowledge is similarly important but often neglected by academic researchers. Digital technologies provide powerful tools for accomplishing both.

This chapter discusses fifteen years of personal research on the 1923 Rosewood Massacre and examines how this research benefits from the use of digital technologies to promote critical public reflection. The following discussion of methods and public outreach have all been conducted or led by me, although as with all such projects numerous team members have joined these efforts at various points. The destruction of Rosewood occurred during a single week. It involved a series of increasingly violent events culminating in the displacement of the town's mostly African American community and the razing of every Black-owned structure in the town. Research with digital technologies continues to provide new evidence about the history of this unincorporated rural community. Archaeological excavation, remote sensing and GIS inform a virtual reconstruction of the town. These efforts are combined with personal testimony to produce documentary videos. This work is oriented towards public outreach. The central goal for fifteen years has been centred on translating scholarly research into public knowledge. The results of this work include new and ongoing engagements between researchers, descendants, landowners and the public, all of which revolve around the ability of digital technologies to share evidence and make transparent the interpretive work common to historical research. The chapter concludes with a brief discussion of how this work has expanded in recent years to include other African American communities. Many of these communities have been largely forgotten, overshadowed by the public attention focused on Rosewood. This expanded research further addresses a different kind of violence resulting from researching difficult histories, the unintended obfuscation of similar events and nearby places.

Brief History of Rosewood

The former site of Rosewood is located nine miles from the Gulf of Mexico in Levy County, Florida (figure 1.1). The town itself was never incorporated. Business directories describe a small settlement in the 1850s, prior to the American Civil War (1861–65). The town experienced rapid growth following the war due to the area's abundant natural resources and the completion of Florida's first cross-state railroad. This railroad ran through the centre of Rosewood and played a crucial role to the community development and spatial patterning.

Although initially settled by White landowners, Rosewood's African American population quickly grew after the 1860s). Initially, a handful of African Americans purchased land from Whites who were either sympathetic, eager to sell after the area's trees were overharvested, or both. These trends resulted in a multidecade transformation, and Rosewood became majority African American by 1900. These families responded to issues like overharvesting by building a mixed economy. Rosewood's residents operated sawmills and market gardens, processed turpentine and raised livestock. The economic fortunes of Rosewood began to slump again in the 1910s, primarily due to the recently constructed Cummer and Sons Lumber Company sawmill in neighbouring Sumner. Sumner was a company town populated in equal parts by White and Black workers and their families. Members of many Rosewood families became employees of this new sawmill during the 1910s (Jones 1997).

Although these economic hardships affected Rosewood, the town's mixed economy and history of Black land ownership allowed its residents to weather such challenges. The economic downturn of the 1910s represented an unfortunate, but not disastrous, challenge for Rosewood. By 1920, Rosewood boasted three churches, a masonic hall, a privately funded school, and a mix of house styles representing the town's different economic classes (Jones et al. 1993).

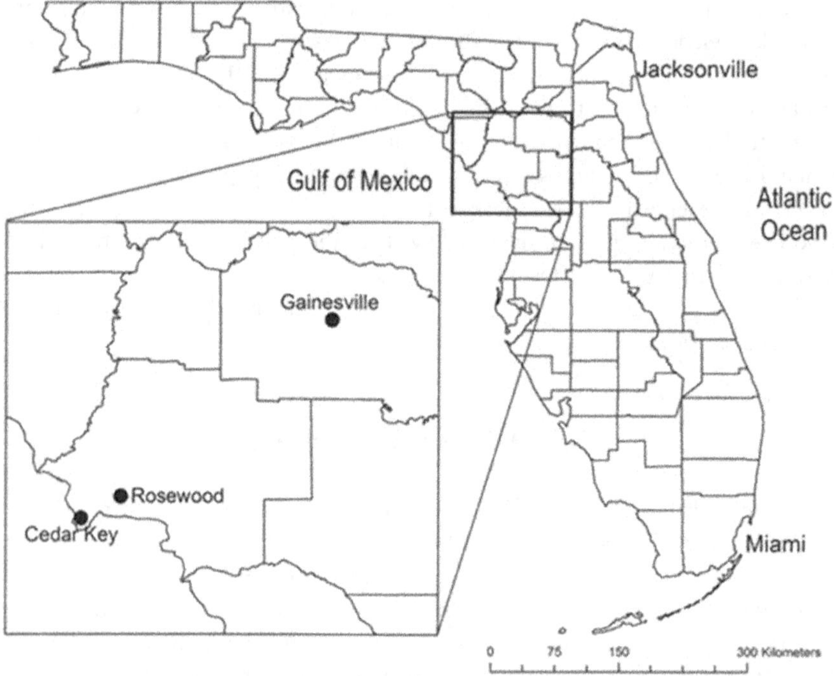

FIGURE 1.1. Location of Rosewood, Florida. Image by the author.

One month prior to the destruction of Rosewood, a group of Whites lynched three Black men in nearby Perry, Florida. These men were accused of killing a White schoolteacher. Following the lynching, the White mob descended upon Perry's Black neighbourhood and burned several homes. Local newspapers ran daily inflammatory accounts of this event for weeks (Jones et al. 1993; Martinez 2008). What is today known as the Rosewood Massacre was in fact a weeklong series of events beginning on Monday, 1 January 1923. That morning, while James Taylor was at work, his wife Fannie claimed a Black man entered their home and attacked her. Sarah Carrier and her granddaughter Philomena, residents of Rosewood, were employed by the Taylor family as laundresses. Sarah Carrier later told family members that she had seen a White man enter the Taylor home that day, and she suggested the assailant was a White man with whom Fannie was having an affair (Jones et al. 1993). Unfortunately, Taylor's accusation resulted in the rapid notification of Sheriff Robert Walker, who quickly organised a posse.

The posse followed bloodhounds towards Rosewood, where they encountered and attacked Aaron Carrier, an African American resident of Rosewood. Sheriff Walker placed Carrier in protective custody and the mob moved on to the home of long-time Rosewood resident Sam Carter (Jones et al. 1993). The mob interrogated Carter by hanging him from a tree by the neck. He admitted to taking a White individual out of the area. When the bloodhounds were unable to pick up the scent, and after Carter was unable to provide additional details, his body was riddled with bullets and the mob hung his corpse from a tree to be discovered the next day (Dye 1996). Carter became the first fatality (Jones et al. 1993). Although Carter's murder was investigated weeks later, a six-man jury found that Carter had been "shot by unknown party [or parties]" (Jones et al. 1993: 38).

No further deaths occurred in Rosewood for nearly three more days. On 4 January a 'party of citizens' went to investigate unconfirmed reports that an unidentified group of Blacks had taken refuge in Rosewood. This party of citizens targeted the home of Sylvester Carrier. Upon arriving at Carrier's home, two members of the mob, Henry Andrews and C. P. 'Poly' Wilkerson approached the house's porch, where they attempted to enter without permission; when they were unsuccessful, the men attempted to burn the house. Carrier and others in his home opened fire on the Whites, and a large gun battle commenced for several hours. The two White men eventually died of their injuries (Jones et al. 1993).

The battle continued into the early morning hours of Friday, 5 January. Dispatches were received in nearby communities, and additional Whites began arriving in Rosewood, including a large number of Ku Klux Klan (KKK) members. While the White mob left the area of the Carrier home for several hours on Friday to replenish ammunition and take care of their wounded, African Americans in Rosewood left their homes and fled into the swamps. Upon returning later that day, the White mob burned down several homes and at least two churches, one African American church and the last remaining White church. When the mob returned and entered the now empty Carrier home, they reportedly found the bodies of Sylvester Carrier and his mother Sarah Carrier. Both had been shot during the previous night's gun battle (Jones et al. 1993). Lexie Gordon, a Black widow of approximately fifty was shot point blank in her face as she fled her burning home on Friday (Jones et al. 1993). Gordon was the sixth recorded death in Rosewood after Sam Carter, Sylvester Carrier, Sarah Carrier, Henry Andrews, and C. P. 'Poly' Wilkerson. The seventh death attributed to the riot took place when Mingo Williams was shot in the head by Whites as they drove through nearby Bronson on their way to Rosewood.

Hearing about the trouble in Rosewood and the African Americans hiding in the nearby swamps, two brothers who worked for the railroad took a train out of Cedar Key in the early morning hours on Saturday, 6 January 1923. The conductors, a pair of White brothers named John and William Bryce, rescued frightened African Americans who had taken refuge in the swamps. Only women and children were allowed on the train, as the brothers feared White vigilantes would kill everyone if they found Black men onboard. The train took survivors to several towns to the east of Rosewood. Members of Rosewood's community disembarked in places like Archer and Gainesville, where descendants remain to this day. Other residents managed to flee the violence through various means. Many walked fifteen or more miles to nearby communities like Gulf Hammock or Otter Creek.

That Saturday, James Carrier, brother of Sylvester and son of Sarah, emerged from hiding in the swamps to bury his recently murdered mother and brother. As he completed his solemn task, a White mob appeared and captured him in Rosewood's Black cemetery, where he was lynched after the mob forced him to dig his own grave near the fresh graves of his brother and mother (Jones et al. 1993). That Sunday, a White mob returned to Rosewood and burned the remaining African American homes and buildings. African Americans never returned to the area, and many of their White neighbours eventually purchased the newly vacated properties. The event remains one of the largest forced displacements of an African American community in US history (González-Tennant 2018). The destruction of Rosewood was not an isolated event. It was only one of dozens of race riots between the years of 1917 and 1923, and of hundreds that have occurred over the past century.

Transdisciplinary Research in Rosewood

In addition to typical challenges facing difficult heritage work, researching Rosewood's past faces additional problems. Much is due to the community's rural location. Rosewood was never incorporated. There are no maps, city directories or other easily accessible documentary records relating to the town's history or spatial layout. Answers that are straightforward in other locations – such as the location of a descendant's ancestral homestead – are more difficult to ascertain in Rosewood. To address these and similar questions, a combination of traditional archaeology supported with intensive documentary research and remote sensing technologies has been necessary. This research began with an approach referred to as documentary archaeology (Beaudry 1988), which is 'an approach to history that brings together diverse source materials related to cultures and societies' (Wilkie 2006: 13). These materials are organised, synthesised and interpreted with archaeological perspectives. In the case of Rosewood, the use of GIS to work with a variety of documentary sources provides the raw materials for a landscape study of the town's history.

This work begins with reviewing thousands of historical property deeds and reconstructing the boundaries for hundreds of properties relating to past residents of Rosewood. The methodology for reconstructing these boundaries involves the following steps: (1) identify the appropriate historic property records, (2) translate the boundary information into a GIS file, (3) identify the owner in the census, (4) add relevant information from census records to the GIS record and (5) overlay this information on other forms of data including aerial photographs, LiDAR and historic maps. This combination of data helps identify locations of both property boundaries and past structures. These steps are repeated hundreds of times for a fifty-year period between the 1870s and 1930, providing an accurate spatial layout of Rosewood through time. A complete description of this process is beyond the scope of this chapter, and readers who are interested in this aspect of the research are directed to the fourth chapter of the author's recent book on Rosewood (González-Tennant 2018).

The results of the GIS mapping act as a predictive model directing traditional archaeological excavations. As of 2020, archaeological research has occurred at more than a dozen locations. These include homesteads, cemeteries, churches, industrial sites and public buildings (e.g. a masonic lodge). This work includes documenting cemeteries, excavating sites and total station mapping. In addition, architectural history work has occurred at standing structures that likely date to before the 1923 riot. The skilful use of various data and methodologies from different disciplines reveals a more complete picture of daily life in Rosewood. Archaeological work uncovers evidence of communal activities at several sites, including the masonic lodge. Excavations at this site began in 2010 and include an assortment of early twentieth-century domestic ceramics. These suggest a variety of community activities, which are further supported by oral histories. A 1993 interview with Rosewood descendant Gretchen Douglas discusses her mother's account of attending 'school at the masonic lodge' (Jones et al. 1993: 194). Such a transdisciplinary approach is vital in Rosewood, where documentary evidence is fragmentary or missing.

Other digital technologies provide additional information about these sites. Low altitude orthomosaics (images with geographic coordinates embedded in them) were collected with unmanned aerial vehicles (UAVs). These high-quality images are added to the above GIS information to better contextualise the results of excavations or to map newly discovered sites that may be located on properties where excavations are not possible. To date, these have been collected for two cemeteries and a large industrial site likely associated with a Black-owned turpentine still. Orthomosaics provide a low-cost method for delivering high-quality aerial images in environments with dense tree canopy. In such locations, the UAV is flown at or beneath the canopy, thus providing important data for areas that are often obscured on publicly available aerial data.

Ground-penetrating radar (GPR) surveys provide additional information. GPR is a geophysical method offering a non-invasive option for archaeological survey. GPR uses electromagnetic waves generated from an antenna from which reflective signals are collected, processed and interpreted. The GPR survey of the Rosewood Cemetery, location of the tragic death and burial of members of the Carrier family in 1923, is revealing a much larger cemetery than previously thought. Work began with a total station map of visible features. These features include depressions associated with potential graves, identified as such because they are oriented east-west, roughly arranged in north-south rows, and longer than wide. The GPR survey verified twelve depressions associated with graves and identified another thirty-six anomalies that are likely unmarked burials. These findings more closely match historical death certificates on file with the State of Florida.

Photogrammetry was also used at several locations to produce accurate 3D models of cultural resources. This included vandalised grave markers in the Rosewood Cemetery (figure 1.2). The choice of which features to document using this technology was dependent on the level of threat facing cultural resources, current or past damage to objects, or the amount of aid doing so would extend to public outreach. Photogrammetry refers to the process of using a series of 2D photographs of an object to create a highly accurate 3D model.

The preceding transdisciplinary research requires methods from different disciplines and the application of these technologies in new ways. The results of this work provide various outputs supporting public outreach efforts. To date, these efforts include annual public talks across the state of Florida, virtual reality applications, a data warehouse at the project's website, and documentary video. These products contribute to new opportunities to engage the public in an ongoing conversation about these kinds of difficult histories in rural Florida, along with their connections to other times and places across the United States. Public outreach is also opening new research potentials and collaborations in Rosewood and nearby places.

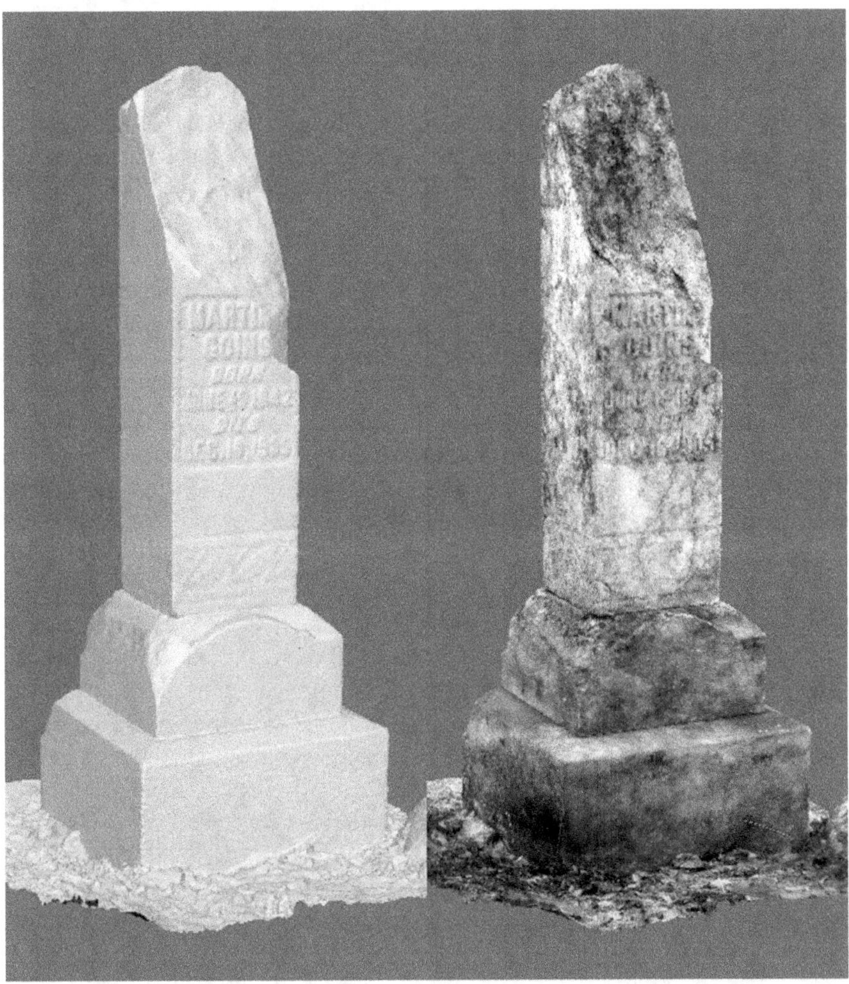

FIGURE 1.2. 3D model of Martine Goins's grave in Rosewood. Image by the author.

Public Outreach in Rosewood and Beyond

The previous section discussed scholarly work associated with developing a nuanced history of Rosewood. Such work is crucial to translating research on Rosewood's history into public knowledge. Many of the outputs – maps, charts and so forth – are more accessible to a public audience than reports, articles or other scholarly works. This section examines additional work centring on the ways these traditional scholarly outputs can be used for public talks, virtual reality applications, digital storytelling and documentary video. The Rosewood Heritage & VR Project (www.virtualrosewood.com) is a mixed-methods approach using various digital tools and media to explore the connections between traditional scholarship, public outreach and social justice (González-Tennant 2013). It is also an engaged project in that it centres the interests of descendants while respecting current property owners and seeking new ways to contribute to public conversations on racial violence in rural American, particularly the area of Florida where Rosewood once stood. My exploration of these tools over the past fifteen years has changed considerably. I no longer maintain a presence in the online, user-created platform Second Life, which has largely fallen out of favour with educators. The following pages focus on a brief overview of the approaches that remain active aspects of this work. The next section discusses how these approaches continue to produce new engagements. This includes expanding the geographic focus of work to explore new contexts in the communities surrounding Rosewood.

One of the first outputs of research in Rosewood was a twenty-five-minute video created in 2010 titled *Remembering Rosewood*. It draws on trends in digital storytelling and specifically the use of digital media to tell personal stories (Lambert 2009). This approach offers many benefits for individuals or small teams engaged in difficult history work. This includes the relatively low cost associated with producing digital media. Whereas traditional film follows an industrial logic (large-scale production studies, expensive equipment costs, necessity of laborers), the use of new media to tell personal stories is a postindustrial method. It is not regulated by mass standardisation, requires less money to produce and can be created with tools that most researchers already own (e.g. personal computers, mobile phones, digital cameras). I was also attracted to digital storytelling because it offers a direct method for engaging the public.

This video centred the concerns of many Rosewood descendants. It was produced for use in educational tours to the area around Rosewood. These tours used to be led by descendants and occasionally included survivors when they were still alive. The last survivor of Rosewood, Mary Hall Daniels, who passed away in 2018, had participated in a single tour in 2009. Although these tours began in the 1990s, most survivors and other descendants were not involved. Daniels was born in Rosewood in 1919. The tours and other efforts by descendants focus on keeping the history of Rosewood alive in the present to combat the intentional erasure of the community in public memory for so many decades. The digital video describes the historical and geographical context of Rosewood from settlement in the mid-nineteenth century until 1923. Of course, the story and community do not stop in 1923. Survivors moved to towns across Florida and eventually throughout the United States. The second half of the video focuses on the lives of two survivors, Robie Morton and Mary Hall Daniels, via oral history interviews conducted in 2009. Robie Mortin, who passed away in 2012, provides a particularly touching moment as she describes meeting her father for the first time after fleeing Rosewood. Robie's father suspected violence would resume after the initial events of Monday, 1 January. He sent Robie, who was eight at the time, along with her older sister to a relative's home in a nearby town. After hearing about the destruction of Rosewood several days later and not being able to reconnect with their father, the sisters assumed the worst and began to look for work. During the following months they worked as migrant fruit pickers, eventually making their home in Riviera Beach, Florida, north of Miami. Fortunately, the sisters did eventually reconnect with their father in Riviera Beach, far from Rosewood. Robie describes the event:

> There was a ditch that separated Riviera Beach from Kelsey City, there was a long ditch there. There had a bridge across it, and of course all the milk houses were there, and the Hearst Chapel AME Church there. They had built that church right on that side of the ditch. So, we went to church, and would you believe our daddy was there, and we didn't know where he was, we didn't know where he was, hadn't seen him in months. We walked into the church that Sunday, and there was our father. (Robie Mortin, private interview with author, 2009)

The emotional impact of her brief story demonstrates the trials and, in this one example, happy surprises that make a life scarred by trauma bearable. The digital video was initially only available to a small group of people, but it was eventually uploaded to YouTube in 2015.[1] It has received forty-two thousand views as of July 2020. Unfortunately, due to numerous hateful statements, comments for the video were disabled after the first year.

In addition to the digital video, a virtual world environment representing Rosewood prior to its destruction was completed in 2011 (figure 1.3). The layout of the virtual world was informed by the spatial template produced with the documentary archaeology and GIS work previously described. This work involved the creation of several dozen 3D models representing historic structures. The appearance of these structures was based on property descriptions, documentation of nearby extant historic structures and oral history accounts. Mary Hall Daniels remembered asking her family about their house in Rosewood. They explained, 'We had a big two-story house and we still lived there after our father died because it was a lot of us children.' Dr. Arnnett Shakir recalled his mother describing the Carriers' home as 'a two-story house with a porch on it, lace curtains and manicured lawns . . . there was a piano in the house.' Earnest Parham, a White man who was eighteen in 1923, remembered substantial houses in Rosewood. Eva Jenkins, a survivor who was thirteen in 1923, described her family's house as having

> three bedrooms and this big hall down the middle and a kitchen and dining room and it was onto the house; a lot of people said theirs were separate from

the house, but ours was all joined, we had front porch and back porch, and two big old Magnolia trees in the front yard, oak tree with a swing on it. But anyhow they had nice furniture. (Eva Jenkins 1993)

Other sources provide additional information. Some historical property deeds include building descriptions. Census records provide a basic idea of the number of people living in a given structure, used to determine general sizes of structures. The size and construction of public buildings like stores, churches, schools and masonic lodges were standard for the time. Photographs and measured drawings of these structures provide additional information for creating an accurate but admittedly conjectural reconstruction of the town.

The above virtual world environment was designed to run in a web browser. It is relatively small and lacks details associated with virtual worlds produced in more recent years.[2] A more recent version was completed in 2020. This updated version is referred to as *Rosewood: An Interactive Experience* as discussed in the next section.

Public lectures remain an important third form of public outreach. To date I have delivered dozens of such talks, typically two to three or more each year since 2011. These talks provide an opportunity to understand how members of the public encounter and respond to difficult histories. These engagements have forced me to reframe aspects of the talk and my research. For example, the knowledge that Fannie Taylor likely fabricated a Black assailant is now a well-established aspect of Rosewood's history. However, most researchers fail to account for the fact that Taylor was undoubtedly a woman who experienced domestic violence. My own reframing of this occurred after a White man in

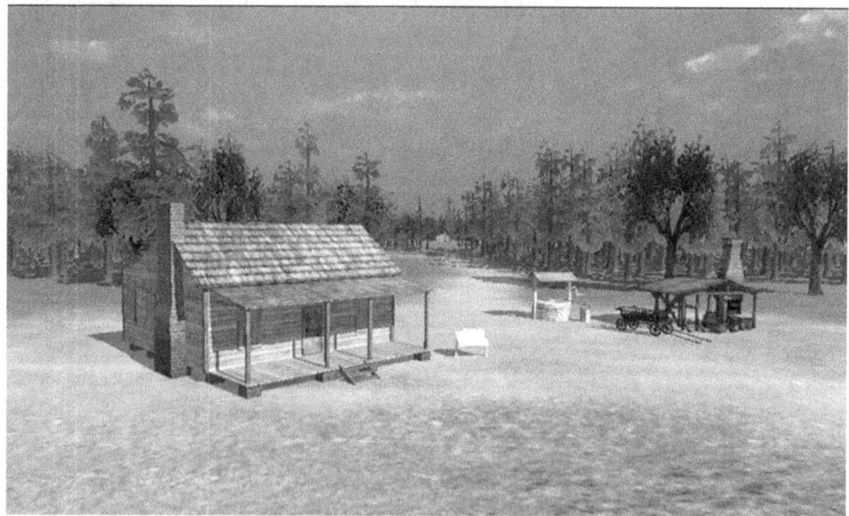

FIGURE 1.3. Screenshot of original virtual world environment. Image by the author.

Levy County encouraged me to speak of Taylor with more sympathy. I did not interpret this as a desire to diminish the larger history of Rosewood but rather to show sympathy to a greater number of people. Public lectures often receive little to no attention in research on difficult heritage, but they remain one of the most direct ways researchers can bring their scholarship alive in socially relevant ways. In the United States, archaeology is often considered a science, and whether we see this sort of research as scientific, humanistic or a mix of both as I do, it remains clear that we need engaging, evidence-based narratives about the past now more than ever (Olson 2019). Of course, speaking on difficult heritage faces challenges, but even the questions that may be framed in hostile or otherwise seemingly insincere ways have often led to new perspectives for me and the public. These engagements with diverse audiences during my public talks have fundamentally and deeply affected not only the way I speak publicly but also how I teach (González-Tennant 2017).[3]

My commitment to remaining transparent during my research and public outreach activities continues to provide new research opportunities by engendering goodwill among descendants and residents of Levy County. The documentary videos, virtual world environments and public talks all align with the goals of survivors, descendants, property owners and the public. This is a difficult balance to strike, but it gets easier each year as new collaborators identify themselves. Over the past ten years, landowners in Rosewood – most of whom moved to the area in the 1980s or after – were often reluctant to have researchers visit their properties. While some landowners simply did not want others on their property, many were reluctant because of previous experiences with researchers. Many of these experiences have been negative, as not all have been honest about their intentions. The individual who owns the property where Rosewood's historic African American cemetery is located has previously worked with several researchers. Most of them have attempted to access his property or apply for public monies to work on his property without his consent. Fortunately, upon reading newspaper accounts of my public outreach work and viewing the digital video, he extended an invitation to visit the property. In the years since then I have returned numerous times, working closely with him to receive state funding to document all the historical resources on his property. His property contains thousands of years of history, including a portion of the historical cross-state railroad, evidence of Native American life dating back thousands of years and Rosewood's African American cemetery. Our collaboration with this landowner has opened up new potentials for research in Rosewood and nearby.

In the past three years, and since the publication of my book in 2018, archaeological work has grown to include several new properties. Documentary research is revealing a more complex African American history in the area. All of this means my own opportunities to engage locally have also grown. Discussing these recent developments is the focus of the next section.

New Engagements in Rosewood and Beyond

The previous sections discuss the recent archaeological work. These include GPR surveys and the use of photogrammetry to document landscapes and graves. Much of the recent archaeological and documentary research is contributing to an updated version of the virtual world environment. This updated version is titled *Rosewood: An Interactive History* (RAIH). It involves updated 3D models, a redesigned user interface, and interactive content (figure 1.4). RAIH is a unique approach to teaching history using video game technologies. It draws users into the rural world of north Florida one hundred years ago. Users interact with various forms of information as they explore a richly detailed 3D world. This includes interacting with the material culture of the period, accessing relevant archaeological and documentary data via the user interface and accessing oral histories of survivors and descendants that describe their lives in Rosewood and beyond. At the heart of this approach is a notes-based system. As users move through the virtual world environment, they collect notes that can then be accessed at any point afterwards. These notes provide brief histories of different locations and how various lines of evidence inform these histories. Readers can access RAIH online via the popular gaming site Itch.io.[4]

In addition to an updated virtual world environment, a second documentary film is nearing completion. A grant from the Florida Division of Historical Resources provided funding to document the archaeological and historical work in Rosewood and Sumner during 2018 and 2019. Videos of fieldwork, historical research, and interviews were recorded in 2019 to document how researchers

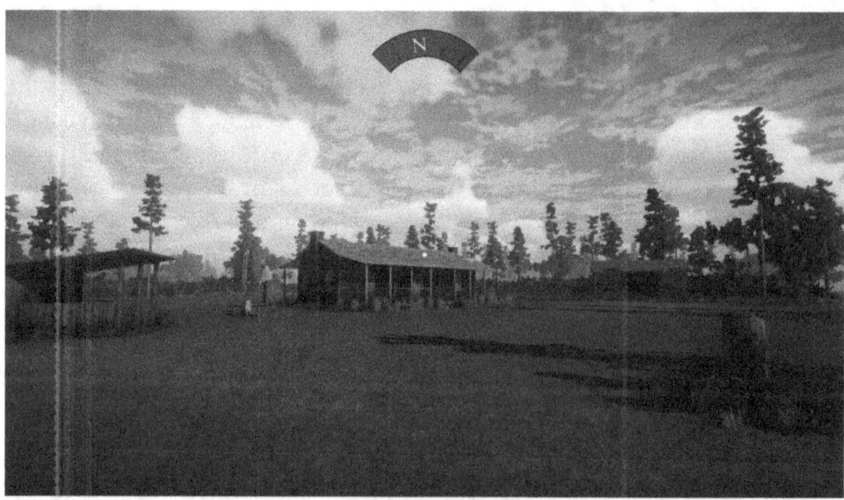

FIGURE 1.4. Screenshot from updated *Rosewood: An Interactive History.* Image by the author.

use various tools to learn more about the past. This second video is a companion to the earlier digital video. It does not include descendant voices but instead describes how archaeology and history reveal new truths about difficult histories. A third documentary is currently being filmed. This third video moves away from the more traditional 'talking head' approach of the initial two videos (Aufderheide 2007). Although well-known to fans of documentary films, these conventions reduce the overall impact of such videos by restricting popular appeal. The third documentary follows several descendants as they visit Rosewood for the first time. This character-driven approach provides a more personal connection to the area's history.[5]

A 2019 GPR survey at the Shiloh Cemetery in Sumner, Florida, further expanded our knowledge of the area's past population. Shiloh contains ten acres, half of which has recently been opened for burials. The mapping and GPR work focused on the other five acres. This cemetery includes some of the oldest marked burials in Levy County. The 2019 work identified seventy-seven unmarked burials and located them into relation to the approximately three hundred marked burials. The Shiloh Cemetery association is using these results to plan future burials, and we are working on making this information public via a web-based interactive map. During our fieldwork, many locals stopped to visit with the group of students working with me, who were paid for their time via external grants administered through the University of Central Florida. Paying students in this way provides new opportunities for underrepresented groups in archaeology and heritage to participate and represents an ethical obligation of researchers who undertake this research. Many of these locals have deep roots in the area and were able to tell us about the individuals buried at the site. This included identifying unmarked graves associated with the two White men who were injured and later died during the gun battle at the Carrier home in 1923. These graves have remained unmarked to this day, but informant knowledge was partly supported when GPR results confirmed the location of unmarked burials at the locations identified as the graves of these two men.

These efforts have set the stage for an expanded form of engagement in the coming years. In April 2020 I was nominated and then elected to serve as president of the Cedar Key Historical Society (a volunteer position). This nonprofit historical society manages the area's oldest local history museum. One of my priorities is to expand the museum's exhibits to include more information about Cedar Key's African American history. This history stretches back to the 1800s and includes events like the election of a Black mayor in the 1870s. Unlike Rosewood, where the African American population was violently displaced in 1923, Cedar Key's African American community persisted until at least the 1940s.

One site we have identified for additional research is the Cedar Key Cemetery. This site is home to a thousand marked burials, none of them African American. Local residents have repeatedly told me that an area in the back of the cemetery is home to the town's African American cemetery. Working together, the historical society has submitted a grant application to conduct a GPR survey of this area. Until recently, we could only assume unmarked burials were associated with African Americans. However, on a recent fact-gathering trip, we uncovered one marked burial in this area. The name and other information were unclear due to weathering of the stone. Photogrammetry provided this information by creating a high-quality 3D model and thereby rendering the engraving legible, perhaps for the first time in decades. This process allowed us to identify the grave as belonging to Adeline Tape (figure 1.5). Tape appears in the 1920 census and is listed as working at the Fiber Factory in Cedar Key, where she worked until her death in 1927. Although the gravestone is still in fair condition, its illegibility has likely restricted efforts to fully document Cedar Key's African American population and related burial ground. Associated research with historic maps and city directories is further illuminating the town's Black history, including an African American section of town with churches, businesses and dozens of homes that persisted until at least the 1940s. The reduction of the area's African American population by this time was part of large social movements restricting most of Florida's Black communities to urban contexts. In places like Cedar Key, social pressures to migrate for employment merged with growing racial intolerance to greatly reduce the majority of Florida's rural African American populations.

Much of the above is occurring in partnership with a growing list of local groups. This expansion of research is in many ways a best-case scenario. When I first began this work in 2005, many locals were reluctant to grant access to their properties, much less support a public conversation on difficult histories

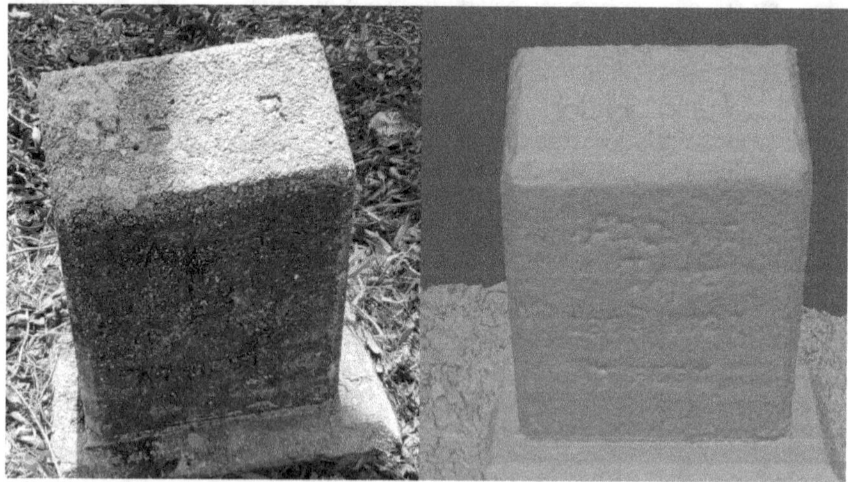

FIGURE 1.5. Results of photogrammetry. Left side of image shows grave of Adeline Tape, right side is of high-quality 3D. Image by the author.

literally located in their backyards. Ultimately, the continued success of this work remains dependent on researcher transparency and an ongoing cultural shift in this and similar parts of Florida.

Conclusion

Digital technologies for difficult history provide a powerful set of tools for addressing the challenges often restricting this work. Crafting a sustainable approach (Agbe-Davis 2010) is vital for realising these positive potentials, which are by no means automatic (Morgan and Pallascio 2016). Engaging the public through digital technologies in substantive ways requires researchers to remain involved, sometimes for years with little to no recognition. I do not know the extent to which my work in Rosewood has contributed to shifting local attitudes. I do know that a continued presence combined with a willingness to *hear* a variety of perspectives has provided me the opportunity to participate in crafting the future of locally produced history in an area where difficult history has engulfed the landscape. Ultimately, any success derived from this approach rests on its ability to address the rational and emotional aspects of difficult history. Finding locally meaningful ways of weaving these strands together is essential. Digital technologies were central in creating these possibilities, and they will remain fundamental for the future of such work.

Edward González-Tennant earned his PhD from the University of Florida in 2011 for research on Rosewood, Florida, the basis for his 2018 book, *The Rosewood Massacre: An Archaeology and History of Intersectional Violence*, published by the University Press of Florida. He is an historical archaeologist who draws on interdisciplinary digital methodologies to investigate the complex intersection between the past and present. He has conducted and published on research in the United States, New Zealand, Norway, China, Peru and the Caribbean. He is currently an Assistant Professor of Historical Archaeology in the Department of Anthropology at Texas State University.

Notes

1. The video is available at https://www.youtube.com/watch?v=_s5kcyBAE6g.
2. The virtual world environment is available online at http://www.virtualrosewood.com/vr/.
3. Readers who would like to see a recent example of my public talks can do so by viewing a 2018 lecture for the Time Sifters Archaeological Society on YouTube at https://www

.youtube.com/watch?v=mnqkBWINfho. This public talk was given to a room of approximately ninety to one hundred attendees, nearly all of them White.
4.   https://digital-heritage.itch.io/raih.
5.   Information about current and future videos is available at http://www.virtualrosewood.com.

References

Agbe-Davis, Anna S. 2010. 'Concepts of Community in the Pursuit of an Inclusive Archaeology', *International Journal of Heritage Studies* 16(6): 373–89.

Aufderheide, Patricia. 2007. *Documentary Film: A Very Short Introduction.* Oxford: Oxford University Press.

Beaudry, Mary Carolyn. 1988. *Documentary Archaeology in the New World.* New York: Cambridge University Press.

Dye, Thomas R. 1996. 'Rosewood, Florida: The Destruction of an African American Community', *The Historian* 58(3): 322–605.

González-Tennant, Edward. 2013. 'New Heritage and Dark Tourism: A Mixed Methods Approach to Social Justice in Rosewood, Florida', *Heritage & Society* 6(1): 62–88.

———. 2017. 'Digital Storytelling in the Classroom: New Media Techniques for an Engaged Anthropological Pedagogy', in Aaron Thornburg and Mariela Nunez-Janes (eds), *Deep Stories: Practicing, Teaching, and Learning Anthropology with Digital Storytelling.* Berlin: de Gruyter Open, pp. 152–69.

———. 2018. *The Rosewood Massacre: An Archaeology and History of Intersectional Violence.* Gainesville: University Press of Florida.

González-Tennant, Edward, and Diana González-Tennant. 2016. 'The Practice and Theory of New Heritage for Historical Archaeology', *Historical Archaeology* 50(1): 187–204.

Jenkins, Eva. Interview by Maxine Jones. September 24, 1993, transcript. Retrieved 18 July 2021 from https://virtualrosewood.com/oral-history/.

Jones, Maxine D. 1997. 'The Rosewood Massacre and the Women Who Survived It', *Florida Historical Quarterly* 76(2): 193–208.

Jones, Maxine Deloris, Larry E. Rivers, David R. Colburn, R. Thomas Dye, and William R. Rogers. 1993. *A Documented History of the Incident Which Occurred at Rosewood, Florida, in January 1923: Submitted to the Florida Board of Regents 22 December 1993.* Tallahassee, FL: Board of Regents.

Lambert, Joe. 2009. *Digital Storytelling: Capturing Lives, Creating Community.* 2nd edn. Berkeley, CA: Digital Diner Press.

Manovich, Lev. 2001. *The Language of New Media.* Cambridge, MA: MIT Press.

Martinez, Meghan H. 2008. 'Racial Violence and Competing Memory in Taylor County Florida, 1922', MA thesis, Department of History, Florida State University.

Morgan, Colleen L., and Pierre Marc Pallascio. 2016. 'Digital Media, Participatory Culture, and Difficult Heritage: Online Remediation and the Trans-Atlantic Slave Trade', *Journal of African Diaspora Archaeology and Heritage* 4(3): 160–78.

Nieves, Angel David. 2009. 'Places of Pain as Tools for Social Justice in the "New" South Africa: Black Heritage Preservation in the "Rainbow" Nation's Townships', in William Logan and Keir Reeves (eds), *Places of Pain and Shame: Dealing with Difficult Heritage.* London: Routledge, pp. 198–214.

Olson, Randy. 2018. *Don't Be Such a Scientist: Talking Substance in an Age of Style*. Washington, DC: Island Press.

Rose, Julia, ed. 2016. *Interpreting Difficult History at Museums and Historic Sites*. Lanham, MD: Rowman & Littlefield.

Wilkie, Laurie. 2006. 'Documentary Archaeology', in Dan Hicks and Mary Carolyn Beaudry (eds), *The Cambridge Companion to Historical Archaeology*. New York: Cambridge University Press, pp. 13–33.

Williams, Raymond. 1977. *Marxism and Literature*. Oxford: Oxford University Press.

Chapter 2

PRESERVING QUEER VOICES

Sharon Webb

Introduction

Oral history interviews and testimonies represent a unique form of cultural heritage. They are a powerful way of capturing lost or silenced narratives, of histories that have been oppressed, contested or difficult to publicly express. They are cathartic for participants and often evoke emotional responses in readers and listeners alike. Given the sensitive nature of both context and content, oral histories often pose a particular challenge in terms of archiving and cataloguing, as well as providing public access in spaces like libraries and museums. These challenges are amplified in the context of oral histories that capture traditionally marginalised voices, as they often reveal complex and difficult histories, recollections and memories. This chapter explores how oral history testimonies from an LGBTQI+ community inspired the creation of an artistic installation, Queer Codebreakers (QC), and how its development, and redevelopment for the community-curated museum exhibition 'Queer the Pier' (QP), highlights the importance of coproduction in museums and other public spaces. QC, a machine that prints and plays curated excerpts from a queer oral history collection, was created as part of a British Academy Rising Star Engagement Award (BARSEA), 'Identity, Representation and Preservation in Community Digital Archives and Collections,' led by the author April 2018–March 2019. The overarching aim of this project was to highlight the problem of long-term digital preservation for community archives (CA) and collections. Therefore, this chapter addresses a number of research activities and practices related to this project and the final output, QC. These are: CA and digital preservation, queer representation in public spaces, and queer archiving and curation. These topics are related to ongoing efforts to archive oral histories carried out by Queer in Brighton (QIB), a queer cultural heritage group in Brighton (UK), in 2012–14. This work, and QC, is a response to the very real threat posed by the fragility of digital formats and environments. It also highlights the need for museums and other cultural institutions using innovative technology to enhance and enrich user experience to think proactively about the long-term sustainability, maintenance and preservation of these pieces and the content therein. A background description of QIB and the problem of long-term digital preservation in relation to community archives will form the first part of this chapter. A discussion of the interactive installation QC, which makes queer oral histories accessible to new publics, then follows. The last section focuses on queer archiving and curation as forms of archival and curatorial activism.

Background: Community Archives and Digital Preservation

Community archives and heritage projects play an important role in creating a diverse and representative historical record. They include archives and projects that collect material related to local histories and interest groups ranging from trade union and associational activity to built heritage and transport. More often than not they are volunteer led, and funding is crowdsourced and/or based on precarious income streams that change periodically. In many cases the imperative to archive is born from a political and societal need to redress past exclusion, erasure or misrepresentation in the historical record and the public sphere. Therefore, in the past decades, in part informed by civil rights, women's liberation and gay liberation movements, DIY and grassroots archival initiatives have transformed into a rich, diverse and important subculture of archive and museum practice, method and research. These initiatives are driven and motivated by a genuine fear – and the historical reality – of being left out of (formal) history, but they are also moved by a need to celebrate and commemorate the stories of traditionally marginalised communities and heritage. Community, grassroots and DIY archives and projects, which represent traditionally marginalised groups, make a unique and crucial contribution to the creation of representative and cohesive historical narratives in cultural heritage across galleries, libraries, archives and museums (GLAM). They challenge hegemonic, heteronormative and patriarchal notions of heritage and invite alternative readings and constructions of mainstream histories. One such project is 'Queer in Brighton'.

QIB initially began as an oral history project to capture the lived experience of the queer community, both past and present, in the city of Brighton and Hove, United Kingdom. The substantive collection includes over seventy oral histories, carried out between 2012 and 2014, and written testimonies as well as collected ephemera donated by community members. In 2014 an anthology, using excerpts from the collection, was published (*Queer in Brighton* (2014), edited by Maria Jastrzebska and Anthony Luvera). The oral history interviews were carried out by trained volunteers, and both interviewers and interviewees were members of the queer community in Brighton. The collection captures a unique moment in the lives of contributors and, given their focus on Brighton, a city rightfully or wrongly labelled as one of the UK's gay capitals, contributes significantly to the narrative of queer heritage in the UK (Browne et al. 2013). QIB's initial funding, through the Heritage Lottery Fund, included provision to train volunteers on oral history methods but made no provision to support archiving activity. Initially, the project website was used to provide access to some of the oral histories, but following a takedown request, all oral histories were removed from the site. As a result, the QIB oral histories were no longer publicly available in any form other than the printed anthology. The collection was initially housed by Lesley Wood, CEO of New Writing South and lead volunteer for QIB, and was later moved to the Marlborough Pub, a queer community social space and hub. In 2018 the collected ephemera and the oral histories were transferred from the basement and office of the Marlborough Pub to the author's office at the University of Sussex. This move enabled a review of the collection and instigated a process of cataloguing and archiving with students and community volunteers. The appraisal and assessment of the collection identified a number of missing files as well as missing and incomplete consent forms. Following the assessment, the oral histories were uploaded to a secure online data store hosted by the university, and access to oral histories for community members was re-established. This process has enabled a reengagement with the collection and inspired reuse in multiple contexts. This assessment highlights the need for projects, and funders, to think carefully about the aftercare of digital assets and objects created through heritage projects and initiatives. It is this digital precariousness, inherent in digital cultural heritage work, exacerbated by underfunding and under-resourcing, that prompted a series of workshops and seminars focused on the broad topic, community archives and digital preservation (funded by the author's BARSEA)

The problem of long-term digital preservation, as defined by the Digital Repository of Ireland (2014: n.p.) is, put simply, 'the volatile nature of the digital medium and the inherent reliance on peripheral resources (e.g. software and hardware) to access and display objects'. In addition to various forms of digital obsolescence, and of significance for CA, is a reliance on third-party services and products (e.g. Dropbox, Tumblr, WordPress) to 'archive' personal and collective histories. This reliance is problematic because of the market tendency to change terms of service and/or withdraw services entirely (e.g. Flickr, Yahoo! Groups, etc.). 'Digital Archives in Communities: Practice and Preservation' (June 2018), held at Sussex Humanities Lab (SHL), University of Sussex, therefore, explored the challenge of long-term digital preservation specifically in relation to CA. The event, and the associated programme of work, was an attempt to bridge the gap between CA and the institutions with the means to provide (digital) infrastructural advice and support. It was influenced by the difficulty that QIB identified of adequately archiving and making accessible their oral history collection. Invited speakers included CA managers and volunteers (e.g. Cork LGBT Archive, Feminist South Archive, the rukus! Archive) and representatives from larger organisations (e.g. London Metropolitan Archives, the Digital Repository of Ireland and the Digital Preservation Coalition).

CA managers and volunteers described the participatory activities they had undertaken to develop collections, which included oral history interviews, object collection days and the creation of digital archives and resources. These activities are not only mechanisms to solidify group identity and community cohesion but are, as Eichhorn (2013: 2) describes, 'cultural interventions' and acts of 'activism in the present'. Framing the work of CA as archival activism is useful but does not represent the full spectrum of work that can also lead to cultural interventions in museums, libraries and other public spaces. Forms of archival activism and community curation, whether queer, feminist, or Black, Asian and Minority Ethnic (BAME) are political acts that seek to redress underrepresentation, and indeed misrepresentation, in historical narratives. They thereby enrich cultural heritage and disrupt prevailing hegemonic power. Significantly, archival activism often leads to community interventions and collaborations with the museum sector, as described later. These representations, which often explore difficult histories or heritage, in public spaces across the GLAM sector can be transformative. In reference to archives, Eichhorn (2013: 4) asserts, they are not merely 'a site of preservation (a place to house traces of the past)' but are also used 'as an apparatus to legitimize new forms of knowledge and cultural production'. It is in this sense that community activities like archiving, co-curating museum exhibitions and conducting oral history interviews represent an act of 'cultural production'. By engaging with the practical imperatives of archiving, of curation, of collecting, community members take ownership of their individual and collective stories and, in doing so, raise the profile of those narratives in contemporary culture and memory. The archive or museum exhibition become not just 'a place to [safely] house the past' but a space to actively challenge it (Eichhorn 2013: 4).

The archival imperative within particular communities, and as described by some of the event participants, is symptomatic of their marginalisation in wider society. Cvetkovich (2003: 8) highlights this in the 'Archive of Feeling' and outlines the fact that

> gay and lesbian cultures . . . have had to struggle to preserve their histories. In the face of institutional neglect, along with erased and invisible histories, gay and lesbian archives have been formed through grassroots efforts, just as cultural and political movements have demanded attention to other suppressed

and traumatic histories, ranging from the Holocaust, to labor and civil rights activism, to slavery and genocide.

The power, or indeed right, to document, record and collect particular histories and narratives resides in the autonomy and independent nature of these groups who often work outside of formal archives and other memory institutions. Yet, it is precisely these characteristics that contribute to their precarity, as many are unable to sustain requisite commitments to maintain collections, digital or otherwise, over the long term. In particular, maintaining digital archives, digital exhibitions and other online digital resources is a complex undertaking that requires significant resources for an indefinite period. It is in this respect that the culture reproduced through these acts of archival activism are at risk.

This difficulty and the subsequent risk of material loss led the Digital Preservation Coalition (DPC) (2019: n.p.), an international advocacy non-profit organisation, to designate 'Community Archives and Community Generated Content' as a 'critically endangered digital species'. Indeed, those most at risk are collections created by traditionally marginalised groups, who, in this context, face double erasure from the historical record and public memory. They are critically endangered because of a number of contributing factors, including: precarious funding streams with inadequate or no provision for digital archiving or digital preservation activities; limited opportunities for volunteers to develop skills to support digital archiving or digital preservation tasks; lack of shared resources and sustainable technical infrastructures; lack of peer support or technical advice; volunteer recruitment and fatigue. Other technical challenges that CA face include hardware and software failures as well as inadequate storage and/or back-ups.

Technology, however, is only one part of the digital preservation problem. As Paul Wheatley (DPC) states, 'The other challenges are organization and resourcing and often these are the most challenging' (Webb 2018). The resourcing problems associated with digital archiving for long-term access is not unique to projects and initiatives like QIB, and it is certainly not unique to the volunteer sector either. While a single solution to resolve these problems may not currently exist, CA can take small steps to mitigate the risk of loss: for example, writing comprehensive, descriptive metadata in standard formats, making multiple copies of digital objects and, where skills allow, actively reviewing digital collections for file corruptions (e.g. carrying out basic digital preservation tasks like checksums or fixity checks). Indeed, as reflected in the following sections, making digital content available to community members and researchers creates an opportunity for this type of work to take place. Facilitating training sessions with community members can be transformative as community members learn the skills required to save their heritage in the long term. This in turn creates dialogue with other institutions, like universities, who can help advocate and negotiate for access to the required resources. Crucially, making content accessible enables new interactions with digital content, which can spur innovative and novel public representations and installations, as exemplified by the installation 'Queer Codebreakers', 1.0 and 2.0.

Queer Representations in Public Spaces: Difficult Histories in Libraries and Museums

'Queer Codebreakers' was a response to an open call for proposals stemming from a collaboration between the Sussex Humanities Lab, Queer in Brighton (Lesley Wood and David Sheppeard) and Laurence Hill, former director of Brighton Digital Festival. The call for proposals asked for work that explored the social, political and cultural implications and impacts of technology on the archive. It looked for submissions that reinvented the way in which oral histories and archival material are represented, to move beyond the grid-based design of most digital archives. Applicants were required to incorporate content from the QIB oral history collection and were asked to be sensitive to the topics and subjects raised in the interviews.

The motivation for this approach stemmed from a desire to challenge the concept of what an archive looks like and to incorporate a playfulness to encourage different types of user/reader engagement with archive collections. The decision to commission an artist instead of a researcher or archivist was based on the desire to explore ways to reanimate the oral history collections and to move away from passive user engagement with the interviews. We wanted to emphasise and centre the diverse voices in the QIB collection so users could experience the 'orality of the oral source' (Portellii 1998:64). Commissioning an artistic piece opened the archive to new interpretations, to new possibilities and, crucially, to new audiences. Since many archives do in fact become 'sites of preservation', we wanted to encourage new formations of the archive to open the collection to users who would not normally visit an archive, digital or otherwise (Eichhorn 2013: 4).

The successful proposal, 'Queer Codebreakers', submitted by London-based computational artist Elle Castle, explored the 'parallels between ciphers, espionage, coded queer communication and the fragility of oral history' (Castle 2018: n.p.). QC, or indeed queer codebreaking, permits a number of interpretations, including coded language used among queer communities to communicate, whether through material culture (e.g. Hanky Codes), coded spoken language (e.g. Polari) or written codes in diaries or journals (e.g. British diarist Anne Lister (1791–1840), made famous after her coded diaries containing details of her lesbian relationships were discovered). It can also refer to the labels and codes used in archival and museum descriptions, which have in the past omitted, misrepresented and 'othered' queer histories and objects. For example, archaic terms in catalogue descriptions include 'gross indecency' and 'unnatural misdemeanors' (Furber 2017: 15). QC also makes explicit reference to computational technology, both in acknowledgement of Alan Turing and the use of digital technology in queer culture and heritage work.

The idea of coding and decoding also resonates with how queer history has been systematically hidden and erased, and with the work required to reveal or decipher those 'hidden' histories. Again, we can think of the work to decode information systems in archives and museums.[1] Indeed, in terms of Alan Turing, described as the father of modern computing, and whose codebreaking feats inspired Castle's work, it is telling that apart from the records that document his work on mathematics and computational thinking there is little historical evidence of his personal life (Doan 2017).

> The 'queerness' of Turing is not lived out in the traces of his life, but in the evidence of his conviction for gross indecency, through the barbaric acts carried out on his body . . . and . . . subsequent reporting and inquest into his death. His everyday 'history' is non-existent. His everyday experiences remain hidden [and] unrecoverable – they are simply not documented (in any known documents currently at least). (Webb 2019: n.p.)

Turing's historical erasure is representative of a particular time and place in which queer history and identity were oppressed in the public domain. It was appropriate, therefore, that QC 1.0 was launched during LGBT History Month (February 2019) and exhibited in a public library. QC 1.0 was an attempt to give new life to the queer voices captured in the QIB oral history collection. It challenged the pervasive decentring of audio in oral history practices and the prioritisation of viewing, presenting and analysing oral histories as textual objects. QC 1.0 was a standalone piece. Users were instructed to locate objects in the library (e.g. a 3D-printed bow tie to represent butch identity), which held a four-digit code, or to answer a riddle secured to the plinth (e.g. the year Section 28 came into force – see figure 2.1). When the user entered the correct code, the machine played a curated extract from the QIB collection and printed the accompanying transcript, enabling users to bring home a piece of the archive (see figure 2.2).

At the launch, Laurence Hill referred to Hito Steyerl's 2018 publication, 'Duty Free Art' and recounted the story of how a Russian separatist group used a tank, which had been placed as a war memorial some years previously, to attack a checkpoint:

> Someone had failed to render the war machine [in]capable of its former function and not recognized, that to be part of a memorial, is to be removed in the world. That story doesn't have a good ending. People died. It raises many

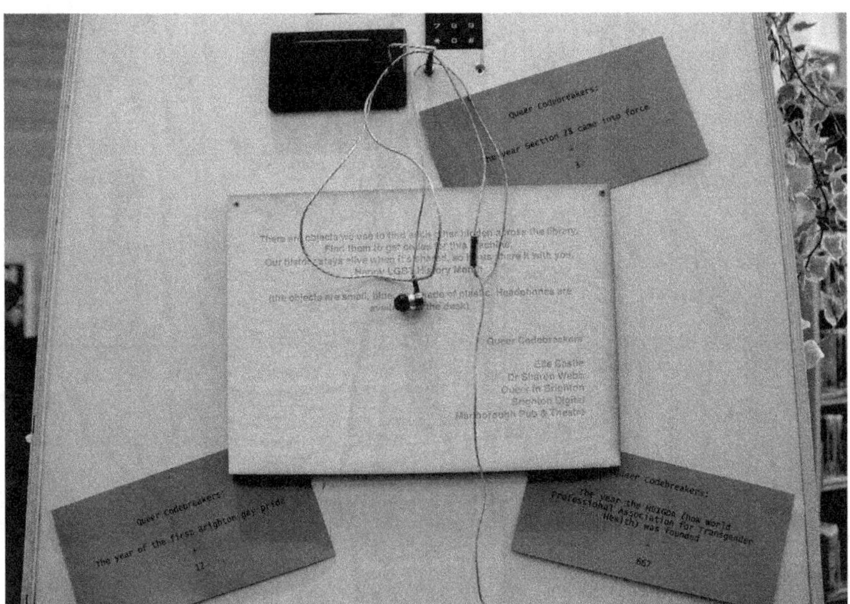

FIGURE 2.1. Queer Codebreakers 1.0 at Jubilee Library, Brighton, UK, February 2019. Image by Elia Habib, CC-BY-SA-NC 4.0.

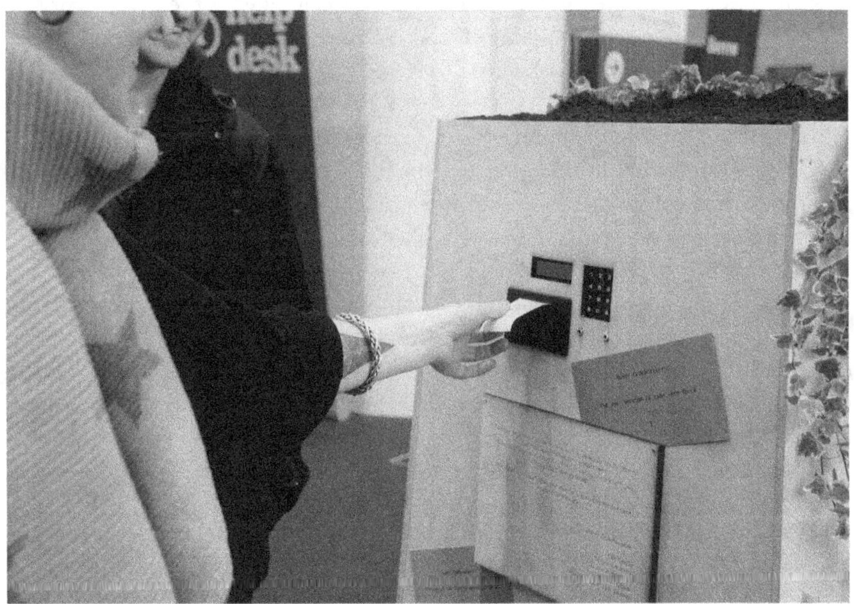

FIGURE 2.2. Queer Codebreakers 1.0, user retrieving a printed oral history extract, February 2019. Image by Elia Habib, CC-BY-SA-NC 4.0.

interesting questions about the meaning of memorials, collections and histories. . . . The idea of de-decommissioning or liberating something that is in a
museum or lodged in a hard drive under somebody's bed is very exciting, and
the digitals that we have make that a possibility, and the liberated artefacts
can have real world impact again. Recommissioning something that properly
belongs to a minority community is, I think, doubly important. (Hill, quoted
in Webb 2019: n.p.).

QC, and the community work to curate and archive, exemplifies this need to
recommission. The 'real world impact' of QC 1.0 was found in the user's engagement with the piece. In particular, at the launch event Webb and Castle spoke
with a number of LGBTQI+-identified young individuals who had gathered
around the piece. The group struggled to answer the question related to Section
28, the Conservatives' 1988 law that banned the promotion of homosexuality
by local authorities and schools in the United Kingdom – a significant moment
in LGBTQI+ history in the country. This prompted the group to search online
for answers. When they retrieved the correct code/answer, the machine printed
transcripts related to Section 28. Listening to and reading a real-life account
instantly reframed their experience of history and had a transformative effect on
their understanding and experience of that history – Section 28 was no longer an
abstract piece of legislation.

As an installation piece, QC 1.0 experimented with how oral history testimonies are presented to the public and explored ways to engage the community in
their collective narratives and stories. QC 1.0 showcased at the Jubilee Library,
Brighton, for four days in February 2019 (see figure 2.3). A year later, QC 2.0
launched during LGBT History Month 2020 as part of the 'Queer the Pier' exhibition at the Brighton Museum & Art Gallery (UK) (see figure 2.4).

QP is a unique exhibition that takes seriously the need to incorporate and
include diverse community voices in the curation process. An overarching aim
of the project was to create an inclusive, accessible exhibition for the queer community. It achieved this goal through a painstaking commitment to community
involvement in all aspects of the build, from design to curatorial decisions. Developed over the course of two years, the exhibition and its various elements were
conceived and built by a team of volunteers and led by head curator E-J Scott,
fashion historian and archivist. As a collaborative, community-led exhibition, it
explores the manifold histories of queer life in Brighton and centres queer representation around the famous Brighton Palace Pier. As the museum website states:

This community curated display peers into local LGBTIQA+ history.
Celebrating the lives of the writers, artists, performers, activists and ordinary
people who have made Brighton & Hove so fabulous, their stories are brought
to life with film and photography, fashion and drag and oral histories (n.d.:
n.p.).[2]

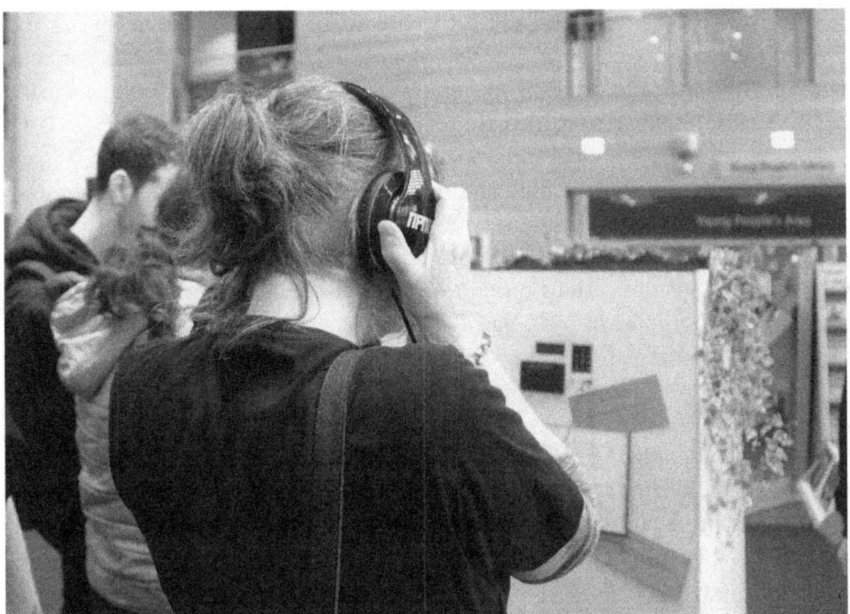

FIGURE 2.3. Queer Codebreakers 1.0, user listening to oral history audio, February 2019. Image by Elia Habib, CC-BY-SA-NC 4.0.

Upon entering the exhibition, visitors are presented with a black-and-white photo of Brighton pier dating from the early 1900s – the caption reads 'Who here on the pier isn't queer?' Scott, curator of QP and the exhibition it replaced, the Museum of Transology, uses this question as a point of reflection and a statement about assumed heteronormativity and queer erasure in history. It is in the context of this wider exhibition that QC 2.0 was developed.

While the functionality of QC 2.0 remains much the same – answer a question, enter the correct code to retrieve audio and/or text extracts from the Queer in Brighton archive – its context within the QP exhibition provided an opportunity to rethink the design and to review the functionality, specifically in terms of accessibility and usability. The technology running the software and hardware remained much the same as version 1.0. We use a Raspberry Pi microcomputer with an Arduino board to control the input and output, and the software was developed using the general-purpose programming language C++. The questions and answers are hard coded into the machine and are therefore stored locally for data-protection purposes, although only anonymised, edited, versions of the text and audio are stored. The Raspberry Pi is Wi-Fi enabled to support remote updates and maintenance, but the Wi-Fi is linked to a device belonging to a team member and thereby only accessible by the project team. User input and output devices include a simple numeric keypad for user input; a standard receipt printer to print out text snippets, with an easy mechanism to replace the printer roll; audio jacks and two sets of headphones. Since QC 2.0 contains significantly more audio files than version 1.0, and the machine will be in situ for over two years, we upgraded the microcomputer from a Raspberry Pi 3 to a 4. This upgrade supports additional storage and increases processing capacity, which stabilises the machine and reduces the risk of software failure and/or processing overload. In addition, we added a high-resolution display screen to present the questions, and a 1980s arcade-style button was added to allow users to scroll through the various questions related to queer history and objects in the exhibition. The inclusion of a high-resolution screen supports a richer user experience and enables the team to update and edit questions on display easily as required. The arcade button supports scrolling in one direction, reducing the complexity of the functionality and thereby making it more user-friendly. Another major upgrade was the casing for the hardware and the graphic design of the overall piece. In keeping with the exhibition's inspiration, Brighton Palace Pier, the casing is a 1980s-inspired arcade game, and the graphics, created by graphic designer Katy Knapp, take inspiration from Alan Turing's enigma machine (see figures 2.4 and 2.5). All combined, this creates a richer user experience as elements of the machine are intuitive and easily understood. Castle remained integral to the concept and build, but acknowledgement should also be made to Scott, Daren Kay (community curator and volunteer), Knapp, Alex Hawkey (designer at the Royal Pavilion & Museums) and not least Kelly Boddington (Royal Pavilion & Museums), who played a crucial coordinating role.

QC 2.0 incorporates objects from the QP exhibition and uses these as explicit reference points for users/visitors to engage with queer history. For example, the exhibition features a scanned copy of pages extracted from Anne Lister's coded diary, the text panel for which includes details of Lister's trip to Brighton in 1826. QC 2.0 includes a question related to this object – 'What year did Anne Lister stay in Brighton?' When the correct year/code is entered, the user/visitor retrieves curated extracts from the QIB collection, which relate to lesbian experiences in Brighton:

Interviewee: . . . some friends of mine who I met in university decided to move to Brighton, and I helped them move. So, I drove the moving van down with them, got to Brighton and I saw some lesbians holding hands on the seafront and I couldn't believe it. I couldn't believe it was safe enough to do that . . .

Interviewer: So actual live lesbians, actually holding hands, actually in public.

Interviewee: Yes, down the seafront. I couldn't believe it; I nearly crashed the van. It was incredible, I mean it was really startling, from going somewhere where you would hide your identity . . . to actually see lesbians holding hands brazenly in the middle of the day, down the seafront, was absolutely gob-smacking to me.

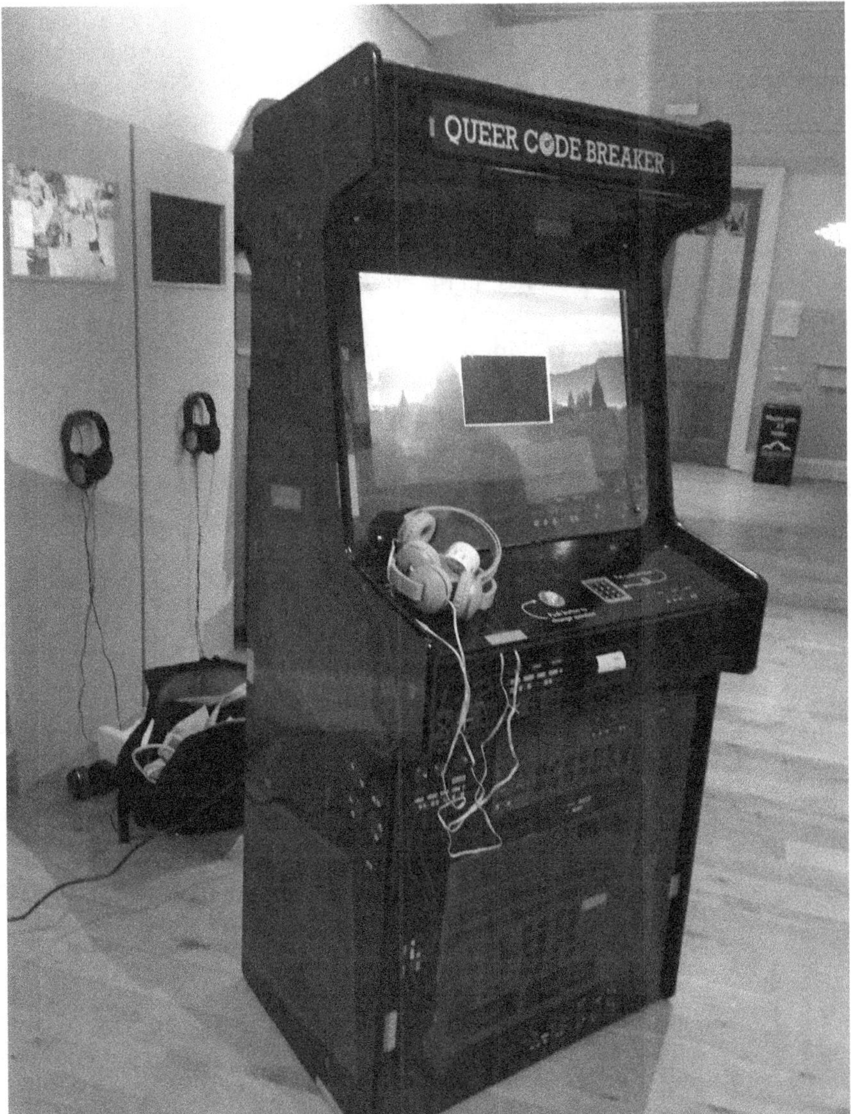

FIGURE 2.4. Queer Codebreakers 2.0 in situ at Brighton and Hove Museum and Gallery (prelaunch), February 2020. Image by the author.

QC 2.0 is a playful, interactive museum installation. It is a relatively simple concept and fairly low-tech build. Despite this, it is an unconventional concept that brings to life intangible heritage and supports a significant range of user engagement with objects, with histories and with archives, and connects all three. The concept of QC and its realisation exemplifies the need to support artistic experimentation and the importance of community engagement. QP, its aesthetic and realisation, would simply not exist without community engagement and involvement. In this regard, Queer in Brighton (Wood, Sheppeard and Roni Guetta), play a pivotal role in supporting and encouraging community members to engage in critical heritage work and experimentation. Initiatives lead by QIB, which include the 'Brighton LGBTQ+ History Club', garner immense community support and encourage wide engagement with local and regional queer histories. QP, and indeed QC 2.0, demonstrates a stated need for marginalised communities to be involved in the creation and presentation of their own histories.

The machine is an access point to the difficult, complex narratives of queer identity, culture and history. It, along with the QP exhibition, confronts previously 'othered' histories and connects museum objects and material culture with oral histories providing users with a rich, multimedia museum experience. Importantly, its development process has opened up a space for community members and volunteers to voice their priorities in terms of the machine's content. The curation process and the work to identify those priorities, as well as guiding curatorial principles, represent a crucial piece of work, which I describe in the next section.

QP launched on 22 February 2020, during LGBT History Month, and will remain in situ for two years. However, one month after the launch, the museum

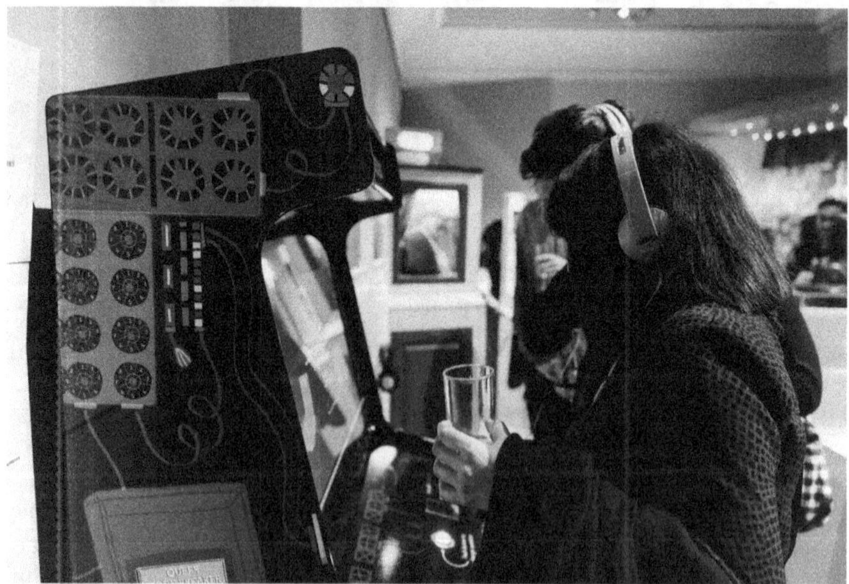

FIGURE 2.5. Queer Codebreakers 2.0, user listening to audio at 'Queer the Pier' launch event, February 2020. Image by Rosie Powell, CC-BY-SA-NC 4.0.

was forced to close because of COVID-19. The exhibition briefly reopened in October 2020 but was closed once again during the UK's third national lockdown (December 2020). At time of writing (July 2021) a lot of COVID-19 related restrictions have been lifted in the UK, and as such the exhibition and the Museum have reopened. However, restrictions remain in place to interactive exhibition pieces such as Queer Codebreakers. As an intervention in queer heritage, with multiple interactive pieces, and as a temporary exhibition that brings to the fore otherwise hidden objects and narratives, the exhibition and the community it represents are disproportionally affected by the closure – a timely reminder that access to public, queer community heritage is vulnerable and precarious.

Archiving and Curating Queer Histories

While QC 2.0 was a technical challenge, the biggest task was curating the oral history content. Content for QC 1.0 was curated by Elle Castle and the author in consultation with QIB. A diverse range of quotes and audio snippets were chosen, but content that identified third parties, which could cause potential harm or which might seem controversial to a non-queer audience, was excluded. When the opportunity to rebuild QC for the community-curated QP exhibition presented itself, it was decided that community members should be involved in the curation process, as such archiving and curating sessions were held to support this.

Archiving the QIB oral histories collection was, and still is, a political act, and as described in the first section a form of archival activism that informs cultural (re)production. In contrast to the objective framework professional archivists work within, QIB archiving sessions were more about listening to and embracing the stories and lived experiences of those interviewed. In many ways, archiving the collection became secondary to experiencing and listening to the queer voices captured in the collection. In the first archiving session (October 2018), participants were guided through the process of writing descriptive metadata (using standard Dublin Core fields) but were encouraged to think beyond the normalised and standardised 'systems and structures' of traditional archiving practices (Kumbier 2014: 3). They were asked to critically evaluate their role as archivist and curator and to consider what constitutes a queer archiving methodology. At a previous event (June 2018), participants were asked to imagine themselves as the subject of an oral history interview. This exercise provided a moment of reflection, allowing for participants to switch from passively consuming oral histories to embedding themselves, their emotions, their experiences into the oral history process. It prompted individuals to evaluate their role as a subject of an oral history interview and subsequently as an archivist of the same object. Thinking critically about how queer history has been documented in the past was an important aspect of these sessions. Participants were made aware of controlled vocabularies for metadata but were not required to use one. Instead, we explored the concept and discussed how some controlled vocabularies provide a limited, often unrepresentative set of terms for queer communities. For example, in the 'Humanities and Social Science Electronic Thesaurus' (HASSET), the preferred term for lesbian is 'female homosexual' – a term problematic for a number of reasons not least because it is trans exclusive and biologically reductionist. In contrast, Homosaurus, 'an international linked data vocabulary of Lesbian, Gay, Bisexual, Transgender, and Queer (LGBTQ) terms' linked to the Digital Transgender Archive, provides a more representative, comprehensive and inclusive list of controlled terms for queer communities and activity (Homosaurus n.d.: n.p.).[3]

Homosaurus 'is intended to function as a companion to broad subject term vocabularies, such as the Library of Congress Subject Headings' (Homosaurus n.d.: n.p.). It not only is more representative of the complexities of queer identity but also acknowledges a broader set of identity markers, including ethnicity, and makes visible sexual practices and acts, compared to other normalised and standardised 'systems and structures' that tend to completely erase these. The vocabulary is applicable to 'libraries, archives, museums, and other institutions . . . [who] . . . are encouraged to use Homosaurus to support LGBTQ research by enhancing the discoverability of their LGBTQ resources' (Homosaurus n.d.: n.p.). This discoverability problem is emblematic of historical categorisations, or lack thereof, of queer history in GLAM catalogues and descriptions. Workshop participants, many of whom are part of the queer community, were free to use their own terms and were able to reference other vocabularies, if necessary, since, as Sandell and Nightingale (2012: 143) assert, 'desire is chaotic and cannot be confined to neat binaries and tidy labels'.

Given the fact that the QIB oral history collection was not fully catalogued, workshop participants had no contextual or background information for the individual oral histories they listened to. Consequently, as they listened to interviews without any visual cues or written context, participants started to profile the voices they heard – assuming gender, ethnicity and other attributes of those speaking. This highlighted a series of unconscious and implicit biases as participants profiled the interviewees' voices based upon their own ethnicity and gender identity. It was not until interviewees explicitly mentioned their gender or ethnicity that participants, or community archivists, realised their bias. In this sense, while archiving and cataloguing prompts us to label for discoverability and reuse, in doing so we place an emphasis on labelling voices, to centre and align them with certain values and belief systems. As Bill Thompson, technology writer, highlights in *Archives Unlocked* (The National Archives 2017: n.p.):

The choices made as we add metadata will embody the beliefs of the archivists as much as the choice of items to preserve, and we must remember this and expose it, as we tell stories on the backs of these new collections. We have told ourselves stories in order to live: we can use a greater understanding of the choices that shape an archive to build ourselves catalogues that will help us thrive.

In this regard, the beliefs and values of the volunteer community archivists become part of the archive. They shape the archive and make editorial decision that influence the historical narrative and also provide crucial context that may otherwise go undocumented. DiVeglia (2012: 71) asserts that archivists determine 'points of access' through, for example, 'subject headings' and subject terms. Controlling these points of access represents a 'significant power over how and why materials will be used by researchers' (DiVeglia 2012: 71). In this sense, community members determine points of access for the QIB collection that may otherwise be omitted. For example, determining that an object (e.g. letter correspondence between two women) describes a 'lesbian relationship' instead of a 'female friendship' makes explicit the queer connotations and is an act of representation that is politically and culturally motivated. An archivist who isn't part of the queer community may not infer the object as such; therefore, working with the community takes the power of inference back to the community the object represents – the possibility of a 'lesbian relationship' is there, but the viewpoint or perspective of the archivist makes that determination. The power and means to control future use and future recognition of queer history is therefore disrupted and shifted when community members write their own records or are involved in the process. The metadata and archival descriptions become part of the archive's history, and community members embed themselves in the archival process. Their interpretations and summaries thereafter provide a glimpse of their priorities and values and are representative of the contemporary, queer moment.

In subsequent workshops, participants were asked to curate excerpts from the QIB oral histories for use in QC 2.0. In these sessions, participants were tasked with devising a list of archiving and curating principles. This task generated, perhaps unsurprisingly, a huge amount of debate and raised a number of challenges related to access and discussion about the nature of archives and the process of curating given the context. Queer history and queer experience contain references to sex, bodily function, protest, love, violence and illegal and illicit behaviour (at least deemed so by those outside of it) – it is messy, complicated and often traumatic. Given historical erasure of queer voices, participants wanted to ensure that oral history interviews were publicly available; however, they also held reservations about sharing information in non-queer spaces, like a public museum, that could be deemed sensitive by the community. They therefore oscillated between a commitment to open access on the one hand and a more restrictive approach to data access and archiving on the other. In this respect, a tension also emerged around the idea that we, as a queer community, were 'sanitising' our queer heritage in order for it to appear more palatable to a generic, public audience. Cvetkovich (2003: 5) reflects upon this de-sanitisation of queer culture in relation to the AIDS crisis and memorials, stating:

> The AIDS crisis offered clear evidence that some deaths were more important than others and that homophobia and, significantly, racism could affect how trauma was publicly recognized. I was not, for example, willing to accept a desexualized or sanitized version of queer culture as the price of inclusion within the national public sphere.

Cvetkovich's work informs a 'public culture around trauma' and makes visible 'the queer response to the ADIS crisis' (Cvetkovich 2003: 5). In a similar vein, the QIB collection includes personal stories of coming out, homophobic attacks, racism, transphobia, biphobia and ostracisation from family, from friends and from neighbourhoods. It includes recollections of protest, police brutality, prostitution and violence. Does this form a public culture centred on trauma? The oral histories represent personal as well as collective traumas, brought about through oppressive legislation like the Sexual Offences Act and Section 28. They also contain personal stories of love, friendship, community and camaraderie, of laughter as well as tears. In this sense, the oral histories represent an 'archive of feeling[s]' (Cvetkovich 2003). Archiving and curating such content is therefore an emotional and complex task.

Within the context of the Queer the Pier exhibition, the private realities and histories of individuals captured in the oral history testimonies become part of wider, public discourse and culture. But what happens when a once-private culture becomes public? When a culture that was once driven underground, through legislation and societal discrimination, is displayed in traditionally heteronormative settings – whose culture should be sanitised and disrupted, or indeed queered? Whose heritage are we representing? If community curators rule out or censor 'criminal' activity, then what of queer culture is dismissed? For example, cottaging, British slang for sex in a public toilet, was once part of the gay scene in Brighton and is described in some interviews. Do we leave this history out of a public exhibition? By selecting 'noncontroversial' material (and noncontroversial by whose standards?), are community curators sanitising, as Cvetkovich (2003: 5) asserts, a 'version of queer culture as the price of inclusion within the national public sphere'? Additionally, if we anonymise material, do we in effect erase queer voices? By censoring content for the public sphere, are we re-enacting and re-performing historical erasure?

As members of the queer community, we archive queer collections to make visible and to weave queer threads into the fabric of history. The archive, as an authentic representation, remains uncensored, and summary information and metadata should include the messiness, the complexities, the nonconformity and the queerness of the content it represents. In developing a digital archive, QIB can implement community protocols to access, acknowledging that the access needs of the community, the queer public, come first and the needs of the general public come second. By acknowledging the existence of two distinct audiences, a queer public and a general public, workshop participants were able to think through and define their curating principles based on the underlying understanding that the museum, as a whole, is not a queer space. In this regard, context and recontextualisation matter. Therefore, curating and selecting oral history testimonies for a public audience was seen not as an act of sanitisation or censoring but as an active curation method designed to respect the oral histories' participants and the context in which they were created. Curated oral history testimonies, and the community work involved, reflect queer culture and queer methodology. If QC were to feature in a queer-only space, then different materials or extracts would be used.

Additional points of discussion included whether a content warning should be displayed; this prompted the group to think about items in a museum and whether they are always age appropriate. Participants took the example of a Greek vase depicting male nudity – is it any different to presenting specifically gay imagery that includes nudity? Perhaps most importantly, the subject of trauma was raised from the perspective of those retelling their trauma and from those listening to or reading it. While not all of the oral histories are centred on trauma, the majority of the interviews explore aspects of the queer experience that can be traumatic – for example, coming-out stories that range from good to bad, stories of protest with both positive and negative public reactions, police brutality, and experiences of racism, homophobia, biphobia and transphobia in public, in the workplace and even among queer communities. There is an emotional labour in the retelling of these narratives, and equally, there is an emotional labour involved in listening to and reading them.

Informed by these discussions, the following curating and archiving working principles were established:

- Archive and curate with empathy; treat an individual's story in the same manner that you would expect someone to treat yours.
- Respect third parties mentioned in interviews and their right to anonymity. This is also a legal requirement under the EU's General Data Protection Regulations (GDPR).
- Consider the life course of the interviewee; individuals interviewed in 2012–14 may, for example, have transitioned since their original interview. Do not assume pronouns.

- Ensure that curated extracts are inclusive and that they reflect the diversity of perspectives, backgrounds, ethnicity and identity. Acknowledge gaps where they exist and question them.
- Assess the appropriateness of curated extracts, particularly in terms of trauma-informed narratives. Consider how a visitor might respond to listening to extracts that contain potentially triggering or retraumatising content. Additionally, consider how the original interviewee would feel hearing it played back in a public space.

These principles guided the curation process for QC 2.0. We selected extracts and developed questions for the machine that covered a broad range of topics, we removed references to third-party names (e.g. if someone mentioned their ex-partner's name, we edited the audio clip), and we assessed how curated extracts might be received by listeners to minimise the risk of (re)traumatisation. Oral history excerpts in QC 2.0 include discussions on lesbian life, bisexual identity and biphobia, gender identity and transitioning, QITPOC experiences of racism and feelings of exclusion from predominately white LGBTQI+ spaces, as well as drag performances and experiences of being 'queer in Brighton'. Importantly, the curated set includes an excerpt that discusses cottaging, a topic some community members were apprehensive about including. Recounting memories of Brighton in the early 1980s, one respondent describes cottaging spaces:

> Interviewee: [They were] like [a] club! If you went to the bushes . . . about 25–30 years ago . . . it was just like a club! Everyone knew each other, you used to take a flask and give everyone a cup of coffee and if there were sandwiches you would get given a sandwich and you could stay there all day and no one would ever bother you. (Queer in Brighton, 2012–14)

The interviewee describes these 'hook-up' spaces as a social environment that provided a much-needed social network for individuals who might otherwise feel isolated and without community. Cottaging is presented as a positive feature both of social life and of sexual liberation and freedom. The need for such spaces is indicative of the broader problem of social isolation, and of social and legislative marginalisation in the period described. Cottaging represents an aspect of queer culture and history, and its inclusion as a topic in the curated extracts was a political act that rejected the need to create desexualised or sanitised versions of queer history.

It is in this sense that we can view, both the machine, QC and the editing of oral history extracts, as well as the wider QP exhibition, as curatorial activism. Furthermore, if we take Kumbier's (2014: 3) definition of *queer* 'as a verb . . . [that] suggests a disruptive, transformational or oppositional practice designed to challenge normalizing systems and structures', then we should view these as forms of *queer* curatorial activism. These interventions explicitly disrupt and challenge heterocentrism in museum spaces and call for a re-evaluation of curation practices that are inclusive of community perspectives. In many respects, the technology used in, for example, QC is secondary to some of these factors. However, as a nonconventional museum piece, the machine is representative of forms of queer interventions that challenge and transform the inclusion of otherwise difficult histories or heritage. Although, we may ask, difficult for whom?

Conclusion

Heritage projects that use technology to make accessible and visible difficult heritage and histories provide necessary and critical interventions in museum spaces. They need not, however, be high-tech solutions. Instead, they should centre on the user experience and the histories they intend to share and on the communities they seek to represent. There is significant opportunity for the museum sector to support community archives and initiatives, such as 'Queer in Brighton', in their endeavours to become more than 'site[s] of preservation' (Eichhorn 2013: 4). But this engagement must acknowledge that significant support is required to ensure the long-term sustainability of such projects. We can ill afford to lose this precious material that counteracts institutional silences and gaps in the historical record.

Preserving queer voices, captured in the contemporary moment, supports ongoing community development and makes a significant contribution to LGBTQI+ heritage. This work recentres the margins and makes them visible to the mainstream. These cultural interventions, online, in the library and in the museum, are 'acts of activism in the present', and they demand attention in the face of historical institutional neglect (Eichhorn 2013: 2). They are also acts of reclamation and subversion, and they demonstrate the utility, as well as the necessity, for museum and other public memory institutions to rethink their engagement with queer histories and narratives, and indeed with other marginalised groups and communities. 'Queer Codebreakers' unlocks queer stories and voices in the archive and encourages broader interactions with queer history and heritage, because, as Castle asserts on the machine's plaque, 'our stories stay alive when they are shared' (see figure 2.1, QC 1.0). But we must acknowledge that community heritage groups and archives require support to ensure these voices are heard in the future. 'Queer Codebreakers', the machine, will require maintenance. In fact, the machine's technology may be more fragile than the printed words it generates – a fact that reminds us of the precariousness of our digital cultural heritage. Given the fragility of the digital medium, community archives and the content they generate are at risk of permeant and irreversible loss. Therefore, digital cultural heritage work across the GLAM sector must come with a commitment to long-term digital preservation and support to ensure the preservation of queer and other marginalised voices and histories.

Acknowledgements

The author would like to acknowledge funding from the British Academy, Rising Star Engagement Award and the Sussex Humanities Lab as a financial contributor to Queer Codebreakers 2.0.

Sharon Webb is a lecturer in digital humanities at the University of Sussex, History Department, and a director of the Sussex Humanities Lab. Sharon is a historian of Irish associational culture and nationalism and a digital humanities practitioner with a background in requirements/user analysis, digital preservation, digital archiving, text encoding and data modelling. Sharon's current research interests include community archives and digital preservation, with a special interest in LGBTQI+ archives, techno-feminism and intersectional digital humanities.

Notes

1. For example, see the Victoria and Albert Museum's LGBTQ Working Group, who "unearth previously hidden or unknown LGBTQ histories in the collections" (available at https://www.vam.ac.uk/info/lgbtq).
2. See https://brightonmuseums.org.uk/brighton/exhibitions-displays/queer-the-pier/ for more details.
3. See https://homosaurus.org for more details.

References

Adair, Joshua G., and Amy Levin K. (eds). 2020. *Museums, Sexuality, and Gender Activism*. New York: Routledge.

Ashton, Jenna. 2017. 'Feminist Archiving [a Manifesto Continued]: Skilling for Activism and Organising', *Australian Feminist Studies* 32: 126–49.

Billey, Amber, and Emily Drabinski. 2019. 'Questioning Authority: Changing Library Cataloging Standards to Be More Inclusive to a Gender Identity Spectrum', *Transgender Studies Quarterly* 6:117–23.

Bly, Lyz, and Kelly Wooten (eds). 2012. *Make Your Own History: Documenting Feminist and Queer Activism in the 21st Century*. Los Angeles: Litwin Books.

Browne, Kath, and Leela Bakshi. 2016. *Ordinary in Brighton? LGBT, Activisms and the City.* London: Routledge.

Castle, Elle. 2018. 'Covert Queer Codebreakers'. Unpublished proposal submission.

Caswell, Michelle. 2014. 'Seeing Yourself in History: Community Archives and the Fight against Symbolic Annihilation', *The Public Historian* 36(4): 26–37.

Cvetkovich, Ann. 2003. *An Archive of Feelings: Trauma, Sexuality, and Lesbian Public Cultures.* Durham, NC: Duke University Press.

Digital Preservation Coalition. 2019. 'The Bit List of Digitally Endangered Species'. Retrieved 15 July 2020 from https://www.dpconline.org/our-work/bit-list.

Digital Repository of Ireland. 2014. 'DRI Factsheet No 4: Long-Term Digital Preservation'. Dublin: Digital Repository of Ireland. Retrieved 15 July 2020 from https://repository.dri.ie/catalog/rr17fc082.

DiVeglia, Angela L. 2012. 'Accessibility, Accountability, and Activism: Models for LGBT Archives'. Master's thesis, University of North Carolina. Retrieved 15 July 2020 from https://cdr.lib.unc.edu/concern/masters_papers/hx11xj81s.

Doan, Laura. 2017. 'Queer History Queer Memory: The Case of Alan Turing', *Journal of Lesbian and Gay Studies* 23(10): 113–36.

Egan, Orla. 2015. 'Dublin Core for LGBT Digital Archive'. Retrieved 15 July 2020 from https://orlaegan.wordpress.com/2015/11/30/dublin-core-for-lgbt-digital-archive/.

Eichhorn, Kate. 2013. *The Archival Turn in Feminism: Outrage in Order.* Philadelphia: Temple University Press.

Furber, Tom. 2017. 'Speak Out London Diversity City: London Metropolitan Archives', *Social History in Museums* 41: 11–18. Retrieved 15 July 2020 from http://www.shcg.org.uk/domains/shcg.org.uk/local/media/downloads/SHCG_eJournal_41.pdf.

High, Steven. 2018. 'Listening across Difference: Oral History as Learning Landscape', *LEARNing Landscapes* 11: 39–48.

Homosaurus. 2020. 'Homosaurus Vocabulary Terms'. Retrieved 15 July 2020 from https://homosaurus.org.

Jastrzebska, Maria, and Anthony Luvera (eds). 2014. *Queer in Brighton.* Brighton: New Writing South.

Kaplan, Elisabeth. 2000. 'We Are What We Collect, We Collect What We Are: Archives and the Construction of Identity', *American Archivist* 63(1): 126–51.

Kumbier, Alana. 2014. *Ephemeral Material – Queering the Archive.* Sacramento: Litwin Books.

Lee, Jamie A. 2017. 'A Queer/ed Archival Methodology: Archival Bodies as Nomadic Subjects', *Journal of Critical Library and Information Studies* 1(2): 1–27. Retrieved 15 July 2020 from https://journals.litwinbooks.com/index.php/jclis/article/view/26/24.

National Archives. 2017. *Archives Unlocked – Releasing the Potential.* London. Retrieved 15 July 2020 from https://www.nationalarchives.gov.uk/documents/archives/Archives-Unlocked-Brochure.pdf.

Portellii, Alessandro. 1998. 'What Makes Oral History Different' in Robert Perks, and Alistair Thomson (eds), *The Oral History Reader.* New York: Routledge.

Sandell, Richard, and Eithne Nightingale. 2012. *Museums, Equality and Social Justice.* London: Routledge.

UK Data Service. n.d. *HASSET Vocabulary.* Retrieved 15 July 2020 from https://hasset.ukdataservice.ac.uk/.

Vincent, John. 2014. *LGBT People and the UK Cultural Sector: The Response of Libraries, Museums, Archives and Heritage since 1950.* Surrey: Ashgate.

Watts, Gina. 2018. 'Queer Lives in Archives: Intelligibility and Forms of Memory', *disClosure: A Journal of Social Theory* 27: 103–11. Retrieved 15 July 2020 from https://doi.org/10.13023/disclosure.27.15.

Webb, Sharon. 2018. '"Digital Archives in Communities – Practice and Preservation": A Summary (or at Least an Attempt)'. Digital Preservation Coalition. Retrieved 15 July 2020 from https://dpconline.org/blog/digital-archives-in-communities.
———. 2019. 'Queer Codebreakers – Preserving Community Archives'. Retrieved 15 July 2020 from http://preservingcommunityarchives.co.uk/blog-post/queer-codebreakers/.
X. Ajamu, Topher Campbell and Mary Stevens. 2010. 'Love and Lubrication in the Archives, or rukus!: A Black Queer Archive for the United Kingdom', *Archivaria* 68: 271–94.

Chapter 3

Women's Metadata, Semantic Web, Ontologies and AI

Potentials in Critically Enriching Carl Sahlin's Industrial History Collection

Anna Foka, Jenny Attemark and Fredrik Wahlberg

Introduction, Background and Aim

In the past two decades, museums and archival institutions have seen unprecedented technological innovations in collections management. Whether technology is used for archiving or curating it has transformed curation and public engagement (Prescott and Hughes 2018). This transformation now extends beyond basic digitisation – the conversion of analogue collections to digital, including related collections management – to digitalisation: the application of digital technologies to enhance data engagement, thus initiating a deeper, core change to curation and information organisation models. This introduction of digitalisation raises new questions on dominant historical, national narratives and organisational legacies (Lowenthal 2015; Smith 2006). While information technology (IT) has revolutionised theoretical possibilities to understanding the human contexts that historical archives carry and to 'democratising' collections (Geismar 2018; Prescott and Hughes 2018), practice proves otherwise (Risam 2018; Thylstrup 2019; Wu 2020). Cultural heritage or other archival collections are made by humans in past lifeworlds and therefore contain critical human narratives (Westin, Foka and Chapman 2018: 283–86). The lack of meaningful and inclusive digitalisation practices risks creating a chasm between collections and curatorial practices (Aldrich 2009: 137–56; Reilly and Lippard 2018).

Digitalisation thus raises new questions around epistemologies, ethics and policy regulations. With emerging technologies such as artificial intelligence (henceforth AI),[1] being mathematical models, there are additional concerns around machine understanding and model interpretation. Mathematical models are systems that have been successfully applied to describe disparate natural phenomena to an unreasonable degree: for example, Newtonian gravity describes both the stability of an arch bridge and the movement of galaxy clusters (Wigner 1960). This success of mathematical modelling has led to important discoveries for humanity. What is not obvious is whether mathematical descriptive models can facilitate the interpretation and curation of diverse human artefacts. In AI, all models are descriptive and approximate, but also quantitative. These models are able to imitate human descriptions, such as the presence of a particular person in a photograph. Given the explosion of available data, mathematical descriptive models have become more accurate in their respective restricted contexts (Halevy, Norvig and Pereira 2009). Connecting the equations and learned parameters to the qualitative aspects of any historical data is an underexplored field – an emerging technology. As such, AI cannot be relied upon for ethically and reliably curating a collection, but it can be of great help in structuring it. The imitation property of an AI algorithm allows for human annotators to change taxonomies (or even work with several in parallel) while letting the computer do the heavy lifting of applying it to a collection. Recently, great strides have been made in letting the AI discover themes in text corpora or finding and differentiating between thousands of objects in images. Even today we have systems that can estimate the year of writing in some collections of manuscripts by using pattern recognition to measure the shape of characters (Wahlberg, Mårtensson and Brun 2016).

Against this backdrop, this chapter moves beyond claims of digital technology alone as means for democratisation of knowledge, by focusing on women's history archival online repositories, targeting a Swedish case study: the collection of the industry leader Carl Sahlin (1861–1943), donated to the National Museum of Science and Technology in Stockholm and digitised within the nationally funded project Digital Models (2016–19). Carl Sahlin was a notorious Swedish business leader and an industry historian, and while the archive is in many ways representative of the twentieth-century history of the Swedish mining industry, women, in Sahlin's collection, often remain invisible. In doing so, our research project examined not only other initiatives and projects on gendered archiving but also current trends in terms of library, information and data science.

The chapter then zooms in to women's presence in Carl Sahlin's collection and discusses the affordances and complexities that arise with its digitisation. We argue that enriching archival collections with metadata is a negotiating process that has the potential to illuminate women's history collections by constituting them as searchable and therefore visible. Ultimately, this chapter contributes a methodology for collection enrichment, including the possibilities and pitfalls of using emerging technologies, specifically AI for classification and enrichment to initiate new critical questions about historical women. Alongside a well-thought metadata ontology, we emphasise the importance of data interoperability in semantic web environments in order to best synthesise and make searchable archival evidence on women's histories for future research. This vision is based on the core assumption that the cultural heritage sector could be benefited by a collaboration between scholarly and technological expertise that both captures and produces more nuanced perspectives around the enrichment of collections and knowledge generation by allowing researchers and the audience to become part of the curatorial process, connecting collections with wider knowledge networks outside of galleries, libraries, archives and museums (often referred to by the acronym GLAM).

(Gendered) Archives in the Digital Age: New Epistemological and Technological Challenges

The study and creation of archives that illuminate women's histories with the purpose of promoting gender equality is growing (for feminist historiography, cf. Severson 2018). Its beginning precedes digital technology and appears as early as 1935, when the World Center for Women's Archives was founded, particularly regarding marginalised groups (Lubelski 2014). The most eloquent example is the Women's History Databases hosted by Harvard University. The collection contains a number of databases that relate to American women's history, such as the American Consumer database; Everyday Life and Women in America, 1800–1920; Gerritsen Collection – Women's History Online, 1543–1945; Women and Social Movements in the United States: 1600–2000; and Women Working, 1800–1930. Especially within the context of European historical archives, women and minorities had their histories and experiences marginalised or even forgotten, and cultural heritage institutions are often part of this process (Lowenthal 2015). Trends such as the Herstory[2] and curatorial activism aim to remedy this (Reilly and Lippard 2018). The cultural heritage sector today embraces intersectionality by inquiring and promoting concepts of gender (Reading 2015), LGBT (lesbian, gay, bisexual and transgender) and Queer Studies (Reilly and Lippard 2018), as well as ethnic and religious minorities (Silverman 2011). Drawing on theories of intersectionality for collection management (Grahn 2011: 222–50) and focusing on gender as a social construct (Levin 2010) are pivotal to any archival research.

From 1980s onwards, feminist museology has brought forward the complexity of issues that arise with the portrayal of cultural notions of gender in museum discourse and in terms of materiality more generally (Alaimo and Hekman 2008;

Bergsdóttir 2016). The Sahlin collection is no exception and thus posed a similar challenge. New forms of digital inquiry have further begun to challenge archival science (Asberg et al. 2015). To uncover and to comprehend how digital technology may illuminate gender in digital archive research, an archive should be digitally transduced with critical questions in mind. In Sweden there are a number of notable platforms that focus on historical materials about gender. These include the Women's Journals database (KvinnSam) and the Gender and Works Database (GaW) that are hosted by the University of Gothenburg and Uppsala University respectively. The GaW repository contains primarily handwritten documents and KvinnSam typewritten text and historical press – yet independent of content or media format, archival categorisation is perceived through the lens of gender (Foka 2019).

The incentive for digitising any historical collections in Sweden since 2016 should ideally comply with the FAIR data principles, as provided by the SND, the Swedish National Data Service.[3] The SND is composed of an academic consortium of a number of institutions that set those guidelines in collaboration. FAIR is an acronym that stands for findable, accessible, interoperable and reusable data. The FAIR principles focus primarily on machine readability but also aim at targeting a human understanding of research data, thus enabling possibilities for reusability. According to the Swedish government incentive, findable research data are assigned a unique and persistent identifier.[4] The openness of historical data is therefore admittedly pivotal to any historical research. With linked open data there is no need for a human to interpret how one piece of data is linked to another – a machine may answer these complex questions online. This presents us with additional epistemological and technological complexities: not only do ICT scholars need to consider how data is linked, but cultural heritage professionals and humanities' scholars now also need to consider how best to enrich online materials to articulate the multivocality of datasets that have been built as manifestations of dominant spatial, gender, ethnicity and status master narratives. Digital and humanities-driven cultural heritage data ontologies ought to be thought through a multitude of humanities and social sciences disciplines, beyond ICT.

The Complexity of a Man-Made Historical Archive

Carl Sahlin (1861–1943) was a Swedish businessman, distinguished industry historian and metallurgist. His historical collection contains about eighteen hundred archive capsules of mining history from the mid-eighteenth century and up to the 1930s. Unpacking and revealing gender in the collection was the first challenge; the complexities that arose when we moved onto digitalisation – the digital organisation and enrichment of the collection – presented us with additional issues that we then had to resolve. The archive itself was an illustration of the exclusion of ethnic diversity and social classes – an issue that is very common in historical heritage archival and heritage collections more generally (Porter 1988). The work of less prominent or foreign women who, for example, offered domestic help to industrial workers and their families has been more or less absent in exhibitions and archival collections, and the Carl Sahlin archive was no exception. The archive, which was donated to the museum in the 1930s, had no thematic categories that relate to women at all. Sahlin's own categorisation list corresponded to an organisational manner in which women were not separately listed. Within this list, there is no mention of women at all, other than perhaps 'Workers and their Families'. In spite of this, Sahlin's archive reflects how he saw his female contemporaries, their lives and activities. During Sahlin's time, labour in Sweden was still largely gendered. It followed early modern models of partnership of working-class families based on mining, agriculture and crafts.

To unveil women in the archive, the project team took several concrete steps in the process. First, Sahlin's archive was examined, precisely targeting scholarship in critical heritage and gender studies and identifying the stark need for women's visibility in historical archives at a time where women are largely invisible from public discourse. Research on women in the past has often argued that women have mainly been presented as subordinate and inferior (Dermineur 2018). The archival norm is that women's roles have been 'hidden'. Household and unpaid work were simply concealed or ignored by (male) officials, so studying these was considered obscure (Ågren 2012). Second, Sahlin's archive was then assessed: it was a mix of pictures, magazines, books, photographs, maps and handwritten and printed text. Third, digitisation and digitalisation practices such as digital rendering, interface, organisation, and enrichment of historical data have also added an additional layer of inquiry by using digital tools to taxonomise and to reveal concepts of critical cultural heritage (see Bergsdóttir 2016).

Our engagement with the Sahlin archive unearthed a number of interesting data. Status appeared overall to be the most important point of reference, and by looking at the archive one can identify that queens' visits to mines were of major political importance. In Sahlin's own documentation, Swedish queen Ulrika Eleonora's 1732 visit to Falun, for example, comes across as a typical prosopography (see figure 3.1). In adding a queen's visit to the mining history archive, Sahlin overall justifies the individual, prominent woman and the diplomatic importance of Swedish queens for Sweden's economic history.

While the higher status of Swedish queens in comparison to other women is something that is agreed upon among contemporary gender and economic history experts (Dermineur 2017) women of lower status are usually found in Sahlin's archive as oppositional narratives, or they are completely discarded. Quite often, data about women in Sahlin's archive are revealed because they are minor

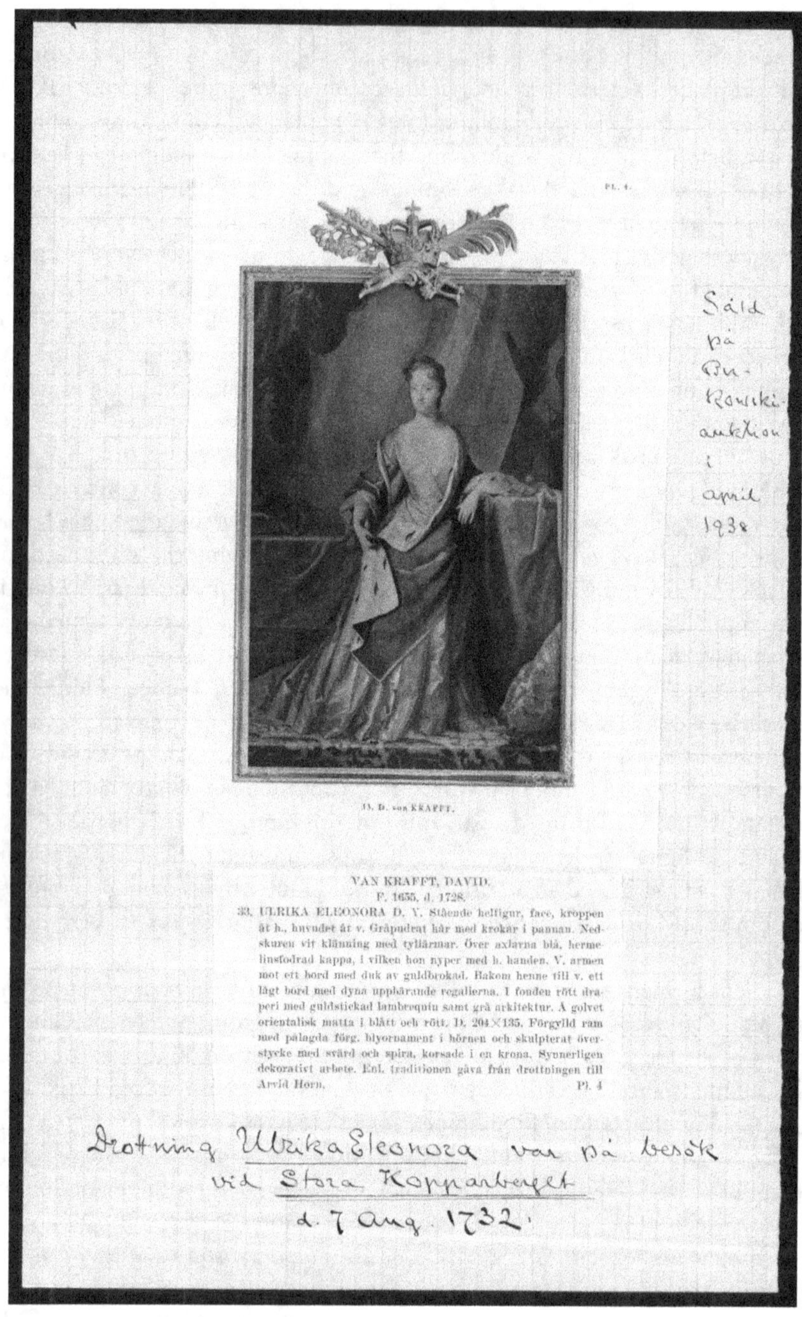

FIGURE 3.1. Queen Ulrika's prosopography from the Sahlin collection with notes from Carl Sahlin himself, available online CS-F1-340-1 012, Creative Commons Attribution 2.0 Generic license.

narratives in a man's story. One prominent example relates to the legendary man "Fet-Mats" (Mats Israelsson), who died by accident from asphyxia in the Falun copper mine in 1677. He vanished one day, and his body was nowhere to be found. The story became a sensation after his body was discovered in 1719, petrified due to the lack of oxygen in the mines, and put on display in Falun for the years to come, inspiring even a Wagner opera at the time. The body was identified by his former fiancée, Margaret Olsdotter, who, as a female figure of lower status and a worker in the mining industry, only became visible in the Sahlin archive because of the man she was associated with (see Foka 2019). In that sense, aside gender, status had to be taken into consideration when digitising. Emphasis was naturally put into enriching materials on prominent women, whereas the stories of less prominent females remained invisible even within the archive.

Additionally, different media formats are present in the archive. The variety of different media made it difficult to implement a coherent digitisation strategy in relation to gender within the Sahlin archive. In this light, given the overall large volume of the collection, digitisation activities followed certain geographies, more specifically areas with factories and mines. After contemplation on the costs and the invariable results of using optical character recognition (thereon OCR) for the electronic recognition of handwritten texts into machine-encoded text, in order to facilitate data entry, the decision was made to actually only digitise printed and typewritten texts (magazines and contracts) and pictures (photographs, maps and paintings). There were also other complexities in the process of digitisation that hindered mass-digitisation of the entirety of the archive; for instance, old hand-painted maps from Gammelbo could not be sent away from the museum because of their delicate quality. The team singled out fifteen archive capsules from the Sahlin archive. These were digitised by different companies in order to compare quality. The private company Devo digitised two capsules from the Sahlin archive and later the national Media Conversion Centre, an initiative of the Swedish National Archive, scanned the majority of the selected archival material. Digitised documents were then inserted into the National Science and Technology Museum's internal database Primus. It was also decided to create a link to the outward database DigitaltMuseum, thus enhancing the media affordance of the materials with visibility to the museum as well as open access to the public.

To conclude, during 2018, a total of almost forty-six thousand items from the Sahlin archive became accessible to the public via DigitaltMuseum. Making gender a structuring principle was a more complex endeavour. As Sahlin did not envision his archive in gendered terms, it became difficult to imagine a novel, gender-illuminating version of his archive. Nevertheless, options for enrichment proved useful in revealing some aspects of gender in this vast and complex archive of nineteenth- and twentieth-century Swedish industrial history.

Emerging Technologies, or Is AI Sexist?

AI technologies are not yet used predominantly for archival science. The reason is that AI models are still immature, requiring infrastructure, time-consuming maintenance, construction and training. However, with the ever-increasing volumes of digital collections, AI has the potential to truly revolutionise archival science. The potential to construct machines that could model and make decisions on their own was formalised in the mid-twentieth century, initiating today's models inspired by the biological brain (Rosenblatt 1958). The inferences made by these models were not hard coded by humans but learned from data, though they were constrained to certain families of flexible mathematical models. However, a drawback was their computational cost, making them a nonviable alternative to more hard coded approaches until the last couple of decades. The descriptive nature of these models is often encapsulated by the quote 'All models are wrong, but some are useful', mentioned at least once in every course on the subject (Box 1976). With the tagged information in some collections being the approximate guess of a human annotator, machine tagging is an imitation of the human annotator together with some generalising and learned prior 'knowledge', to the extent made possible by the underlying mathematics. The qualitative understanding of more successful and more complex models – sometimes referred to as 'black box' models – is opaque to the user. This leads to problems when applying these AI models to artifacts or objects where qualitative aspects that cannot be quantitatively approximated are the focus. Models do not comprehend the data in a human sense but concern themselves only with a mathematical representation of the world. This lack of transparency in the underlying model, and, consequently, our ability to identify dangerous edge cases, is why some models can have better-than-human capacity in identifying malignant skin growths in an image yet can also fail to be approved for clinical use (Esteva et al. 2017).

Due to the nature of creating a collection of anything human-made, cultural and social bias will be present in the material and thus embedded into the AI model. As machine learning gives the computer the ability to learn statistical relations by itself, the responsibility for ethical performance is often pushed from algorithm development to the process of collecting and annotating data. An illustrating example is how word embeddings, a core part of modern machine translation, can reproduce sexist stereotypes. A word embedding is a high-dimensional vector space representation of words where a distance metric can be trained to correlate with a qualitative semantic 'distance' between words (Firth 1957) (e.g. a geometry where 'car' is closer to 'truck' than 'dolphin'). This is done by letting an AI process huge amounts of text, find words and work out similar contexts (Mikolov et al. 2013). This follows from a distributional interpretation of semantics often described as 'you know a word by the company it keeps'. The modern classic paper 'Man Is to Computer Programmer as Woman Is to Homemaker', where the authors look at word embedding relations, illustrates this with its title (Bolukbasi et al. 2016). In the learned embedding space, when the 'work' relation, found between the 'man' and 'programmer', was applied to 'woman', the machine found the concept 'homemaker'. AI has no moral or human understanding of what words entail in a social context. AI is based on correlations so if the data contains sexist stereotypes, the algorithm will likely pick up on those. A significant body of literature exists in trying to 'de-bias' embeddings from irrelevant or detrimental relations (Vanmassenhove Hardmeier and Way 2019). Turning this obvious problem into a strength, the data material does not have to explicitly state the woman-to-homemaker relation. This relation is inferred from context, opening up possibilities to look beyond the explicitly stated (or clearly visible) to find more 'hidden' relations between artefacts, e.g. finding families of semantic use across collections of letters. Another example is the ever-evolving language of hate speech, where dedicated users might find euphemisms or variations for words that become socially unacceptable that only the 'initiated' can recognise. Given enough data, a semantic embedding can pick up on new usage or re-emergence of words taking the place of the old word (e.g. in the context of a less subtle dog whistle where one word has simply replaced another).

For almost a decade, neural networks have been the dominant way of recognising heterogeneous objects in images (Krizhevsky, Sutskever and Hinton 2012; He et al. 2014). There are two major factors that have made this possible: increased computing power and the availability of data. These models have been extended to be able to infer relations between objects, generate natural language descriptions of the image content (Karpathy and Fei-Fei, 2015) and treat labelling as a taxonomy (Esteva et al. 2017). These neural models require millions of parameters, making qualitative interpretations hard on the numbers level. However, significant work has been done on trying to make the model tell the user where it draws its information from, so-called 'explainable AI'. A popular technique called 'neural attention' gives the model the ability to clearly show where in an image or text document information is drawn for a specific part of a translation or recognition (Bahdanau, Cho and Bengio 2014; Xu et al. 2015). An example is how an image-captioning system describes an image that could be described as, 'A child, with long hair and dressed in a skirt and shirt, holding an umbrella jumps in front of a steel bench with a brick wall in the background and terracotta gravel'. The system inferred the sentence 'a *little girl* sitting on a *bench* holding an *umbrella*' (italics show the main words focused on by the AI model). Some objects (girl, bench, umbrella) and relations (in front, above) were recognised but the sentence context is inferred by statistically conditioning on the recognised objects from some larger general text corpus (Lu et al. 2017). Hence, the long-haired child in a skirt is assigned a female gender. Though likely correct in a maximum likelihood sense, the autogenerated description cannot currently be trusted to make the final call for archival descriptions in complex and historical socio-cultural contexts. Given the growth of digital archival data, often with large photo collections, this technology provides a potential for searching that would require huge undertakings if done through only tagging and metadata.

Not all AI models are created equal, and some families of machine learning models are better suited for linking equations to qualitative aspects of the data. In recent years, topic models have been increasingly popular in digital humanities and the social science scholars (Blei 2012; Meeks and Weingart 2012; Wiedemann and Wiedemann 2016). In these models, each document in a collection is treated as a mixture of different content topics or themes, where each topic (and their number) is identified by the AI model. This can be a completely machine-driven process (i.e. unsupervised learning) or guided by a human annotator (Wang et al. 2016). The result is a soft clustering of the documents under a number of content topics. Currently, the dominant approach for topic modelling is based on Bayesian statistics (Blei, Ng and Jordan 2003). Bayesian topic models lend themselves well to qualitative interpretation in the sense that most of the parameters and model parts have real-world equivalents. They also allow for overlapping categorisations and quantification of attribution uncertainty. This goes far beyond the binary approach of standard tagging practices and is more suited for archival collections where categorisation usually is highly ambiguous.

To conclude, scholarship shows how the reproduction of human tagging, or metadata enrichment in AI technologies, raises important ethical and practical questions for GLAMs (Ashar and Cortesi 2018). With increased awareness and regulations about data usage in wider society, GLAMs have approached AI with caution (Padilla 2019; Stark and Crawford 2019). There is also a lack of digital expertise and funds available for most museums to engage in digital developments (Murphy and Villaespesa 2020). But given the extraordinary increase of collection data, exploring, critiquing and understanding the usability, sustainability and ethical implications of AI within a GLAM context is becoming an increasingly pressing need. Human-centred approaches to AI serve the dual objective of aiding human understanding of AI processing systems while enriching the technology with better (human) capabilities and knowledge on diverse user perspectives. This two-way relationship is essential to developing accurate and sensitive AI, which can be deployed in a data context as complex and nuanced as the digital curation of heritage collections. Developing ethical and inclusive AI is as much about building ethical principles into AI processing systems as it is about enabling human users to use AI systems ethically and with diversity and inclusion in mind.

Unveiling by Digital Organisation and Enrichment: Zooming in Ebba Augusta Hägerflycht as a Female Foundry Proprietor

Scholarship on women and the industry argues that women's presentation within the workforce has been, in its majority, presented as 'subordinate and inferior in the nexus of labour and economics' (Dermineur 2018: 10–29). In early modern Europe, women's finances are historically delineated in context and by factors such as resources, skills, and status. A woman's work, its type and form, locations and structures have, therefore, been largely gendered and dependent on status. Indeed, this is evident in Carl Sahlin's archive, where women have been, in many ways, absent from records of the workforce. In order to enrich documents that contain information about women, in that light, the archive or database needed to be made searchable by keyword. We studied the best approach to unearth gender in the archive, to crowdsource a simple model of semantic tagging of the selected digitised capsules – based on aforementioned categories such as status, age and social role. An envisioned ontology for tagging was then created, with a metadata structure where critical and relevant subcategories would be applicable. In doing so, and given the complexity of semantic web environments as well as the Swedish government requirements for open research data as identified above, we proceeded in enriching the archives utilising both URIs (Uniform Resource Identifiers) and persistent URLs (Uniform Resource Locators).[5] The terms are related in the sense that a URI can be a name, locator or both for an online resource where a URL is simply the locator – in other words an actual web location. A URL is a subset of URIs. While all URLs are URIs, not all URIs are URLs. For example, the name Ebba Augusta Hägerflycht can be a URI because it identifies the person, but a URL is, for example, the web page that refers to her genealogy.[6] This URL then is both a URI and a URL as it both identifies the person as well as providing a web location. In using both URIs and URLs when enriching an archival item we ensure that data is open, accessible for verification and re-use and even interoperable, thus maximising the technical affordances of an item, and in turn its social affordance, following the FAIR Guiding Principles for scientific data management and stewardship. The principles emphasise machine actionability (i.e. the capacity of computational systems to find, access, interoperate and reuse data with none or minimal human intervention) because humans increasingly rely on computational support to deal with data as a result of the increase in volume, complexity and creation speed of data.

Generating a plan for open data access allows us to outline how data may be preserved and to determine the nature of the metadata we collect and organise. The European Commission's principles make research data, methods, guidelines, reports and products broadly available to the public under CC0 1.0 and CC BY 4.0 licenses while protecting confidential participant information.[7]

Given the nature of the archive itself and in relation to our critical heritage approach with a focus of unearthing, organising, enriching and thus making searchable data about historical women, the first category of structured URI data would be:

'Persons' in which subcategories would be as applicable:
1. Name – or names before and after matrimony – including relevant open URLs as applicable
2. Gender
3. Age, by which the information could be described as relative (for example twenty-six years old) or absolute (mid-twenties), or different ages referring to this particular archival item if there is more than one description of age
4. Citizen status (referring to the countries of origin or placement, by proxy)
5. Social status (married, widowed, single, unidentified/other)
6. Professional status (position, property)

'Place' in which several subcategories would be applicable, such as:
1. Geographic information mentioned, such as place names, including co-ordinates, if available
2. Geographic information related to events (see above)

In relation to space – and given that there is a number of structured vocabularies for space (although there is no Scandinavian one), otherwise known as space gazetteers (Barker, Foka and Konstantinidou 2020; Foka et al. 2020) – an option here is to include the URLs from the global gazetteer Geonames.[8] The process enables interoperability with other resources (Geonames) and actual geographic coordinates when applicable.

'Time' in which several subcategories would be applicable, such as:
1. Relative historical date, including chronology: for example, nineteenth century
2. Absolute historical date (if available): for example, 1867

In relation to studying and organising time, there is a number of structured vocabularies, with the most complete, open-access URLs at the moment being those of periodO.[9] Such an ontology would target a number of categories and make gender an essential classification marker, thus enabling searchability and accessibility of the archive through technical affordance. Moreover, it would, in the same breath, provide the researchers with further information, such as the spatiality of women – for example, how many women appear in one given place – and chronologies, signifying events that relate to industrial history, including their social and professional role, if applicable.

While the project time and funding did not allow us to delve into every single case study, we decided to concentrate on particular archival cases, zooming in to data about female foundry proprietors (*kvinnliga brukspatroner*, in Swedish) more precisely. These were prominent women in a Swedish context who oversaw land property that contained mines or was associated with the mining industry more generally. These women were highly central figures of the Swedish mining industry, and very little is written about their history (Westerlund 2004). Data about prominent women, besides Swedish queens, were scattered across Carl Sahlin's collection.

Zooming in to one case study, we found out that employing ontologies described above was a more complex issue in practice. For a pilot tagging study, we looked at material pertaining to women foundry proprietors, specifically the case of files found in Åkers Styckebruk, and attempted to extract information about Ebba Augusta Hägerflycht, a prominent Swedish woman who is presented throughout Sahlin's archive as a female foundry proprietor. The information we receive from the collection concerning Ebba Augusta Hägerflycht comes from disparate parts of discussions about Åkers Styckebruk, a cannon manufacturer's town founded around 1580 by King Karl IX of Sweden. The cannon manufacture in the cannon foundry lasted between 1588 and 1866. The ore was sourced from nearby Skottvång's mine and Utö. The mill has been given the name of the entire community, which later also included Åker's gun mill. Ebba Hägerflycht, according to the archive, inherited part of the mining and cannon mill industry through her marriage to Martin Berg. In the archives she appears throughout the collection pertaining to Åkers Styckebruk with three different names, interchangeably, often with variable spelling. According to the archive, Ebba Hägerflycht changed her name three times, marrying a different man each time, and lived most of her life not in Åkers Styckebruk but in the Taxinge-Näsby castle where she came to rule as Mrs Majoress Berg (or otherwise in the archives Bergh – between 1862 and 1881, Mrs Countess Posse (between 1886 and 1901) and Lady Gosling (between 1904 and 1911 – thus under 49 years [1862–1911]). Accordingly, if we were to classify one item of the collection (see figure 3.2), say the very prosopography of Hägerflycht, the chart would look as follows:

Persons' in which subcategories would be as applicable:
1. Name or names before and after matrimony: Ebba Augusta Hägerflycht, Ebba Augusta Berg (otherwise Ebba Augusta Bergh), Ebba Augusta Posse, Ebba Augusta Gosling.
2. Gender: female

3. Age, by which the information could be described as relative (for example twenty-six years old) or absolute (mid-twenties) or different ages referring to this particular archival item, if there is more than one description of age: relative – young, middle aged
4. Citizen status (referring to the countries of origin or placement, by proxy): Swedish
5. Social status (married, widowed, single, unidentified/other): single, married, widowed, majoress, countess, lady
6. Professional status (position, property): foundry proprietor, *brukspatron*

'Place' in which several subcategories would be applicable, such as:
1. Geographic information mentioned, such as place names, including co-ordinates, if available
2. Geographic information related to events (see above)
(the option here would be: Taxinge Castle)

'Time' in which several subcategories would be applicable such us:
1. Relative historical date, including chronology: for example, nineteenth to twentieth centuries
2. Absolute historical date (if available): for example, marriage to Arvid Posse, 1886
3. Structured temporal data (insert relevant link from PeriodO)

In the same breath, and taking into consideration interoperability, other online open data about Hägerflycht could also be used to enrich the collection. Research revealed that there exist URLs that could be used to enrich information available in Carl Sahlin's archival collection. However, these URLs are of generic character and do not contain actual information about the female foundry proprietor, thus hindering the aforementioned enrichment ontology. The majority of such existing URLs refer to online genealogies, while some point to a small number of materials and artefacts donated by Ebba Augusta Hägerflycht to other organisations.[10] Most genealogical information as a noble and prominent woman of the time also appears incomplete online only in relation to her marriage to the Swedish prime minister Posse, whose presence online is greater than his wife's.[11]

To conclude, while there seems to be some information about Ebba Augusta Hägerflycht available online, data available do not illuminate her role as a foundry proprietor. However, data do render some more general information on her background and prominent family and, more specifically, her husbands, the men she was associated with. Naturally, while there is little analogue and digital information about Ebba Augusta's leadership skills, at least the technical affordances of digitalisation with structured data can help unearth some information

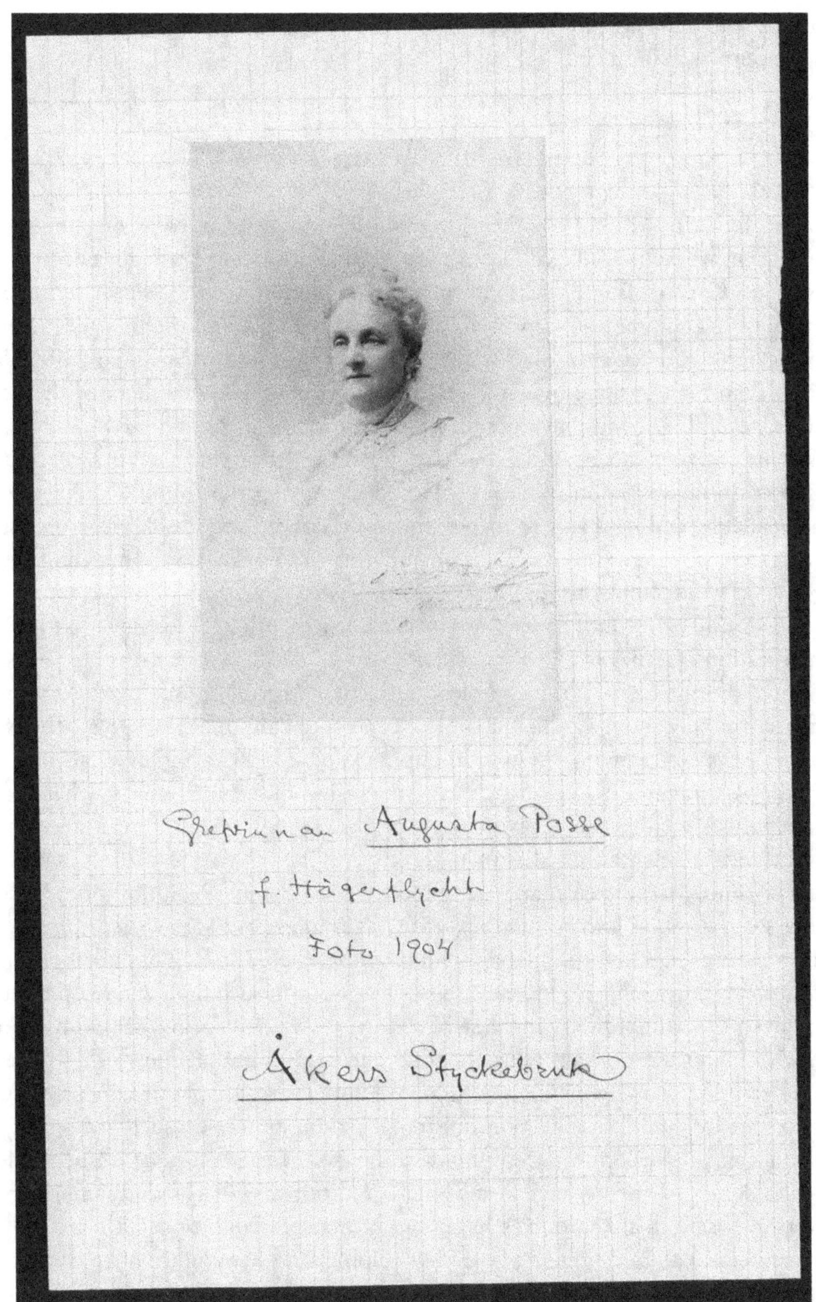

FIGURE 3.2. SEQ Figure * ARABIC 2: Augusta Hägerflycht as found in Carl Sahlin's Collection available online, CS-F1-431B 120, Creative Commons Attribution 2.0 Generic license.

and make it searchable for researchers and the public by keeping URIs and URLs in the same web location.

Conclusions and the Future

To conclude, in the light of other, international initiatives of collecting and tax-onomising women's historical data as found in archival and heritage collections, digitising Carl Sahlin's collection has been an interesting exercise. In terms of digitisation, the type and condition of archival material and media determined both careful and selective digitisation (for example, choosing printed materials rather than manuscripts), while estimated technical affordances dictated the usage of accessible, open and interoperable platforms and prompted enrichment with meaningful and critical URIs and URLs when applicable. In short, our digitisation/digitalisation process succeeded in making the Sahlin archive open and available, and thus able to inspire further research in the field. Nevertheless, the process of thinking about and implementing ontologies, taxonomies and categories in gendered terms was indeed complicated. In Sahlin's archive, women did obviously exist, but gender was not explicitly mentioned, let alone used as a classification category in the physical archive.

An additional issue is the complexity of using AI for automatic subject classification. The way forward is for subject experts to train machines to synthesise critical perspectives with the use and application of AI technologies. Unlocking the AI potential for a nuanced and inclusive curation of cultural heritage collections is a laborious yet worthy enterprise. In doing so, a future scientific significance of such an endeavour is threefold. First, given the nascent state of human-centric AI, the cultural heritage sector could benefit by innovation. With increased awareness and regulations about data usage in wider society, archives and museums have approached AI with caution. There is a lack of digital expertise and funds available for most museums to engage in such digital development. But given the extraordinary increase of collection data, exploring, critiquing and understanding the usability, sustainability and ethical implications of AI is becoming an increasingly pressing need for the heritage sector. Second, by using AI to diversify an archival collection, meaning-making processes, such as diversity, equality and inclusion, for the human audiences of the future could be made visible. While AI for heritage is still uncharted territory, it has the potential to diversify past human narratives by targeting heritage collections that are built as manifestations of dominant, national, colonial and heteronormative layers of interpretation. By analysing the compliance of AI methods and tools with FAIR and international data standards, and their reflection of diversity and ethics, both the field of AI and cultural heritage studies could benefit. Third, mapping current practices, as well as anticipated futures of AI deployed for heritage, would directly impact the industry, resulting in AI-generated descriptions of heritage images and texts and scholarly deliverables on how collections can be enhanced in meaningful ways. This is as much about building ethical principles into AI processing systems as it is about enabling human users to use AI systems and collections with diversity and inclusion in mind.

Anna Foka is Professor of Digital Humanities at Uppsala University, Department of Archival Studies, Library and Information Studies, and Museums and Cultural Heritage Studies (ALM). Her research explores how artificial intelligence, data infrastructures, and digital technologies shape cultural history, heritage, and memory, with a particular focus on ethics, bias, and critical approaches to technology in the humanities. She is the author of a number of scholarly works, including articles in AI & Society, Digital Scholarship in the Humanities, Digital Humanities Quarterly, Heritage, and the International Journal of Heritage Studies. Her recent publications include AI and Image by Cambridge University Press.

Jenny Attemark is a project manager and curator at the Swedish National Museum of Science and Technology in Stockholm. She worked as the coordinator of a digitisation and research project, 'Digital Models', a collaboration between the museum and Umeå University. She is also a cowriter and editor of the anthology *Digitala modeller: Teknikhistoria och digitaliseringens specifi citet* (ed. Attemark-Gillgren and Snickars, Lunds universitet, 2019). She has previously worked at Centrum för Näringslivshistoria and Armémuseum in Stockholm.

Fredrik Wahlberg is a researcher in digital humanities and a senior lecturer in computational linguistics at Uppsala University. He earned his PhD in computer science in 2017 with the thesis 'Interpreting the Script', presenting work on machine vision for medieval manuscripts. His current research concerns developing machine learning techniques within paleography and philology for scribal attribution and estimation of production years.

Notes

1. The borders between similar and overlapping fields such as AI and machine learning are not fixed. As to not fall into a lengthy discussion about field definitions, we will use the AI loosely to represent everything from machine learning to machine cognition/intelligence/vision
2. The term often denotes separatism and is an Anglocentric reading of the word 'historia', which literally means 'knowledge by investigation' and is a feminine noun in Greek.

3. https://snd.gu.se/en.
4. For more information at a global and local level see the following links:
   The Swedish National Library's evaluation criteria for FAIR publications (in Swedish): http://www.mynewsdesk.com/se/kungliga_biblioteket/documents/vetenskapliga-pub likationer-och-fair-principerna-bedoemningskriterier-och-metod-foer-att-kunna-foelja-utvecklingen-mot-ett-oeppet-vetenskapssystem-86176.
   The EU project Fostering Fair Data Practices in Europe (FAIRsFAIR):https://www.fairs fair.eu/.
   Final Report and Action Plan from the European Commission Expert Group on FAIR Data: https://ec.europa.eu/info/sites/info/files/turning_fair_into_reality_1.pdf.
5. On digital curation and URLs, see Yakel (2007: 335–40).
6. https://www.geni.com/people/Ebba-Hägerflycht/6000000006127131752.
7. Commission Decision of 22 February 2019 adopting Creative Commons as an open license under the European Common's reuse policy.
8. https://www.geonames.org.
9. https://perio.do/en/.
10. For example, in Åkers Styckebruk's Sörmland Museum there is a collection called "Åkers herrgård vid styckebruket, enstaka minnen från Augusta Posse född Hägerflycht" (Åker's manor at the piece mill, single memories from Augusta Posse, neé Hägerflycht), which actually includes items that had been in her possession, such as tools (https://sokisamlingar.sormlandsmuseum.se/collections/show/40) or her own bed (https://sokisamlingar.sorm landsmuseum.se/items/show/287785?collection=40&query=&sort_field=added&sort_dir=d&ref=%2Fcollections%2Fshow%2F40%3Flayout%3Dlist). The Swedish National Heritage Board's K-samsök portal and its portal to Europeana, includes a drawing of the memorial to Ebba Augusta from the church in Taxinge: https://www.europeana.eu/portal/sv/record/91622/raa_kmb_16000200100795.html?q=ebba+augusta#dcId=155 4272167283&p=1. The National Museum of Sweden has a donated painting listed as given by Augusta Bergh, neé Hägerflycht in 1882: http://www.europeana.eu/portal/sv/record/2064116/Museu_ProvidedCHO_Nationalmuseum__Sweden_24097.html?q=h%C3%A4gerflycht#dcId=1554271036255&p=1. One may also find the crest of the noble Hägerflycht family: https://www.europeana.eu/portal/sv/record/91622/raa_kmb_16000200080915.html?q=h%C3%A4gerflycht#dcId=1554271036255&p=1.
11. http://www.forsling.eu/ms/pc2275571.html. Compare this to her second husband's personal file (http://www.forsling.eu/ms/p4da998a6.html) as there is, as expected, more detailed information. On Kulturnav, another online initiative, there is no information at all about Ebba Augusta, only of her second husband Count Posse: http://kulturnav.org/b807e13f-6f67-4faa-bd64-18ea1efc7a34. On the Projekt Runeberg web page, the will of Arvid F. Posse is open and readable, where one may find information about the property and other belongings of his widow: http://runeberg.org/millionar/7/0082.html. Historical information on the Taxinge Castle property has also limited information relating to the history of the castle. https://www.taxingeslott.se/historik/.

References

Ågren, Maria. 2012. 'Genus Och Arbete i det Tidigmoderna Sverige', *Historisk tidskrift: Svenska historiska föreningen*, Stockholm, 132(1): 2–11.

Alaimo, Stacy, and Susan Hekman. 2008. *Material Feminisms*. Bloomington: Indiana University Press.

Aldrich, Robert. 2009. 'Colonial Museums in a Postcolonial Europe', *African and Black Diaspora: An International Journal* 2(2): 137–156.

Asberg, Cecilia, Kathrin Thiele and Iris Van der Tuin. 2015. 'Speculative before the Turn: Reintroducing Feminist Materialist Performativity', *Cultural Studies Review* 21(2): 145.

Ashar, Amar, and Sandra Cortesi. 2018. 'Why Inclusion Matters for the Future of Artificial Intelligence', Medium. Retrieved 30 August 2020 from https://medium.com/berkman-klein-center/why-inclusion-matters-for-the-future-of-artificial-intelligence-2cb9d3b1b92b.

Bahdanau, Dzmitry, Kyunghyun Cho, and Yoshua Bengio. 2014. 'Neural Machine Translation by Jointly Learning to Align and Translate', arXiv [cs.CL]. Retrieved 30 August 2020 from http://arxiv.org/abs/1409.0473.

Barker, Elton, Anna Foka and Kyriaki Konstantinidou. 2020. 'Coding for the Many, Transforming Knowledge for All: Annotating Digital Documents', PMLA. MLA, 135(1): 195–202.

Bergsdóttir, Arndis. 2016. 'Museums and Feminist Matters: Considerations of a Feminist Museology', *NORA – Nordic Journal of Feminist and Gender Research* 24(2): 126–139.

Blei, David. 2012. 'Probabilistic Topic Models', *Communications of the ACM* 55(4): 77–84.

Blei, David, Andrew Y. Ng and Michael I. Jordan. 2003. 'Latent Dirichlet Allocation', *Journal of Machine Learning Research: JMLR* 3: 993–1022.

Bolukbasi, Tolga, Kai-Wei Chang, James Zou, Saligrama Venkatesh and Adam Kalai. 2016. 'Man Is to Computer Programmer as Woman Is to Homemaker? Debiasing Word Embeddings', in D. D. Lee et al. (eds), *Advances in Neural Information Processing Systems* 29: 4349–57.

Box, George E. P. 1976. 'Science and Statistics', *Journal of the American Statistical Association* 71(356): 791–99.

Dermineur, Elise Marie. 2017. *Gender and Politics in Eighteenth-Century Sweden: Queen Louisa Ulrika (1720–1782)*. London: Taylor & Francis.

———. 2018. 'Rethinking Debt: The Evolution of Private Credit Markets in Preindustrial France', *Social Science History* 42(2): 317–42.

Esteva, Andre, Brett Kuprel, Roberto A. Novoa, Justin Ko, Susan M. Swetter, Helen M. Blau and Sebastian Thrun. 2017. 'Dermatologist-Level Classification of Skin Cancer with Deep Neural Networks', *Nature* 542(7639): 115–18.

European Commission. 2018. *Final Report and Action Plan from the European Commission Expert Group on FAIR Data*. European Commission website. Retrieved 30 August 2020 from https://ec.europa.eu/info/sites/info/files/turning_fair_into_reality_1.pdf.

Firth, Rupert John. 1957. 'A Synopsis of Linguistic Theory, 1930–1955', *Studies in Linguistic Analysis*. Basil Blackwell. Retrieved 30 August 2020 from https://ci.nii.ac.jp/naid/10020680394/.

Foka, Anna. 2019. 'Women's (In)visibility: In the Carl Sahlin Archive', in J. Attemark-Gillgren and P. Snickars (eds), *Digitala modeller: Teknikhistoria och digitaliseringens specificitet*. Lund: Lund University, pp. 95–106. Retrieved 30 August 2020 from https://uu.diva-portal.org/smash/get/diva2:1307768/FULLTEXT01.pdf.

Foka, Anna, Coppélie Cocq, Philipp I. Buckland and Stefan Gelfgren. 2020. 'Mapping Socio-ecological Landscapes: Geovisualization as Method', in Kristen Schuster and Suart Dunn (eds), *The International Handbook for Research Methods in Digital Humanities Methods*. New York: Routledge, pp. 203–17.

Foka, Anna, Jonathan Westin and Adam Chapman. 2018. 'Introduction to Special Issue: Digital Technology in the Study of the Past', *Digital Humanities Quarterly* 12:3. Boston: Northeastern University Press. Retrieved 30 August 2020 from http://www.digitalhumanities.org/dhq/vol/12/3/000396/000396.html.

'GeoNames'. 2020. GeoNames website. Retrieved 30 August 2020 from https://www.geonames.org/about.html.

Geismar, Haidy. 2018. *Museum Object Lessons for the Digital Age*. London: UCL Press.

Grahn, Wera. 2011. 'Intersectionality and the Construction of Cultural Heritage Management', *Archaeologies* 7(1): 222–50.

Halevy, Alon, Peter Norvig and Fernando Pereira. 2009. 'The Unreasonable Effectiveness of Data', *IEEE Intelligent Systems* 24(2): 8–12.

He, Kaiming, Xiangyu Zhang, Shaoqing Ren and Jian Sun. 2014. 'Spatial Pyramid Pooling in Deep Convolutional Networks for Visual Recognition', in *Computer Vision – ECCV 2014*. European Conference on Computer Vision. London: Springer (Lecture Notes in Computer Science), pp. 346–61.

Karpathy, Andrej, and Li Fei-Fei. 2015. 'Deep Visual-Semantic Alignments for Generating Image Descriptions', in *Proceedings of the IEEE Conference on Computer Vision and Pattern Recognition, Boston MA*: 3128–37. Retrieved 30 August 2020 from https://www.computer.org/csdl/proceedingsarticle/cvpr/2015/07298932/12OmNywfKEQ.

Krizhevsky, Alex, Ilya Sutskever and Geoffrey E. Hinton. 2012. 'Imagenet Classification with Deep Convolutional Neural Networks', *Advances in Neural Information Processing Systems* 25: 1097–105.

Levin, Amy K. 2010. *Gender, Sexuality and Museums: A Routledge Reader*. London: Taylor & Francis.

Lowenthal, David. 2015. The Past Is a Foreign Country – Revisited. Cambridge: Cambridge University Press.

Lubelski, Sarah. 2014. 'Kicking Off the Women's "Archives Party": The World Center for Women's Archives and the Foundations of Feminist Historiography and Women's Archives', *Archivaria* 78: 95–113.

Lu, Jiasen, Caiming Xiong, Devi Parikh and Richard Socher. 2017. 'Knowing When to Look: Adaptive Attention via a Visual Sentinel for Image Captioning', in *Proceedings of the IEEE Conference on Computer Vision and Pattern Recognition, Honolulu, Hawaii*: 375–83. Retrieved 30 August 2020 from https://ieeexplore.ieee.org/document/8099828?denied=.

Meeks, Elijah, and Scott B. Weingart. 2012. 'The Digital Humanities Contribution to Topic Modeling', *Journal of Digital Humanities* 2(1): 1–6.

Mikolov, Tomas, Ilya Sutskever, Kai Chen, Greg S. Corrado, and Jeff Dean. 2013. 'Distributed Representations of Words and Phrases and Their Compositionality', in Christopher J. C. Burges et al. (eds), *Advances in Neural Information Processing Systems*. New York: Curran Associates, Inc., 26:3111–19.

Murphy, Oonagh, and Elena Villaespesa. 2020. *AI: A Museum Planning Toolkit*. London: Goldsmiths, University of London.

Padilla, Thomas. 2019. 'Responsible Operations: Data Science, Machine Learning, and AI in Libraries'. OCLC Research, Dublin, Ohio. Retrieved 30 August 2020 from https://www.oclc.org/content/dam/research/publications/2019/oclcresearch-responsible-operations-data-science-machine-learning-ai.pdf.

'PeriodO'. 2020. PeriodO website. Retrieved 30 August 2020 from https://perio.do/en/.

Porter, Gaby. 1988. 'Putting Your House in Order: Representations of Women and Domestic Life', in Robert Lumley (ed.), *The Museum Time Machine: Putting Cultures on Display*. London: Routledge, 102–27.

Prescott, Andrew, and Lorna M. Hughes. 2018. 'Why Do We Digitize? The Case for Slow Digitization', *Archive Journal*. Louisiana State University Press. Retrieved 30 August 2020 from: https://eprints.gla.ac.uk/165726/7/165726.pdf.

'The Project'. 2020. FAIRsFAIR: Fostering Fair Data Practices in Europe website. Retrieved 30 August 2020 from https://www.fairsfair.eu/the-project.

Reading, Anna. 2015. 'Making Feminist Heritage Work: Gender and Heritage', in Emma Waterton and Steve Watson (eds), *The Palgrave Handbook of Contemporary Heritage Research*. London: Palgrave Macmillan UK, 397–413.

Reilly, Maura, and Lucy R. Lippard. 2018. *Curatorial Activism: Towards an Ethics of Curating*. London: Thames & Hudson.

Risam, Roopika. 2018. *New Digital Worlds: Postcolonial Digital Humanities in Theory, Praxis, and Pedagogy*. Evanston, IL: Northwestern University Press.

Rosenblatt, Frank. 1958. 'The Perceptron: A Probabilistic Model for Information Storage and Organization in the Brain', *Psychological Review* 65(6): 386–408.

Severson, Pernilla. 2018. 'The Politics of Women's Digital Archives and Its Significance for the History of Journalism', *Digital Journalism* 6(9): 1222–38.

Silverman, Helaine (ed.). 2011. *Contested Cultural Heritage: Religion, Nationalism, Erasure, and Exclusion in a Global World*. New York: Springer.

Smith, Laurajane. 2006. *Uses of Heritage*. London: Routledge.

Stark, Luke, and Kate Crawford. 2019. 'The Work of Art in the Age of Artificial Intelligence: What Artists Can Teach Us about the Ethics of Data Practice', *Surveillance & Society* 17(3/4): 442–55.

'Swedish National Data Service'. 2020. Swedish National Data Service website. Retrieved 30 August 2020 from https://snd.gu.se/en.

'Swedish National Library's Evaluation Criteria for FAIR Publications'. 2019. Swedish National Library website. Retrieved 30 August 2020 from http://www.mynewsdesk.com/se/kungliga_biblioteket/documents/vetenskapliga-publikationer-och-fair-principerna-bedoemningskriterier-och-metod-foer-att-kunna-foelja-utvecklingen-mot-ett-oeppet-vetenskapssystem-86176.

Thylstrup, Nanna. 2019. *The Politics of Mass Digitization*. Cambridge MA: MIT Press.

Vanmassenhove, Eva, Christian Hardmeier and Andy Way. 2019. 'Getting Gender Right in Neural Machine Translation', arXiv [cs.CL]. Retrieved 30 August 2020 from http://arxiv.org/abs/1909.05088.

Wahlberg, Fredrik, Lasse Mårtensson and Anders Brun. 2016. 'Large Scale Continuous Dating of Medieval Scribes Using a Combined Image and Language Model', in 2016 12th IAPR Workshop on Document Analysis Systems (DAS). Santorini, Greece: IEEE, pp. 48–53. Retrieved 30 August 2020 from https://ieeexplore.ieee.org/document/7490092/citations#citations.

Wang, Shuai, Zhiyuan Chen, Geli Fei, Bing Liu and Sherry Emery. 2016. 'Targeted Topic Modeling for Focused Analysis', in *Proceedings of the 22nd ACM SIGKDD International Conference on Knowledge Discovery and Data Mining*. New York: Association for Computing Machinery (KDD '16): 1235–44.

Westerlund, Kerstin. 2004. *Kvinnliga brukspatroner*. Stockholm: Tekniska museet Forlag.

Westin, Jonathan, Anna Foka and Adam Chapman. 2018. 'Humanising Places: Exposing Histories of the Disenfranchised through Augmented Reality', *International Journal of Heritage Studies* 24(3): 283–86.

Wigner, Eugene P. 1960. 'The Unreasonable Effectiveness of Mathematics in the Natural Sciences: Richard Courant Lecture in Mathematical Sciences Delivered at New York University, May 11, 1959', *Communications on Pure and Applied Mathematics* 13(1): 1–14.

Wu, Katherine. J. 2020. 'Smithsonian Releases 2.8 Million Images into Public Domain', *Smithsonian Magazine*. Retrieved 30 August 2020 from http://www.smithsonianmag.com/smithsonian-institution/smithsonian-releases-28-million-images-public-domain-180974263/?.

Xu, Kelvin, Jimmy Ba, Ryan Kiros, Kyunghyun Cho, Aaron Courville, Ruslan Salakhudinov, Rich Zemel and Yoshua Bengio. 2015. 'Show, Attend and Tell: Neural Image Caption Generation with Visual Attention', in *International Conference on Machine Learning*, pp. 2048–57. Retrieved 30 August 2020 from https://arxiv.org/abs/1502.03044.

Yakel, Elizabeth. 2007. 'Digital Curation', *OCLC Systems & Services: International Digital Library Perspectives* 23(4): 335–40.

Part II

ELICITING AFFECTIVE AND EMPATHETIC RESPONSES

Chapter 4

New Realities for New Museum Experiences

Virtual and Augmented Realities for Difficult Heritage in Iraq

Rozhen Kamal Mohammed-Amin

Introduction

Throughout history and across cultures, museums have needed to change and adapt. The needs are shaped by changing societies' preoccupations and expectations (Parry and Sawyer 2005). Museums' adaption to the zeitgeist (though limited in some places and cases) has contributed to their survival and relevancy (Burton and Scott 2003). The digital transformation of the third industrial revolution has accelerated the embracing of digital technologies by museums (Griffiths 2003). Most recently, state-of-the-art emerging technologies like augmented reality (AR) and virtual reality (VR) have found a home, real or simulated, in a growing number of museums worldwide. AR and VR mediate novel multisensory museum experiences through innovative visual, auditory, kinaesthetic or, even, olfactory engagements. More than any of their predecessors and digital relatives, AR and VR are pushing the *physical* and *virtual* boundaries of museums into new territories and engagements. Evidence on the impact of AR and VR on different levels of informal learning and engagement is accumulating across many fields and applications, including cultural heritage and museums. The growing findings on their effective ability in eliciting emotions and empathy make them a focus for innovative engagement with heritage, especially difficult heritage, in or outside museum walls. This chapter discusses the intersection of AR and VR technologies, museums and difficult heritage. It first provides an overview of the growing AR and VR uses in or by museums for attracting, edutaining and engaging visitors. It then focuses on AR and VR uses and impacts in the context of difficult heritage. Through a case study in the context of Iraq, the chapter elaborates on the *what*, *why* and *how* components of a VR-mediated experience and engagement with difficult heritage.

New Realities and New Museum Experiences and Engagements

The two *realities* technologies of AR and VR are like portals to other real or imagined worlds, places and times (Merritt 2016). In the 'Reality-Virtuality continuum' (Milgram et al. 1995), VR appears at one end, while AR stands in a middle ground between the virtual and physical (real) environments or realities. VR detaches users from their surrounding real environment and immerses them in a real-time simulated environment, which is a recreation of the real world or an imaginary one (Perry Hobson and Williams 1997). In this immersive virtual world, users can interact through 'multiple sensorial channels', including sight, hearing, touch, smell and taste (Burdea and Coiffet 2003). In addition to immersion and interaction, imagination is the third characteristic of VR technology because it enables users to 'perceive nonexistent things' (Burdea and Coiffet 2003). Instead of replacing it, AR enhances users' surrounding real environment with computer-generated (virtual) objects by combining real and virtual worlds. Such an enhanced hybrid world borrows from both the materiality of the real world and the dynamism and high interactivity of the virtual world. In addition to coexistence, AR enables real-time interactions with both real and virtual objects in the same place and time (Tillon, Marchal and Houlier 2011).

Each of AR and VR has specific abilities and limitations, which make them fit or unfit for different purposes and with different design and development considerations. VR's full immersion and wide field of view come with some yet to be overcome limitations, including restricting users' interactions with their surrounding real environment and people, reducing their mobility, and causing motion sickness–like symptoms (known as *VR sickness*) in some users. The trade-offs for AR's interactive enrichment of physical reality, compared to VR, are less immersion in the virtual world and a smaller field of view. In addition to technical challenges associated with underlying hardware and software, AR and VR's wide adoption are still challenged by cross-platform compatibility and content accessibility. Still, AR and VR can empower users, producing innovative experiences resembling those imagined in science fiction.

As 'an adaptive medium', the museum has always been shaped by its information and communication technologies (ICT) (Parry and Sawyer 2005). AR and VR, as new ICT, create new realities for museum experience and engagement. In the last decade, a growing number of museums around the world have started to experiment with innovative VR and AR experiences. Some museums have already incorporated these technologies into their learning programs and spaces (Rae and Edwards 2016; Denver Museum of Nature & Science n.d.). VR enables full immersive virtual tours through time and space for remote or on-site museum visitors. In such transformative experiences, users can walk in/ by scaled or full-size 3D or 360-degree restorations or creations of collections, rooms, buildings or even cities from the past, the present, or even imagination (Shieber 2015). Many of these VR-mediated experiences and interactions are impossible to replicate in the physical reality of the museum.

Some museums integrate VR experiences and time and space travel into their physical premises and on-site visitor engagement activities. The first permanent VR-based exhibition of the National Museum of Natural History in Paris time travels visitors through evolution history (National Museum of Natural History n.d.). Another VR experience at the British Museum's Great Court enabled visitors, alone or in groups, to time travel to an imaginary Bronze Age site from 3500 BC (Rae and Edwards 2016).

Instead of time traveling in a fully simulated virtual world, AR enables such travel in a hybrid world where real and virtual objects and worlds are bridged in real time. The *Terracotta Warriors* application developed for a special exhibition in the Museum of Asian Civilizations time-travels terracotta warriors from the 200s BC into the exhibition space to re-enact historic events and dramatised stories from the rise and fall of the Qin dynasty (Thian 2012).

Both VR and AR technologies can innovatively borrow additional features and capabilities from the immateriality of the virtual world to facilitate transformative experience and engagement with museum collections and spaces. VR and AR enable the animation of static collections and allow visitors to enter inside of them. They can be like 'magic wands', revealing invisible things around us beyond what is possible in the real world (Merritt 2016). The *Mona Lisa: Beyond the Glass* VR experience immerses visitors inside the interactive virtual world and unheard stories of this famous painting (VIVE Arts n.d.). The *Jurassic Flight* multisensory VR experience at the Denver Museum of Nature and Science takes the VR-based experience to a whole new level. This solo full-body VR simulation enables visitors to fly amongst dinosaurs from the Jurassic period in prehistoric skies and landscapes (Denver Museum of Nature & Science n.d.). Instead of flying with virtual dinosaurs, the *Ultimate Dinosaurs* AR application at the Royal Ontario Museum (ROM) in Canada enables its visitors to revive the real skeleton of the dinosaurs on display by layering virtual flesh and skin on them and then animating them (Royal Ontario Museum n.d.). The *Perpetual Garden* AR application combines real and virtual worlds to animate real dioramas and gardens at the Carnegie Museum of Natural History, Pittsburgh, Pennsylvania. This real-time contextualised animation helps the museum explain a complex ecological phenomenon to its visitors. The AR application creates context-sensitive experiences with perceptual, emotional and cognitive impact (Harrington et al. 2019).

New Realities and Difficult Heritage

In the people-centred mission of twenty-first-century museums, visitors' experience has become a keyword and measure for success. Visitors' experience is a 'combination of sensory, aesthetic, intellectual, and social factors' (Peng 2019: n.p.). Within visitors' experience, affective experience and learning, such as inducing a new interest, attitude or value, serve modern museums' missions better than mere cognitive examples, such as recalling facts or comprehending basic principles and ideas (Lord 2014). Therefore, effective museum exhibitions 'must be excellent at generating enthusiasm, challenging long-held opinions, affecting attitudes, arousing interest, raising awareness of specific issues, or generating deep – often long-held – emotional responses' (Dexter Lord 2014: 40). Deeper levels of learning and emotional engagement in affective experience can also elicit empathy and inspire action.

Museums and memorial centres, where visitors are often exposed to difficult heritage, therefore, are increasingly exploring new strategies to trigger visitors' imagination and evoke their emotional response. In doing so, their goal is to 'elicit empathy for and/or moral engagement with historical events and actors portrayed through an exhibition' as well as to induce 'historical empathy' (Savenije and de Bruijn 2017: 832). Historical empathy becomes particularly important for presenting, interpreting and engaging with sensitive difficult heritage topics and events. After all, museums are 'stable, safe, pleasant spaces with a certain amount of social responsibility' (Janes 2007; Bedigan 2016: 88). They have an authoritative and legitimising status and a role as symbols of their communities (Burton and Scott 2003).

Interactive, multisensory and immersive AR and VR technologies have been showing the potential for creating affective experiences and penetrating deeper into informal learning levels, beyond cognitive learning and enjoyment, or edutainment. Although these technologies are still emerging and more studies are necessary, scientific evidence on the effectiveness of AR and VR for education – including informal education, emotional engagement, empathy eliciting, changing behaviour and inspiring action – is growing in the cultural heritage field, among others. For example, empirical evidence from a study by Stanford University shows that VR can evoke people's empathy and alter their attitudes. In this experimental study, Stanford researchers found that the participants who underwent their *Becoming Homeless* experience in the immersive VR mode were likely to develop more empathy and prosocial behaviours in short and long-term periods in comparison to those who underwent the experience in more traditional ways, such as reading a narrative or using a desktop computer (Herrera et al. 2018). The study also found a statistically significant difference between the VR and non-VR participants with regards to taking action after the experience, which was signing a petition to support affordable housing for the homeless (Herrera et al. 2018).

VR's potential in translating empathy to action made it a target by the UN for developing VR experiences like *Clouds Over Sidra* as part of its VR program. The experience immerses users in the daily life and schooling struggles of a twelve-year-old girl in a Syrian refugee camp in Jordan (UNVR n.d.). The *Clouds Over Sidra* VR experience was used by policymakers and donors during a fundraising conference for Syrian refugees (Anderson 2015; Harris 2015). The conference raised US$3.8 billion, over 70 percent more than the projected US$2.3 billion (Robertson 2016). In another VR experience, 'Project Syria VR', users are virtually transported to a refugee camp in the city of Aleppo to witness a rocket blast and other war tragedies (WIRED n.d.). VR technology has also been used to relive and engage with difficult heritage from distant history. The 'Sandby Borg – A Virtual Connection' project time travels users to a fifth-century Iron Age fort on a Swedish island, where they behold the sights and sounds of a bloody massacre (RISE n.d.). Called the 'Ultimate Empathy Machine', VR technology enables people to see through the eyes of others or 'experience any situation from any point of view' (Herrera et al. 2018: 1).

Although less immersive than VR, at least in terms of full immersion in the virtual world, AR's real and virtual blending, real-time interactivity and location-based capabilities make it a powerful medium for provoking emotion and empathy. These capabilities become even more promising for experiencing and encountering difficult heritage in which physical context plays a significant role in heightening an *authentic* sense of presence and contextualisation. In the itinerant AR experience of 'With New Eyes I See' (WNEIS), the participants playfully and unexpectedly projected, literally and metaphorically, untold stories and inaccessible archival materials from the First World War onto the surface of relevant historic buildings, including the National Museum of Wales and spaces at Cardiff's Civic Centre (Kidd 2019). The contextualised encounter and interaction through WNEIS not only created a new narrative and perception about familiar places and buildings to the local participants but also empathetically connected most of the participants to the story character from a distant past (Kidd 2019). The 'Talk to Sarai Tour' (TST) is a self-guided AR experience that enables Sarai Museum visitors to listen to stories from the difficult history of Sulaimani (also spelled as Slemani) city, the cultural capital of the Kurdistan Region of Iraq and a UNESCO Creative City in literature. In this interactive experience, mobile AR technology brings the historic Sarai building and eyewitnesses back to life to recount their memories on important historic events from the period of British colonialism and the early postcolonial era. Through a blend of despair and hope stories, TST aims to elicit cross-generational awareness, emotion and dialogue about Sulaimani's difficult history.

Nobody's Listening VR Experience

Nobody's Listening (NL) is an exhibition project that combines art, technology and advocacy to commemorate and memorialise the Yazidi genocide by ISIS (Islamic State of Iraq and Syria) and inspire action. The exhibition includes four components: artworks (crowdsourced paintings and sculptures by Yazidi, Christian and Assyrian survivors and artists in Iraq), photography (portraits of survivors and prominent individuals working to bring ISIS to justice), models and reliefs of tangible cultural heritage destroyed by ISIS, and an immersive VR experience about the Yazidi genocide. The virtual NL VR experience is the centrepiece component of the exhibition. It aurally and visually immerses users in a virtually reconstructed world where the horrors of the Yazidi genocide can be seen, heard and felt. VR technology spatially and temporally teleports users to Yazidis' homeland, Sinjar region, where many dark historical moments of the twenty-first century have taken place. The NL VR experience enables users to hear accounts of real horror stories and testimonies narrated by fictitious Yazidi and ISIS fighter characters. The project aims to raise awareness and educate about the Yazidi genocide and continued hardships, as well as advocate for recognition, justice and action for Yazidi and other minorities in Iraq.

Background and Motivation

In August 2014, tens of thousands of defenceless people from the Yazidi minority in Northern Iraq suddenly found themselves fleeing their home, many on foot, to the difficult terrain of the nearby Sinjar Mountains (Heartland Alliance 2017). To make the difficult, hot summer journey in the shortest time, many Yazidis had to leave everything behind and go towards an uncertain fate. For some, this even meant leaving behind loved ones, old and sick relatives with limited mobility (Sly 2014). Hunger, thirst, exhaustion, blisters, bloody feet and death from trekking through and being stranded in the mountains (McDonnell 2014) soon proved to be the least of the horrors and sufferings Yazidi women, men and children had to endure. As many more were preparing to escape their homes, ISIS arrived at the Yazidi heartland and villages in their full force with mortars and heavy weapons. This was part of a wider campaign of cruelty and a series of war crimes by ISIS between 2014 and 2017 across Nineveh Province and towards the Kurdistan Region in northern Iraq that swept through ethnic and religious communities, including Christian communities and especially that of the Yazidi (UNAMI-OHCHR 2018). The Yazidi ethno-religious minority are predominantly Kurdish in their ethnicity, and Yazidism is their religion. About 750,000 of them live in the northwest of Iraq in Nineveh Province, while close to 250,000 Yazidis are scattered across some neighbouring and other countries worldwide (Dege 2018). Misunderstandings about their ancient religion and worship of Melek Tawwus or Peacock Angel (a fallen angel) have subjected them to marginalisation, discrimination, prosecution and genocide throughout history, as far as Ottoman ruling (Jalabi 2014).

While strict and extremist Muslims called them 'devil worshippers' or 'infidels' (Jalabi 2014; NBC News 2014), the Yazidi community was systematically targeted by the ISIS extremist group (UNAMI-OHCHR 2016). In just ten days, UN Human Rights reported the displacement of 250,000 members of the Yazidi community (UNAMI-OHCHR 2016). Since 2014, it is estimated that 5,500 Yazidis have been killed by ISIS and over 6,300 Yazidis, mostly women and children, have been abducted, detained, tortured, enslaved and sexually assaulted. Yazidi women and girls were sold and bought as spoils of war in ISIS slave markets in Iraq and Syria (UNAMI-OHCHR 2016). All the Yazidis under ISIS control were forced to convert to Islam, and many Yazidi boys were indoctrinated, trained and used in hostilities (OHCHR 2016). Fathers, sons and brothers of many were executed and mass murdered, while captive family members were forced to witness the killings (OHCHR 2016). About two years after the ISIS atrocities, a Human Rights Council report revealed that over 3,200 Yazidi women and children were still held by ISIS (OHCHR 2016). Many young Yazidi women who could not endure their constant and ruthless rapes by ISIS fighters committed suicide (Dakhil 2015). ISIS's cruelty and calculated ethnic cleansing did not stop only at the Yazidi people themselves but also extended to their ancient and rich tangible and intangible cultural heritage, from sacred places and temples to traditions, memories and customs (RASHID International 2019).

Today, most of the displaced Yazidis remain in IDP (internally displaced people) and refugee camps (UN-HABITAT 2015) in the Kurdistan Region of Iraq and Syria, unable to return to the ruins of their homes because of lack of stability, security and reconstruction in the area. Remains of thousands of unidentified victims, including Yazidis, in over two hundred mass graves in ISIS-controlled areas have been recovered as of 2018 (UNAMI-OHCHR 2018). Post-traumatic stress disorder and perceived social rejection and stigma are at an alarming rate among the women and girls who survived ISIS sexual enslavement and genocide (Ibrahim et al. 2018). With 70 percent of the buildings in the region damaged, the few families that decided to go back to what is now the ghost town of Sinjar are living in dire conditions and despair (Peyre-Costa and Jenssen 2018). The psychological tolls of ISIS horrors on the Yazidi survivors and their community are vastly unresolved and still unfolding. Almost every displaced Yazidi family has 'male relatives who have been killed and women who have been kidnapped'

(UN-HABITAT 2015: 14). About six years after the genocide and three years after the victory declaration over ISIS in Iraq, the Yazidi minority still feels helpless and hopeless. Although a growing number of states and entities have recognised ISIS atrocities against Yazidis as *genocide* (YAZDA n.d.; UN-OHCHR 2016), the UN is yet to formally recognise it as such. What has been done for the struggling Yazidis appears to be too little too late. In 2017, Amal Clooney, a high-profile human rights lawyer, and Nadia Murad, an ISIS survivor of sexual enslavement and Nobel Peace Prize laureate, called out the UN on its failure and inaction in tracking down 'the perpetrators of genocide and put[ting] them on trial' (Morrow 2017: n.p.).

A multidisciplinary team from human rights activists, legal professionals, Yazidi genocide advocates and VR producers felt an urgency for new and *different* ways of advocacy for Yazidis, beyond reports, statements and traditional media in a world that is becoming desensitised to genocide. Taking into account VR technology's effective use in other difficult heritage contexts, they saw in it the potential to present and remind people of the scale and magnitude of the Yazidi genocide, as well as to amplify their unheard voices and continued struggles. The outcome was the NL exhibition and its emotionally engaging VR experience. Initiated by Ryan Xavier D'Souza (a human rights advocate working on genocide prevention), the exhibition is a multinational and cross-disciplinary collaboration between Yazda, an international Yazidi charity, and Surround Vision, an award-winning 360-degree and VR film studio based in London. Other international and Iraqi partners have joined the project, among them the Digital Cultural Heritage (DCH) Research Group based at the Sulaimani Polytechnic University (*Nobody's Listening* 2019b).

Although the exhibition is currently mobile, in that it can be experienced anywhere, and is part of a worldwide advocacy campaign, it is planned to be installed as a permanent exhibition in the proposed Yazidi Memorial Centre/Museum in Sinjar. This will make the NL the first ever VR-based exhibition in an Iraqi museum. The mobility of such VR-based exhibitions can extend local museums' accessibility and international outreach. Local museums' mediated VR exhibitions have high potential to increase access to and engagement with Iraq's inaccessible difficult, and nondifficult, heritage.

In the NL VR experience, users virtually travel to witness the consequences of ISIS genocide and its devastating effects on Yazidi people and their cultural heritage, focusing on the horrific incidents that took place in Kocho, one of the hardest-hit Yazidi villages in Sinjar. The first-person immersive time travel experience along with the exhibit's narration pull users and their emotions deeply into the Yazidi stories and wounds. Such timely and multisensory difficult heritage experience is necessary not only for raising awareness, engaging emotions and invoking empathy but also for inspiring actions and justice for Yazidis. The VR experience and its impacts can potentially support reconciliation and peace efforts among Iraqi communities, which cannot be achieved or sustained without truth, recognition, justice and empathy for the victims and survivors. After all, many of the ISIS perpetrators were Iraqis from other ethnic and religious groups. Some were even from the cities, towns and villages neighbouring to Sinjar.

Experience Storyline

The NL VR experience is accessed through VR headsets like Oculus Quest, which teleport users to the NL virtual world where they encounter its sights and sounds. First, a disclaimer warns users about the content of the experience and the recommended age (sixteen years or over) to view it. The disclaimer also warns Yazidis who have directly suffered under ISIS not to go through the experience without expert supervision to avoid any emotional triggers caused by post-traumatic stress disorder. Users are then transported to a 'new world'. In the entrance to this world, users find themselves in a bird's-eye view of an Iraqi map where the Yazidis' homeland and Sinjar mountains are visually indicated. The voice of a Yazidi woman briefly introduces users to the ancient history, culture and religion of the Yazidi community and their geographic and historic ties to Sinjar mountains. The voice then directs users' attention to a distant view of Kocho, one of the hardest-hit Yazidi villages, where the horrific enslavement and courageous survival stories of Nadia Murad and many other women started.

The woman narrator then invites users to walk through the frame of a portrait of a Yazidi woman. The portrait works as a virtual portal to move users to the next scene. Once users physically move to walk through the virtual portal, they are transferred to the ruins of one of the seven Yazidi holy temples destroyed by ISIS. While there, the narrator briefly explains the ISIS destruction of their holy temples and introduces them to Yazidi religion's symbolism in the temple's architecture by referring to the remains of the temple. When users go through the next portal, they see Kocho village in its current devastation and ruin. High-quality 360-degree video with VR immersion makes it possible to look and move around to view the landscape in different ways, just like in real life. The voice narration continues to explain the simple life and works of two hundred families living in the village before the ISIS attacks. Through another portal, users enter a 360-degree video of a chaotic scene of an abandoned house in Kocho, Nadia Murad's house. There, the narrator introduces herself as Shereen, a genocide survivor. Her character in the VR experience is a composite based on real stories of Yazidi women. Shereen continues by recounting her family's and her own everyday life and routines before ISIS. She then goes on to recount the fatal night of the ISIS attack and the gunfire sounds that changed her life forever. Another virtual portal transports users to the front of the school where ISIS atrocities and genocide at their full scale started and endured for months and years to come.

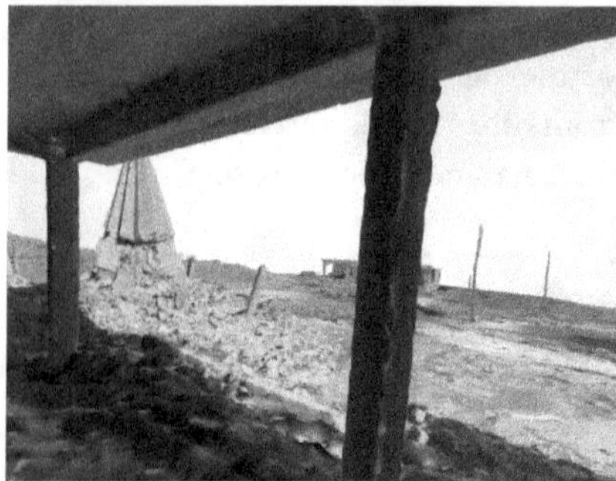
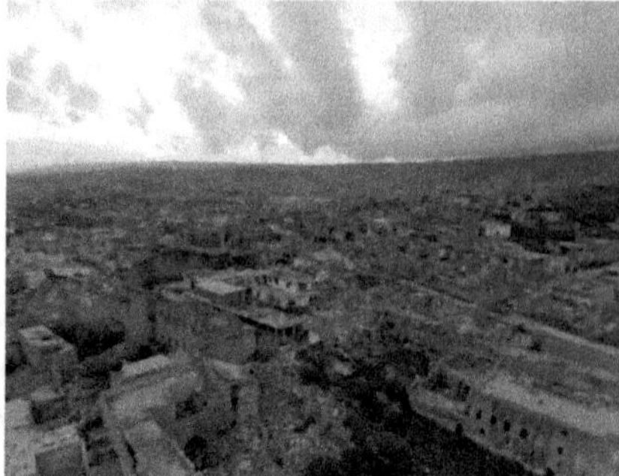
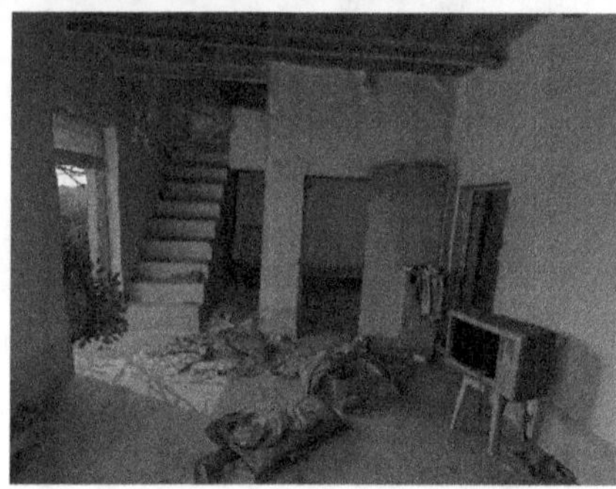

FIGURE 4.1. Virtually reconstructed scenes from the temple site, Kocho village and a Yazidi family house in the NL VR experience. Screen captures by the author.

In the next part, the VR experience invites users to choose to follow the story of one of the three presented characters (three branches). At this point, silhouettes of a Yazidi woman (Shereen), a Yazidi man (Shamo), and an ISIS fighter are presented side by side. Upon choosing a character, users are transported to the virtual world of that character. Shereen and Shamo narrate their stories, one as a survivor of sexual enslavement and the other as a massacre escapee. The detailed recounting of the events, scenes, and feelings and the 360-degree scenes of surrounding devastation from real buildings and streets immerse users in the stories. They also engage users' emotions as they see and feel, in a way, the terrifying experiences that so many Yazidis had as ISIS fighters were unleashing their cruelty.

The anonymous ISIS fighter, who is also a local man from a village close by, talks from the perpetrator's point of view. He first recounts his motivations to join ISIS: revenge against the Iraqi government's prior persecution of his people and attraction to ISIS's extreme ideologies and propaganda against Yazidis. The fighter then continues with recalling the cruelties and crimes he witnessed or partook in then as a "proud" ISIS fighter.

At the end of each character's story, users are taken to a virtual reconstruction of a Yazidi tent in one of the camps. Shereen's voice welcomes users, 'the guests' in her word, and offers them drinks, modelling Yazidi tradition and generosity towards their guests. By looking and moving around the 360-degree reconstruction of the tent, users can see the dire living conditions of the Yazidi families.

Shereen continues by giving statistics regarding the killed, displaced, enslaved, indoctrinated and missing Yazidis. She also shows users videos of real Yazidis and their living conditions in the camps before transporting users to scenes of more ruins in Kocho and one of the many mass grave sites in their homeland. Despite all the crimes and horrors, Shereen says that 'not a single ISIS fighter has been prosecuted in Iraq for attacking Yazidis' and that those in jail 'are low-level fighters accused of other crimes'. Shereen then explains that despite media and governments' awareness about their atrocities, and even though Nadia Murad was awarded a Nobel Peace Prize, the Yazidi cause has not yet been formally recognised as a genocide. She finishes by sombrely complaining, 'Nobody is listening to us – are you?' As the NL virtual world turns black around users, two hashtags (#WeAreListening and #TimeForJustice) appear in front of the users, promoting calls for action.

Design and Development

The NL VR experience harnesses the power of VR technology, emotional first-person storytelling, and 360-degree videography and photography to sensitively reconstruct the scenes and events of the dark history of the ISIS genocide of Yazidi people and heritage and to immerse users in it. Intrigued by his own emotional response and increased empathy level in using 'Clouds over Sidra' and UNMAS's VR for Somalia, two VR-based advocacy experiences, D'Souza saw an opportunity to explore using VR technology to advocate for Yazidis. The exhibition name, *Nobody's Listening,* is a verbatim phrase from a Yazidi activist that insightfully articulates the helpless feeling expressed by the many Yazidis that D'Souza and his team met. The VR experience storyline was developed and directed by Mary Matheson from Surround Vision, an advocate of VR for Good and director of the Female Planet 360-degree VR series for Google Daydream (*Nobody's Listening* n.d.).

The creatively crafted branching storyline blends facts about Yazidi culture and tradition with real stories from publicly accessible testimonies of Yazidi survivors and interviews with imprisoned ISIS fighters. The composite nature of the characters' stories and hypothetical names of the Yazidi characters conceal identities and make the real stories unidentifiable. For ethical considerations and in order not to interfere with local authorities' investigations, the ISIS detainees interviewed in the local prisons were not asked about any potential crimes they perpetrated. The interviews focused on their background and pre-ISIS life. This was to ensure that they did not face any recriminations as a result of speaking to the project team, who were warned by human rights organisations that they might be speaking under duress. Due to the sensitivity and intensity of the Yazidi genocide, the delivery of this difficult history VR experience required even more careful planning and content selection and development. The script was not only reviewed by a clinical psychologist and a legal analyst who were working closely with the Yazidi community but also by several prominent human rights organisations based in the Middle East, the United States and the United Kingdom.[1] To avoid causing emotional stress and overwhelming users and to comply with the 'Do No Harm' principle, the VR experience does not include scenes or narrations that are overly graphic (Johnston 2019). The scenes do not include blood or dead bodies. The narration also avoids direct mention of sexual violence (Johnston 2019). Instead, sexual enslavement is implied and inferred through the stories of the three characters.

The VR experience uses various techniques and effects to immerse users and 'put them in the shoes' of the characters. The use of 360-degree videos and photos of real scenes from the destroyed homes and village virtually transport users into the actual places where some of the genocide events took place. Most of these sites are still inaccessible or unsafe to visit in person, making a museum-mediated VR-based exhibition an accessible and effective medium for interpreting and displaying inaccessible difficult heritage. Users' viewing angles in the NL virtual world match the viewing angles in the real world. In addition to looking around, users are able to move around the virtually reconstructed 360-degree scenes and to get closer to the marks and evidence of the destruction. The use of a wireless Oculus Quest VR headset for the delivery of the experience increases mobility when navigating the virtual space.

Mixing the videos and static photos of the real scenes with computer-generated animations makes the scenes more engaging and like a living environment. This can lead to a higher sense of presence and emotional impact. For example, the integration of clouds moving, nightfall and flying firefly time-lapse animation with the static house scenes visually reinforces Shereen's account as a peaceful day turns to the fatal night of the ISIS attack. The virtual trees swaying in the wind in front of the broken door and window of the house and at the front of the school further heighten the sense of immersion and the impression of being

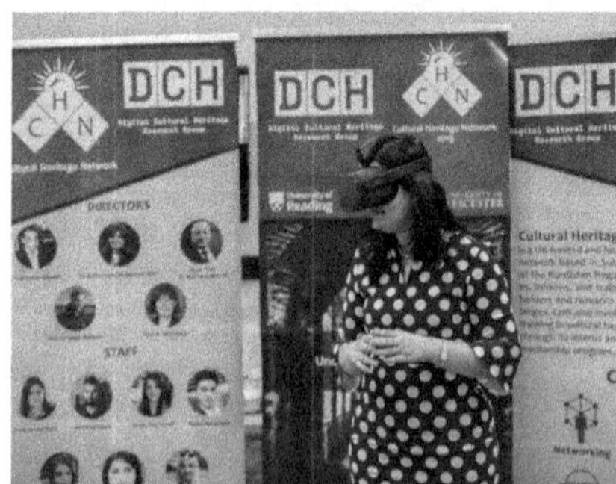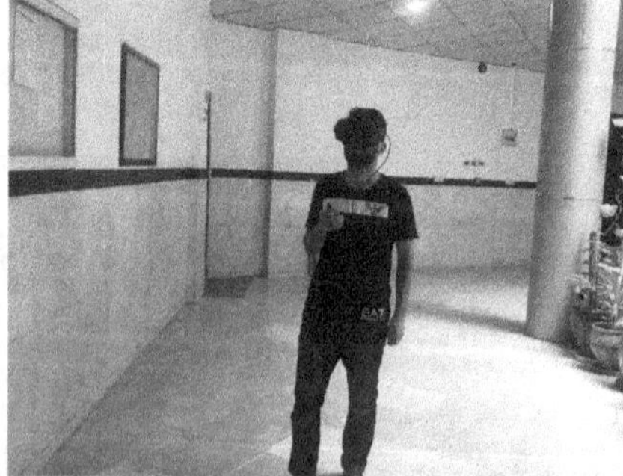

FIGURE 4.2. DCH members trying the NL VR experience in different locations with a wireless Oculus Quest headset. Images courtesy of DCH.

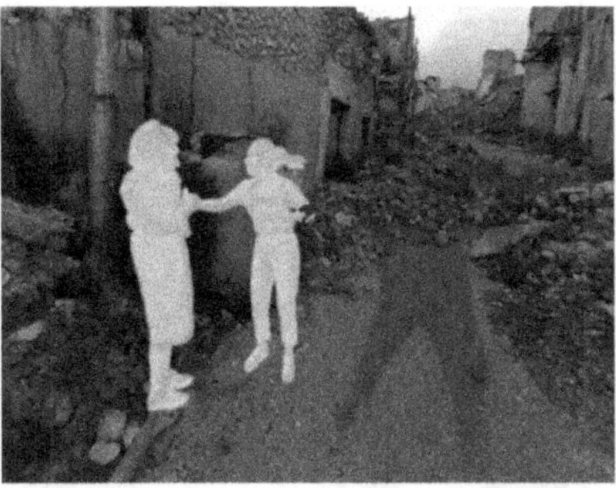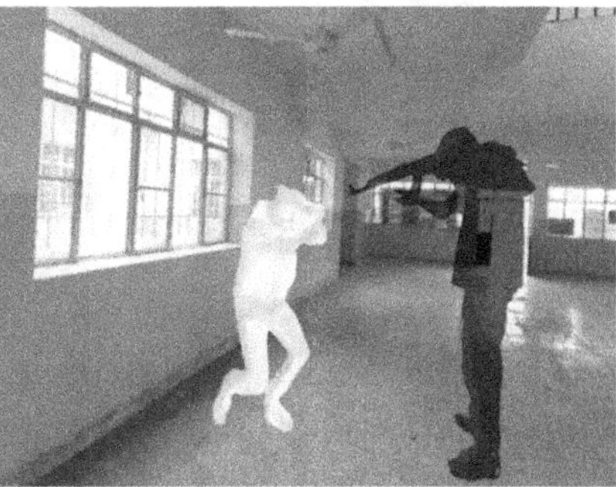

FIGURE 4.3. Blending virtual reconstructed scenes from Kocho village and the school with animated silhouettes in the NL VR experience. Screen captures by the author.

in a living environment. The sway of the ceiling fan in the 3D-reconstructed tent engages users in the virtual space and draws their attention to discomfort conditions of such a tent, where many Yazidis are still living in the unbearably hot summers of Iraq. Animated silhouettes of Yazidis and ISIS fighters in the houses, school and village effectively, cautiously and facelessly show users some of the criminal acts in place. Soundscapes in the background of some of the 360-degree scenes mentally intensify the devastation events and conditions. The experience also makes use of photogrammetry-based 3D reconstruction models of the site of the destroyed temple and tent. The 3D model of the temple was lent by the Turner Prize–nominated 'Forensic Architecture' based in London. The model was developed as part of a documentation project of the destruction of Yazidi tangible cultural heritage to be used as part of the genocide prosecution by the UN as well as future preservation and restoration efforts (Forensic Architecture 2018). Transitions between the scenes and stories in the VR experience are mediated through the portals (virtual frames). These portals serve as a visual reference for easy navigation and direction in the virtual world. The NL VR experience was developed in Unity, which is a cross-platform game engine that enables the development of 3D and 2D VR and AR visualisations. The experience was designed to last approximately twelve minutes, though users can choose to stay longer and further explore a scene before moving to the next one through a portal.

Public Launch

In August 2019, a demo version of the NL VR experience along with the other components of the NL exhibition was softly launched in Baghdad during Yazda's fifth annual conference to commemorate the anniversary of the genocide. Prior to, during and after the launch, many high-profile local and international human rights advocates, diplomats, government officials, academics, professionals and members from the local community tried the demo version of the VR experience in an informal evaluation of the experience. Their written or verbal reactions were observed, collected and shared with the author by Ryan X. D'Souza. Some described it as a 'powerful reminder', a 'moving exhibition', 'an incredibly moving, affecting exhibition'. Others explained that it 'plung[es] you into the awful, appalling world ISIS created for their Yazidi captives' and that it is a 'journey of suffering where you discover the inhumanity of ISIS and also at the same time the courage of the Yazidis who never lost hope' (*Nobody's Listening* 2019a).[2] The testimonies and feedback suggest affective engagement, beyond the cognitive engagement of learning and remembering. The uniqueness of the experience appears in such feedback as, 'It takes you beyond what pictures and oral testimonies can do'.[3] Several European diplomats, who are architects of their country's foreign policy towards Iraq, pointed out the usefulness of the experience for accessing the sights and level of destruction in Sinjar, an area that they have never been to before[4].

Most of the users are affected by this multisensory experience in one way or another. The majority came out of the experience with sadness and empathy, which appeared in their facial expression and verbal feedback. Many of the users became curious about the Yazidis, while others had more questions about the fate of the Yazidi people and the current situation. A handful of users, especially non-Iraqis, came out interested and excited, less about the story and more about the technical aspects of the storytelling. This appeared from how they described the experience: 'amazing' or 'cool' were some of the words used.[5] Some other users could not complete the experience and soon took off their headsets, either due to unresolved technical glitches they experienced in the demo version or from VR sickness, which affects some people in virtual environments.

D'Souza noticed differences in the reactions to the VR experience depending on the location and ties to the Yazidi community. He noticed that most of the people in Baghdad wanted to try the NL despite its depressing content. This pre-NL usage curiosity seemed to be more about the novel technology and interest in knowing what is inside the high-tech headset. This observation suggests that the novelty of the NL may have been the main draw for attracting local non-Yazidi users to try it. There has been an overwhelming response from the Yazidi community to the NL. Some of them saw opportunities in the VR experience for reminding and educating Yazidis and non-Yazidis about the genocide because some had already forgotten this dark and unresolvable difficult history from 2014.

Another indication for the potential of the NL exhibition and its VR experience for advocacy appears in its attraction of a growing number of local and international supporters, funders, donors and partners. Several prominent organisations worldwide have invited the NL exhibition and, particularly, its VR experience to display at their location. The UK government had invited the project to display the NL VR experience in the 'Preventing Sexual Violence Initiative Conference'. The UN undersecretary-general for genocide prevention has also invited the NL team to show the experience to the UN secretary-general during a high-level event in New York to commemorate the victims of genocide. The experience also gained the attention, welcoming or funding of other European, North American, African and Australasian organisations and institutions.[6] So, in addition to raising awareness, empathy and advocacy, the NL VR experience is showing strong potential to work as an effective fund- and donation-raising tool from local and international organisations and governments for such humanitarian projects and/or the Yazidi cause.

After fine-tuning the VR experience and translating its content to the two formal languages in Iraq (Arabic and Kurdish), a systematic formal evaluation of its cognitive and affective impact will be undertaken in Iraq at the end of 2020. This evaluation will be carried out with local users by the DCH Research Group in collaboration with the NL project and some of its partners. The evaluation and two public outreach events in Iraq will be funded by UN IOM (International Organisation for Migration) and USAID.

Conclusion

In AR- and VR-mediated museum experiences, users (museum visitors in the real or virtual world) are not passive consumers of *facts*. Instead, they become active participants in the making of the experiences through their actions, interactions and reactions in the interactive virtual or hybrid worlds. With higher sensorial engagements, these experiences enable museums to dive deeper into users' emotions, minds and actions. Deeper engagement with heritage creates unprecedented opportunities to powerfully recreate, reveal, see, listen to or even touch untold difficult stories and memories from history. AR and VR experiences also present opportunities for engaging those who are disengaged, raising awareness, increasing public dialogue and seeing through the eyes of 'others', for making distant or recent difficult heritage accessible and relevant to everyone. The NL VR experience and others presented in this chapter demonstrate some of the many imaginary possibilities these *realities* technologies can make *real* for engaging with and experiencing recent and distant difficult heritage. They also highlight some of the challenges to be overcome or managed with the adoption and integration of such technologies by or in museums.

Unlike the gaming and entertainment industry, cultural heritage institutions like museums often have authoritative and legitimising powers. The influence of these powers appears even stronger in presenting and interpreting multifaceted and high-stakes difficult heritage topics and events. Therefore, AR and VR technologies' persuasive power needs to be responsibly and sensitively exploited during the design, development and delivery of AR and VR experiences for difficult heritage engagement. Informed, inclusive and participatory content selection, design and production are even more essential for AR- and VR-mediated difficult heritage experiences.

As more museums are developing unintegrated 'Big Shiny Projects' using cutting-edge technologies like AR and VR, long-term vision and maintenance become a necessity (Weinard 2018). Lack of digital integration and maintenance planning and funding raises serious questions about the sustainability of these technology-based experiences in museums with limited technical infrastructure and resources. In general, AR and VR experience developments consume time and resources and require multidisciplinary collaborations. These needs are further intensified in developing AR and VR experiences for the sensitive and complex ecosystem of museums (real or virtual) with higher social responsibilities and lower budgets. Also, like any other museum technologies, they require maintenance. Currently, many of the AR and VR project developments and maintenance are outsourced by museums. As AR and VR research and development communities strive to make these technologies more accessible and easier to develop, museums and other users across the cultural heritage sector need long-term investment in their technical infrastructure, resources and skills.

Aside from the practicality challenges of AR and VR adoption by museums, the long-term impact of these technologies on the dynamic relationship of museums and their diverse audiences requires in-depth understanding. The cognitive and affective impacts of attracting museum visitors to new immersive and interactive *realities* with difficult and nondifficult heritage need more research. As more are yet to be revealed, it is clear that the emerging technologies of AR and VR bring new realities and novel experiences to the ever-changing museums and a growing tech-savvy population.

Rozhen Kamal Mohammed-Amin is an academic with an interdisciplinary background and research interest in the confluence of digital technology, architecture, and cultural heritage. She holds BSc in architectural engineering from the University of Sulaimani in the Kurdistan Region of Iraq and a master's and Ph.D. degrees in computational media design and environmental design from the University of Calgary in Canada. She is currently an Associate Professor at the Kurdistan Institution for Strategic Studies and Scientific Research (KISSR), and a co-founder of the Cultural Heritage Organization (CHO). From 2020 to 2024, she co-directed the Nahrein Network at University College London (UCL), where she remains an Honorary Research Fellow. She has undertaken professional and scholarly activities in 23 countries across North America, Europe, Asia, Australasia, and the Middle East. She is a recipient of numerous national and international appreciations, scholarships, awards, and fellowships , and has (co)led multiple internationally funded projects.

Notes

1. Ryan X. D'Souza, Skype interview with author, 4 May 2020.
2. Ryan X. D'Souza, email to author, 10 December 2019.
3. Ryan X. D'Souza, email to author, 10 December 2019.
4. Ryan X. D'Souza, email to author, 10 May 2020.
5. Ryan X. D'Souza, Skype interview with author, 4 May 2020.
6. Ryan X. D'Souza, email to author, 9 February 2020.

References

Anderson, Mark. 2015. 'Can Tearjerker Virtual Reality Movies Tempt Donors to Give More Aid?' *The Guardian*, 31 December 2015. Retrieved 12 May 2020 from https://www.theguardian.com/global-development/2015/dec/31/virtual-reality-movies-aid-humanitarian-assistance-united-nations.

Bedigan, Kirsten M. 2016. 'Developing Emotions: Perceptions of Emotional Responses in Museum Visitors', *Mediterranean Archaeology & Archaeometry* 16(5): 87–95.

Burdea, Grigore C., and Philippe Coiffet. 2003. *Virtual Reality Technology*. Hoboken, NJ: John Wiley & Sons.

Burton, Christine, and Carol Scott. 2003. 'Museums: Challenges for the 21st Century', *International Journal of Arts Management* 5(2): 56–68.

'The Cabinet of Virtual Reality'. n.d. The National Museum of Natural History website. Retrieved 10 May 2020 from https://www.mnhn.fr/en/visit/lieux/cabinet-realite-virtuelle-cabinet-virtual-reality.

'A Call for Accountability and Protection: Yezidi Survivors of Atrocities Committed by ISIL'. 2016. UNAMI-OHCHR website. Retrieved 11 May 2020 from https://www.ohchr.org/Documents/Countries/IQ/UNAMIReport12Aug2016_en.pdf.

'Clouds Over Sidra'. n.d. UNVR website. Retrieved 18 June 2020 from http://unvr.sdgactioncampaign.org/cloudsoversidra/#.XvDIBudS-Uk.

Dakhil, Vian. 2015. 'Iraq's Only Female Yazidi MP on the Battle to Save Her People'. Agora-parl website. Retrieved 05 May 2020 from https://agora-parl.org/news/vian-dakhil-iraqs-only-female-yazidi-mp-battle-save-her-people.

Dege, Stefan. 2018. 'Who Are the Yazidis?' DW website. Retrieved 19 June 2020 from https://www.dw.com/en/who-are-the-yazidis/a-43324003.

Denver Museum of Nature & Science. n.d. 'VR Arcade'. Retrieved 10 May 2020 from https://www.dmns.org/visit/exhibitions/vr-arcade/.

Dexter Lord, Gail. 2014. 'Museum Specific Evaluation Criteria' in Barry Lord and Maria Piacente (eds), *Manual of Museum Exhibitions*, 2nd edn. Lanham, MD: Rowman & Littlefield, pp. 27–29.

'Destroying the Soul of the Yazidis'. 2019. RASHID International website. Retrieved 19 June 2020 from https://rashid-international.org/publications/report-destroying-the-soul-of-the-yazidis/.

'The Destruction of Yazidi Cultural Heritage'. 2018. Forensic Architecture website. Retrieved 7 May 2020 from https://forensic-architecture.org/investigation/the-destruction-of-yazidi-cultural-heritage.

'Emerging Land Tenure Issues among Displaced Yazidis from Sinjar, Iraq'. 2015. UN-HABITAT website. Retrieved 5 May 2020 from https://unhabitat.org/sites/default/files/documents/2019-04/emerging_land_tenure_issues_among_displaced_yazidis_from_sinjar_iraq.pdf.

Griffiths, Alison. 2003. 'Media Technology and Museum Display: A Century of Accomodation and Conflict', in David Thorburn and Henry Jenkins (eds), *Rethinking Media Change: The Aesthetics of Transition*. Cambridge, MA: MIT Press, pp. 375–89.

Harrington, Maria C. R., Markus Tatzgern, Tom Langer and John W. Wenzel. 2019. 'Augmented Reality Brings the Real World into Natural History Dioramas with Data Visualizations and Bioacoustics at the Carnegie Museum of Natural History', *Curator: The Museum Journal* 62(2): 177–93.

Harris, Blake J. 2015. 'How the United Nations Is Using Virtual Reality to Tackle Real-World Problems'. Fast Company website. Retrieved 12 May 2020 from https://www.fastcompany.com/3051672/how-the-united-nations-is-using-virtual-reality-to-tackle-real-world-problems.

Herrera, Fernanda, Jeremy Bailenson, Erika Weisz, Elise Ogle, and Jamil Zaki. 2018. 'Building Long-Term Empathy: A Large-Scale Comparison of Traditional and Virtual Reality Perspective-Taking', *PLOS One* 13(10): e0204494. Retrieved 7 May 2020 from https://doi.org/https://doi.org/10.1371/journal.pone.0204494.

Ibrahim, Hawkar, Verena Ertl, Claudia Catani, Azad Ali and Frank Neuner. 2018. 'Trauma and Perceived Social Rejection among Yazidi Women and Girls Who Survived Enslavement and Genocide', *BMC Medicine* 16(1): 154. Retrieved 9 May 2020 from https://www.ncbi.nlm.nih.gov/pmc/articles/PMC6136186/.

'Immersive Exhibition'. 2019a. *Nobody's Listening* website. Retrieved 7 May 2020 from https://www.nobodys-listening.com/exhibition.

'International Recognition of the Yazidi Genocide'. n.d. YAZDA website. Retrieved 6 May 2020 from https://www.yazda.org/genocide-recognition.

Jalabi, Raya. 2014. 'Who Are the Yazidis and Why Is Isis Hunting Them?' *The Guardian*, 11 August 2014. Retrieved 19 June 2020 from https://www.theguardian.com/world/2014/aug/07/who-yazidi-isis-iraq-religion-ethnicity-mountains.

Janes, Robert R. 2007. 'Museums, Social Responsibility and the Future We Desire', in Simon Knell, Suzanne MacLeod, and Sheila Watson (eds), *Museum Revolutions: How Museums Change and Are Changed*. Abingdon, Oxon: Routledge, pp. 134–46.

Johnston, Holly. 2019. '*Nobody's Listening*: A Fresh Approach to Help Iraq's Forgotten Minorities?' *Rudaw*, 4 December 2019. Retrieved 7 May 2020 from https://www.rudaw.net/english/culture/04122019.

Kidd, Jenny. 2019. 'With New Eyes I See: Embodiment, Empathy and Silence in Digital Heritage Interpretation', *International Journal of Heritage Studies* 25(1): 54–66. Retrieved 7 May 2020 from https://doi.org/10.1080/13527258.2017.1341946.

Lord, Barry. 2014. 'The Purpose of Museum Exhibitions' in Barry Lord and Maria Piacente (eds), *Manual of Museum Exhibitions*, 2nd edn. Lanham, MD: Rowman & Littlefield, pp. 27–29.

McDonnell, Patrick J. 2014. 'Iraqi Yazidis Describe Flight from Islamic State Militants'. *Los Angeles Times*, 10 August 2014. Retrieved 04 May 2020 from https://www.latimes.com/world/middleeast/la-fg-iraq-yazidis-20140810-story.html.

'Meet the Team'. n.d. *Nobody's Listening* website. Retrieved 7 May 2020 from https://www.nobodys-listening.com/team.

Merritt, Elizabeth. 2016. 'Me/We/Here/There: Museums and the Matrix of Place-Based Augmented Devices'. American Alliance of Museums website. Retrieved 9 May 2020 from https://www.aam-us.org/2016/05/01/meweherethere-museums-and-the-matrix-of-place-based-augmented-devices/.

Milgram, Paul, Haruo Takemura, Akira Utsumi and Fumio Kishino. 1995. 'Augmented Reality: A Class of Displays on the Reality-Virtuality Continuum', *Proceedings of the Telemanipulator and Telepresence Technologies*, Boston, 21 December 1995. Retrieved 3 May 2020 from https://www.spiedigitallibrary.org/conference-proceedings-of-spie/2351/1/Augmented-reality--a-class-of-displays-on-the-reality/10.1117/12.197321.short.

'Mona Lisa: Beyond the Glass'. n.d. VIVE Arts website. Retrieved 11 May 2020 from https://arts.vive.com/us/articles/projects/art-photography/mona_lisa_beyond_the_glass/.

Morrow, Adrian. 2017. 'Amal Clooney Denounces UN's Inaction as Genocide of Yazidis by IS Continues'. *The Globe and Mail*, 9 March 2017. Retrieved 6 May 2020 from https://www.theglobeandmail.com/news/world/human-rights-lawyer-amal-clooney-denounces-uns-inaction-as-genocide-of-yazidis-by-is-continues/article34262535/.

'On the Road to the Mountain, They Stopped Us'. 2017. Heartland Alliance website. Retrieved 5 May 2020 from https://www.heartlandalliance.org/on-the-road-to-the-mountain-they-stopped-us/.

Parry, Ross, and Andrew Sawyer. 2005. 'Space and the Machine: Adaptive Museums, Pervasive Technology, and the New Gallery Environment', in Suzanne MacLeod (ed.), *Architecture, Design, Exhibitions*. Oxon: Routledge, pp. 39–52.

'Partners'. 2019b. *Nobody's Listening* website. Retrieved 7 May 2020 from https://www.nobodys-listening.com/partners.

Peng, Jingyu. 2019. 'How Does This Exhibition Make You Feel? Measuring Sensory and Emotional Experience of In-Gallery Digital Technology with GSR Devices', *Proceedings of the Annual Conference of Museums and the Web*, Boston, 2–6 April 2019. USA: Museum and the Web (MW). Retrieved 3 May 2020 from https://mw19.mwconf.org/paper/how-does-this-exhibition-make-you-feel-measuring-sensory-and-emotional-experience-of-in-gallery-digital-technology-with-gsr-devices/.

Perry Hobson, J. S., and Paul Williams. 1997. 'Virtual Reality: The Future of Leisure and Tourism?' *World Leisure & Recreation* 39(3): 34–40. Retrieved 7 May 2020 from https://doi.org/10.1080/10261133.1997.9674077.

Peyre-Costa, Tom, and Thale Jenssen. 2018. 'Close to 200,000 Yazidis Remain Displaced'. Norwegian Refugee Council website. Retrieved 5 May 2020 from https://www.nrc.no/several-hundred-thousand-yazidis-remain-displaced.

Rae, Juno, and Lizzie Edwards. 2016. 'Virtual Reality at the British Museum: What Is the Value of Virtual Reality Environments for Learning by Children and Young People, Schools, and Families', *Proceedings of the Annual Conference of Museums and the Web*, Los Angeles, 6–9 April 2016. USA: Museum and the Web (MW). Retrieved 3 May 2020 from https://mw2016.museumsandtheweb.com/paper/virtual-reality-at-the-british-museum-what-is-the-value-of-virtual-reality-environments-for-learning-by-children-and-young-people-schools-and-families/.

Robertson, Adi. 2016. 'The UN Wants to See How Far VR Empathy Will Go'. *The Verge*, 19 September 2016. Retrieved 12 May 2020 from https://www.theverge.com/2016/9/19/12933874/unvr-clouds-over-sidra-film-app-launch.

'Sandby Borg – Difficult Heritage Brought to Life with VR'. n.d. RISE website. Retrieved 18 June 2020 from https://www.ri.se/en/our-stories/sandby-borg-difficult-heritage-brought-life-vr.

Savenije, Geerte M., and Pieter de Bruijn. 2017. 'Historical Empathy in a Museum: Uniting Contextualisation and Emotional Engagement', *International Journal of Heritage Studies* 23(9): 832–45. Retrieved 8 May 2020 from https://doi.org/10.1080/13527258.2017.1339108.

Shieber, Jonathan. 2015. 'Museum Collections Enter VR with the Launch of the Woofbert VR App for Samsung Gea'. Tech Crunch website. Retrieved 10 May 2020 from https://techcrunch.com/2015/11/17/museum-collections-enter-vr-with-the-launch-of-the-woofbert-vr-app-for-samsung-gear/.

Sly, Liz. 2014. 'Exodus from the Mountain: Yazidis Flood into Iraq Following U.S. Airstrikes'. *Washington Post*, 10 August 2014. Retrieved 3 May 2020 from https://www.washing tonpost.com/world/exodus-from-the-mountain-yazidis-flood-into-iraq-following-us-air strikes/2014/08/10/f8349f2a-04da-4d60-98ef-85fe66c82002_story.html.

'The Ultimate Dinosaurs: Giants from Gondwana'. n.d. Royal Ontario Museum website. Retrieved 12 May 2020 from https://www.rom.on.ca/en/exhibitions-galleries/exhibitions/the-ultimate-dinosaurs-giants-from-gondwana.

'They Came to Destroy: ISIS Crimes Against the Yazidis'. 2016. OHCHR website. Retrieved 7 May 2020 from https://www.ohchr.org/Documents/HRBodies/HRCouncil/CoISyria/A_HRC_32_CRP.2_en.pdf.

Thian, Cherry. 2012. 'Augmented Reality—What Reality Can We Learn From It?' *Proceedings of the Annual Conference of Museums and the Web*, San Diego, 11–14 April 2012. USA: Museum and the Web (MW). Retrieved 3 May 2020 from https://www.museumsandtheweb.com/mw2012/papers/augmented_reality_what_reality_can_we_learn_fr.

Tillon, Anne Bationo, Isabelle Marchal, and Pascal Houlier. 2011. 'Mobile Augmented Reality in the Museum: Can a Lace-like Technology Take You Closer to Works of Art?', *IEEE International Symposium on Mixed and Augmented Reality-Arts, Media, and Humanities*, Basel, Switzerland, 26–29 October 2011. IEEE. Retrieved 3 May 2020 from https://ieeexplore.ieee.org/document/6093655.

'UN Commission of Inquiry on Syria: ISIS Is Committing Genocide against the Yazidis'. 2016. UN-OHCHR website. Retrieved 05 May 2020 from https://www.ohchr.org/EN/HRBodies/HRC/Pages/NewsDetail.aspx?NewsID=20113&LangID=E.

'Unearthing Atrocities: Mass Graves in Territory Formerly Controlled by ISIL'. 2018. UNAMI-OHCHR website. Retrieved 11 May 2020 from https://www.ohchr.org/Documents/Countries/IQ/UNAMI_Report_on_Mass_Graves4Nov2018_EN.pdf.

'Virtual Reality, Empathy and the Next Journalism'. n.d. WIREDwebsite. Retrieved 18 June 2020 from https://www.wired.com/brandlab/2015/11/nonny-de-la-pena-virtual-reality-empathy-and-the-next-journalism/?fbclid=IwAR0ckVwGvhqk4XyavDUnTNk-hHdy-K6gg F9R0ZPqUu3eE4gsNZu7JztWZSA.

Weinard, Chad. 2018. 'Maintaining' the Future of Museums'. Retrieved 20 June 2020 from https://medium.com/@caw_/maintaining-the-future-of-museums-d72631f6905b.

'Who Are the Yazidi, and Why Is ISIS Targeting Them?' 2014. *NBC News*, 8 August 2014. Retrieved 19 June 2020 from https://www.nbcnews.com/storyline/isis-terror/who-are-yazidi-why-isis-targeting-them-n175621.

Chapter 5

DIMENSIONS IN TESTIMONY

Affect, Holograms and New Curatorial Challenges

Elena Stylianou

'How can we get people to use the lessons of the past to transform the future – to build empathy and an understanding of our common humanity . . . working towards a day when "never again" is a reality for all people?' The answer is combining historical storytelling with technology.
　　　　　　—Illinois Holocaust Museum and Education Center Facebook page [1]

Museums and Emerging Technologies: What Is All the Fuss About?

The last few decades have witnessed a widespread use of technologies in museums, ranging from handheld devices, tablets, interactive kiosks and screens to smartphone applications and videos. More recently, emerging technologies such as virtual reality (VR), augmented reality (AR) and mixed reality (MR) have also started appearing in museum settings.[2] These are technologies that provide 'sensory experiences through various combinations of real and digital content' (Kassahun et al. 2018: 2) and are used for different purposes in museum exhibitions. Whether they are deployed for familiarising visitors with the collection, enhancing engagement with the stories on display, filling in the blanks in history making and/or the reconstruction of artefacts, or making a temporary exhibition more attractive[3] and increasing visitor numbers, the adoption and use of these technologies is no longer an unexpected or surprising event in museums. The ease of deployment and affordability of these technologies, coupled with museums' ongoing concerns about sustaining their relevance, has led to the inclusion of more and more sophisticated emerging technologies in museum displays.

Visitors' developing familiarisation with technologies – including AR and VR – both inside museums as well as in their everyday life, from films and video games to educational settings and personal mobile applications, acts as incentive for museums to adopt interactive and multimedia technologies. This is perceived as a way of attracting audiences and retaining numbers. Susan Marenoff-Zausner, president of the Intrepid Sea, Air & Space Museum, says that not only do their artefacts and the physical experience of touring around the space shuttle in the museum 'create this exciting and tactile opportunity', but the adoption of different types of technologies is also in fact seen as a necessity in order to sustain the interest of the current generation by engaging them 'in the language they're speaking' (cited in Pardes 2018: n.p.). Sree Sreenivasan, chief digital officer, and Loic Tallon, deputy chief of digital, at the Metropolitan Museum of Art, similarly explain that the main aim of the museum's expansive Digital Department (over seventy employees) is to remain relevant and keep pace with the changing expectations and habits of their audiences (as cited in Dodge 2016).

The extensive use of technology is part of our society's behaviour, a 'new normal', and museums owe it to their communities to embrace that behaviour in their strategic planning if they wish to avoid seeing their visitors seeking that seamless experience elsewhere, in other attractions and entertainment sites (Murphy 2015). In any case, museums need to decide when, how and to what extent they should invest valuable time and resources for the design and implementation of emerging technologies in their collections, as technology's relevance to and impact on museum narratives and displays remains seminal.

This chapter specifically focuses on this aspect of the use of emerging technologies in museums: the impact on museum narrative structures, but also the implications for both audiences and the museum's own process of defining itself and its social role. Particular emphasis is given to the use of holographic technology – until recently still undeservingly seen as a technology of the future[4] – yet increasingly adopted by museums worldwide. The next section briefly analyses holographic technology and its history and lays the groundwork for an in-depth analysis of a specific case of holographic application in museums: *Dimensions in Testimony*, an initiative developed by the University of Southern California (USC) Shoah Foundation, in association with the Illinois Holocaust Museum, which uses 3D holography to capture and preserve survivor testimonies.

Museums and Holography: A Technology of the 'Future'

Holography is not something new. It has a long history dating back to the late 1940s, when Hungarian émigré and research engineer Dennis Gabor conceived a technology that could improve image quality in electron microscopy. Initially called 'holoscopy', it was adopted in various fields and took several forms over the next decade before it was judged as limited and categorised as a white elephant by the same industrial laboratory that initially pursued its development (Johnston 2005). Interest in holography was revived in the early 1960s by electrical engineers and physicists who combined findings in information theory and optics with newly developed lasers. A key moment was when Emmett Leith, a research engineer at the Willow Run Laboratories of the University of Michigan, presented a coauthored paper (with Juris Upatnieks) at a conference in Washington, DC, in early 1964 and demonstrated an extension of Gabor's ideas (Johnston 2005, 2009). A journalist recorded similar demonstrations in a hotel suite in Boston that same year; scientists and engineers had gathered to play with a toy locomotive that, according to the journalist, 'wasn't really there at all' (cited in Johnston 2005). The reconstruction of the toy train was made using gas laser projected onto a special photographic plate; an early, yet accurate, reproduction of a three-dimensional object and the basis of future experimentations with holographic technology.

Holographic technology, an optical technology that literally means 'I describe everything' (Pietroni et al. 2019: 4) is essentially based on a two-step imaging process. Sean Johnston provides a clear description of the process in his historical overview of holography:

> First, an interference pattern (the 'hologram') is recorded by superimposing two beams of light, one reflected from the subject and the other traveling directly from the light source. . . . Since 1963 holograms have almost exclusively been recorded using lasers, but other light sources . . . have adequate coherence for some purposes. The interference pattern of the hologram is recorded on a photosensitive material. . . . The second step of the imaging process is the reconstruction of the wave front of light by illuminating the hologram with a suitable light source. (2005: 79; see also figure 5.1)

The diffracting beams of laser light produce a three-dimensional light field as a reproduction of an original object or scene. The resulting holographic images, although seemingly three-dimensional, were until recently and most frequently, simply two-dimensional renditions, as they were viewed 'on the flat screen of a display monitor or projected onto a flat surface such as a wall or sheet of glass' (Corning 2019). These projections currently tend to be classified as false holograms or fauxlography.

Nevertheless, holography captured popular imagination by awakening an old attraction to magic and the mysterious (Johnston 2017). 'Like a magic show, the disorientation, surprise and charm of viewing holograms reduced even experts to a state of unsophisticated wonder' (Johnston 2017: 494). The dematerialisation of the image, the opening up of a window to another world, and the poten-

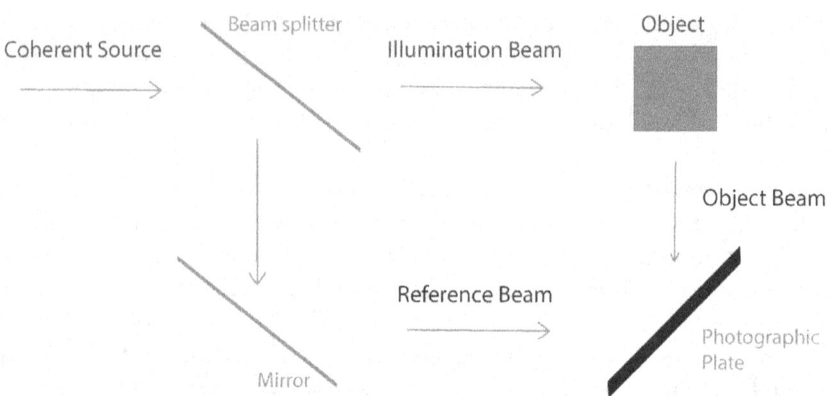

FIGURE 5.1. Illustration of how holographic technology works. Diagram by the author.

tial of the viewer to interact with the produced holographic scene and/or image were among the elements that enthused audiences, but they were also left perplexed about its workings. The ability of holography to cause childlike wonder and surprise, as much as its mysterious and intuitive properties, led to the adoption of technology that could produce holographic-like displays mainly by the entertainment industry, for example at Disneyland in the late 1960s (Johnston 2017). The infamous Haunted Mansion projected ghostly floating images. Over the next few decades, 'Pepper's Ghost', as the effect was known, familiarised the public extensively with holography, and although not actually being holography it masqueraded as such for the decades to come (Johnston 2017: 494).

It was not long ago that the industry was finally able to overcome its technological limitations and design three-dimensional holographic objects that are colourful and low static while also maintaining volume, coming close to fulfilling what previously remained a science fiction fantasy, only possible in films such as *Star Trek*. One such process involves the recording of three-dimensional information by filming an object from multiple angles, using a number of cameras that each take an image of the object every second. These views are then processed into

> holographic pixel data by a computer, which sends a signal to two pulsed laser beams that then write the data into the recording material. During the writing process, the two beams combine to create an interference pattern of light and dark patches in the recording material. Firing another light at the pattern reconstructs the 3D image. (Merali 2010: n.p.)

More recently, another solution was developed at Brigham Young University that uses lasers to trap tiny particles and controls their movements to create an image. This technique, although still not safe to be used outside the laboratory, seems to come closer to how holograms were popularised in the media in the second half of the twentieth century. It produces holographic images that can 'be projected into thin air – also called "volumetric images" – [and can] be viewable from all sides with 360-degree visual dimensionality' (Corning 2019).

A lack of generally accepted collective terms for these fast-changing technologies – holographic[5] as well as AR and MR (Kassahun et al. 2018) – means it is difficult to determine what belongs under this category; nevertheless, holograms today are in most cases 3D images shown on a 2D surface (Corning 2019). Many argue that true holograms are only those that require no headset technology and allow the viewer to see the three-dimensional object from every perspective. For the purposes of this chapter, however, holography and holograms are viewed more broadly, encompassing anything that uses the principles of holographic technology in any manner described above. This can include holographic projections with which a user can interact in an MR environment wearing headset technology, such as Microsoft's HoloLens,[6] as well as holographic displays that provide a dynamic three-dimensional representation without the need for a headset, such as the ones used in *Dimensions in Testimony* (to be discussed in the following sections).

Ultimately, the chapter explores the ways in which holography is used by museums as a means of establishing a more direct dialogue and stronger links between digital content, real collections and museum visitors. It is especially concerned with visitors interacting with people and objects that are not really there, engaging with stories that were left behind or experiencing an environment that is long gone in the physical world, all the while still being in the museum and among the real exhibits (Pietroni et al. 2019). At the Intrepid Sea, Air & Space Museum, for instance, a hologram of Dr Mae Jemison,[7] the first woman of colour to go into space, gives a tour of the Space Shuttle *Enterprise*. Visitors wearing a HoloLens headset can listen to Jemison while exploring both real and virtual artefacts. The hologram of Jemison introduces space history but also presents previously marginalised narratives by talking about the women who have historically made significant contributions to space exploration.

The Kyoto National Museum also demonstrates how holographic technology can be used to enhance the visitor experience. The museum collaborated with hakuhodo-VRAR (a specialised factory that produces Japan's latest VR and AR technologies) to create a hologram of a Zen Buddhist monk that tells the story of the 'Folding Screen of Fujin and Raijin' (otherwise known as 'the Wind God and Thunder God Screens') painted by Tawaraya Sōtatsu over four hundred years ago (Hansen 2018). The holographic monk guides users inside Kennin-ji, the oldest Zen Buddhist temple in Japan, providing a narrative about the painting, making connections with other artists inspired by Sōtatsu and the theme of the gods of wind and thunder, and showcasing 3D renditions of these artworks that are physically dispersed in other museums.

Holographic technology is sometimes used as a form of theatre to produce characters that talk to visitors, encouraging them to engage with the exhibits on display, as in the 'Treasure Seekers' exhibit at the Tampa Bay History Center. Holographic pirates appear on a life-sized pirate ship giving visitors instructions as to how and when to fire virtual cannonballs at other ships. Utilising the effects of theatre is, of course, not new. Rather, several historic examples showcase the power of the surrounding or immersive image to create the effect of illusion, of feeling that you are actually there. Theorist Oliver Grau (2003) has extensively discussed the historicity of these image spaces of illusion that aimed to surround the viewer and has traced their history in various examples from the European art historical tradition. These image spaces appear as early as in the cult and garden frescos in Italy, the Renaissance perspectival rooms and the ceiling panoramas in Baroque church architecture, as well as in panoramas and cycloramas of the nineteenth century (Grau 2003).

One of the most popular cases is the Battlefield of Gettysburg Cyclorama, one of two remaining cycloramas in the United States. Originally painted by Paul Dominique Philippoteaux, the four-hundred-foot-long, fifty-foot-high painting was inaugurated in 1884 in a huge cyclical room, after the French artist spent months interviewing survivors and sketching on site. His realistic rendering of the event created a spectacular tableau that provides the illusion of being at the battle of Gettysburg, while actual props in the foreground like dirt, debris and cannons complete the illusion. Visitors feel immersed in the actual battlefield. While acknowledging the varying degrees of success in achieving a feeling of immersion, Grau highlights the significance of the human desire to consistently 'produce maximum illusion with the technical means at hand' (2003: 5). Thus, it is not surprising that more than a hundred years later, the cyclorama would be revived in a multimedia exhibition to enhance the illusion.

In February 2019, multimedia interactives at the Atlanta History Center were used to recover the other surviving cyclorama: the Battle of Atlanta. The Atlanta History Center aimed to bring to life this old form of art and entertainment by overlaying it and enhancing it with a panoramic multi-projector film that included different points of view, offering the opportunity for an expansive critical perspective about the ways in which history is made. Through this exhibition, the centre affirms the importance of questioning the ways in which 'perceptions, memory and interpretations [can] be shaped, or misshaped, by a combination of art and entertainment, myth and memory, cultural context, and current events during different eras'.[8] At the same time, the multimedia projection was designed so that alternative voices from people equally affected by the Civil War, but not originally depicted in the painting, such as African Americans and women, were represented, included and heard.[9]

Dimensions in Testimony, a collection of testimonies by genocide survivors, is exemplary in its adoption of holographic technology to produce holographic images that one can see without needing a headset and in its similarity in function to the multimedia interactive described above: it reanimates the past and makes visible and public stories that were previously obscured, silenced or concealed – sometimes by the survivors themselves who were often reluctant to share their stories.[10] Primarily funded by the USC Shoah Foundation, which was established by Steven Spielberg in 1994 following his award-winning film *Schindler's List*, the project was developed in association with the Illinois Holocaust Museum, and it aims 'to document first-hand accounts of the Holocaust for future generations' (O'Brien 2017: n.p.). More recently, it expanded to collect what Spielberg calls 'living testimony' from modern genocide victims from places like Cambodia, Armenia, Guatemala and the Central African Republic (Popescu 2018).

Beyond an acknowledged potential of such technologies to offer museum experiences that are entertaining, educative and awe-inspiring, holography also opens up the possibility of engaging audiences with difficult histories in alternative and meaningful ways. At the same time, such technological applications raise questions about the impact holographic technologies in museums have on memory and affect, as much as they do about processes of memorialisation and spectacularisation. The sections that follow will focus on *Dimensions in Testimony* as a prime example of how holographic technologies can be both valuable and problematic, as they can equally foster empathy and give prominence to trauma.

Technology and Affect: *Dimensions in Testimony*

Dimensions in Testimony cannot be interpreted in isolation from portrayals of the Holocaust across history, politics, literature, visual culture and art, a phenomenon that has led many to speak of the saturation and even commercialisation of the Holocaust. Cultural and critical theorist Andreas Huyssen has talked about it as an event historically established as unique among other examples of ethnic cleansing and the resulting risk in the hierarchisation of suffering (Patrick 2018). He further identifies the surfacing of this issue in 'claims of Holocaust uniqueness [that] have been instrumentalised, either for political purposes or for a last-ditch aesthetic defense of a now untenable modernist theory of unrepresentability' (Huyssen in Patrick 2018: n.p.). Other theorists, such as Reesa Greenberg (2007), claim instead that many would prefer to forget the Holocaust or believe the event and its repercussions are behind them. Aaron Breitbart, a senior researcher at the Simon Wiesenthal Center – a human rights organisation that has worked with the USC Shoah Foundation since the 1990s – claims that the foundation has made a significant contribution to the memory of the Holocaust, because not only are some willing to forget but, even worse, there are those who are willing to deny it (Popescu 2018).[11] Thus, the narratives of the survivors in *Dimensions in Testimony* have a dual function, both as testimony and concrete evidence of an event that actually happened and as a form of memorialisation, ensuring that it will keep being remembered. This aligns with a more generally acknowledged desire of survivors to 'document and testify to the existence of the Holocaust in the face of Holocaust deniers' (Witcomb 2010: 43) and to use testimony as an integral process of remembering and perseverance (Witcomb 2013).

This can also be seen alongside a widespread fascination with trauma and the emergence of trauma theory, often put on par with memory. Memory discourses that emerged in the wake of decolonisation and as part of the 1960s Western avant-gardism in search of alternative and revisionist histories were in the 1980s 'energized by the broadening debate about the Holocaust' and of the testimony movement: the rise of autobiography, the proliferation of historical documentaries on television, memoir writing, confessional literature and the spread of visual memory practices centred on photography (Huyssen 2000: 22). As Andreas Huyssen argued in an interview (in Ganito and Agostinho 2013), the turn to memory over recent decades has to do less with our anxiety around an uncertain future and more with a political process of working through traumatic histories – such as the Holocaust, apartheid, genocide – in the present. Traumatic histories and trauma can be individual and collective, personal and political and refer to an event that cannot be assimilated, because it is opposed to our sense of self, similarly to Julia Kristeva's (1982) notion of the abject. It is thus in this relationship to memory that the paradox of trauma lies: 'Trauma is felt but not understood; it is memorized and recalled, but not necessarily experienced; it defies language, but insists on being communicated; it refuses to be incorporated into normality but goes on perpetuating itself in memory' (Resende and Pudryte 2014: 2). At the same time, it is in trauma's remembrance that traumatic histories can be dealt with in the present.

When addressing difficult histories, museums often document and memorialise trauma through the portrayal of atrocities, pain and victimhood, which can result in the triggering of intense emotions (Stylianou 2019). The intense emotions caused by testimony and remembrance facilitate a level of engagement that, according to Rachel Perry (2017), might be the only means of avoiding the sensationalist exploitation of death, violence and suffering that could ultimately revictimise the victim (a common characteristic in exhibitions that negotiate difficult histories). More so, disremembering or denying the reality of others' trauma and suffering can lead to defusing our sense of responsibility, restricting solidarity and allowing others to suffer alone (Alexander 2004). That said, numerous Jewish and Holocaust museums and memorials around the world have recently shifted their focus from what Theodor Adorno (1973) has described as a moral predicament, i.e. how one can continue to write poetry, make art, even exist after Auschwitz, to the centrality of the Holocaust's representation in displays through the personal account (Katsaridou 2017). Shying away from the death paradigm (explicit displays of atrocity and death), museums nowadays often place their emphasis on personal and individual voices, favouring 'an ethical imperative to experience Holocaust memory by identification and empathy' (Katsaridou 2017: 48). This bottom-up approach in processes of history telling has now been embraced by many museums as an alternative yet equally powerful form of evoking emotion.

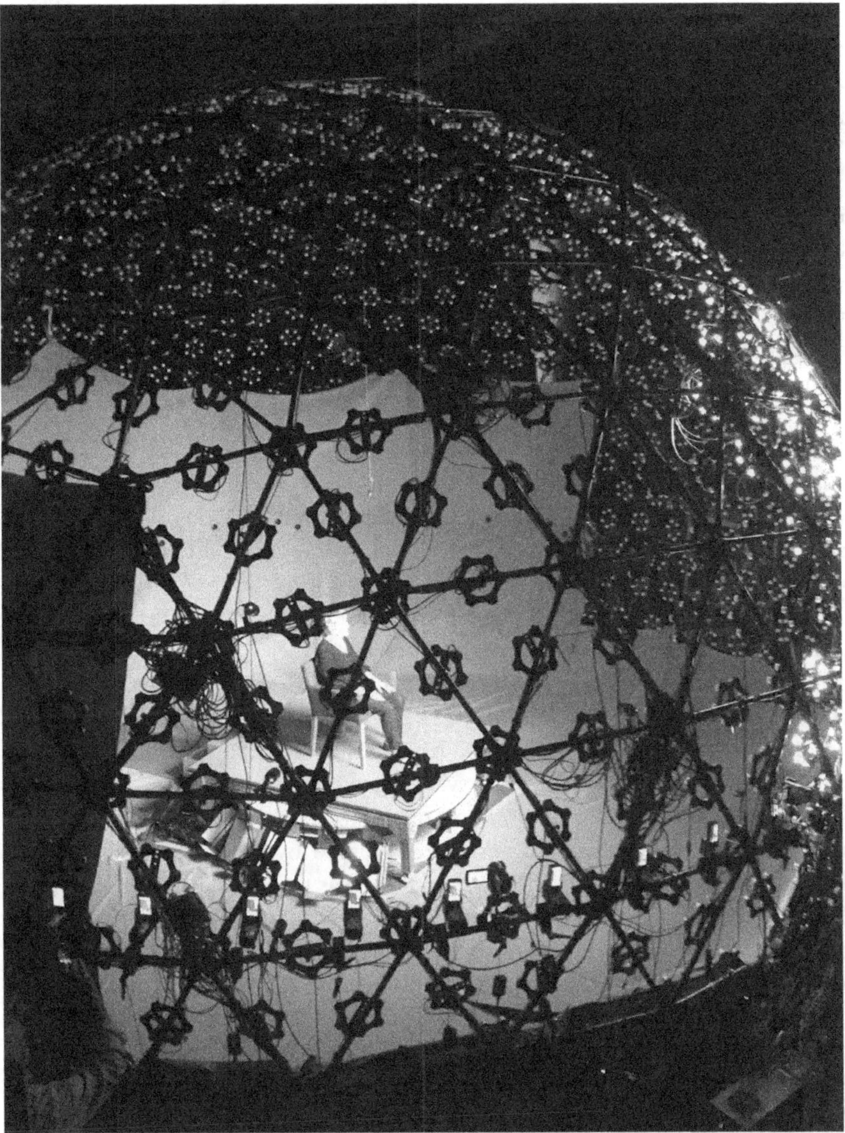

FIGURE 5.2. Holocaust survivor recording her testimony for the Survivor Stories Experience, featuring *Dimensions in Testimony*, developed by the USC Shoah Foundation in association with the Illinois Holocaust Museum. Image courtesy of the Illinois Holocaust Museum.

Returning to the idea of the image space of illusion and immersion in technologically constructed environments, Oliver Grau recognised that in these attempts rests a desire to minimise the 'psychological distance' between the image space and the observer (2003: 6). In a similar manner, creating the conditions of feeling close to the survivor through their own testimony and listening to a personal narrative in real time minimises the psychological distance between the victim/survivor and the visitor. And when distance is eliminated, one can become the other, be in the other's position. 'Now you have a piece of me, and I have a piece of you. We're joined together now', says Holocaust survivor Pinchas Gutter, who was one of the first to be interviewed in 2014 for *Dimensions in Testimony* (McMullan 2016). Andrea Witcomb added that 'testimonies are predicated on the possibility of empathic listening', as the act of listening creates the hope of reconstituting the victim as whole again (2013: 261). No longer alone, victims regain a sense of self that was once damaged by the denial of their humanity. Andrea Witcomb and Alexandra Bounia (2019), in their analysis of the Museum of Refugee Memory on the Greek island of Lesvos, describe the process of making a group of people whole again, by healing their collective trauma, as one of restoration.

The creators of *Dimensions in Testimony* claim that the project is about the authenticity of the voice of the individual and the recording of those voices that would otherwise get lost as survivors age and pass away. Creating this database as a form of documentation and of archiving the Holocaust raises concerns about the use of the event 'as a universal trope for historical trauma' (Huyssen 2000: 23). This centrality of the Holocaust might prevent us from considering local particularities, politics and histories, but it can also serve as proof of our failure to live with otherness (Huyssen 2000). Emphasis has also been put on creating the conditions for intimacy (Smith in O'Brien 2017) and immediacy (Smith in Goode 2017) as a way of 'understanding empathy and using testimony to shine a light' (Popescu 2018: n.p.) on the event as a whole.

Testimonies by Pinchas Gutter and other survivors included their responses to more than 1,500 questions and were recorded by 116 cameras in over 20 hours of interviewing time. The large database was then used by the USC Shoah Foundation in a way that would conceal the meticulous and complex technical aspects of the project behind fully functioning interactive holograms of the survivors. When holograms are asked a question, the responses are generated using automatic speech recognition and natural language processing to locate the most appropriate answer for the question asked, giving the illusion of a real-time one-to-one and face-to-face dialogue. Stephen Smith, the executive director of the USC Shoah Foundation, claims that these conversations are about the visitors and what they want to learn from the Holocaust survivors.[12] It is a self-driven learning process based on the power of conversation, that moment of dialogue that deeply and meaningfully engages the visitor, as well as on the belief that

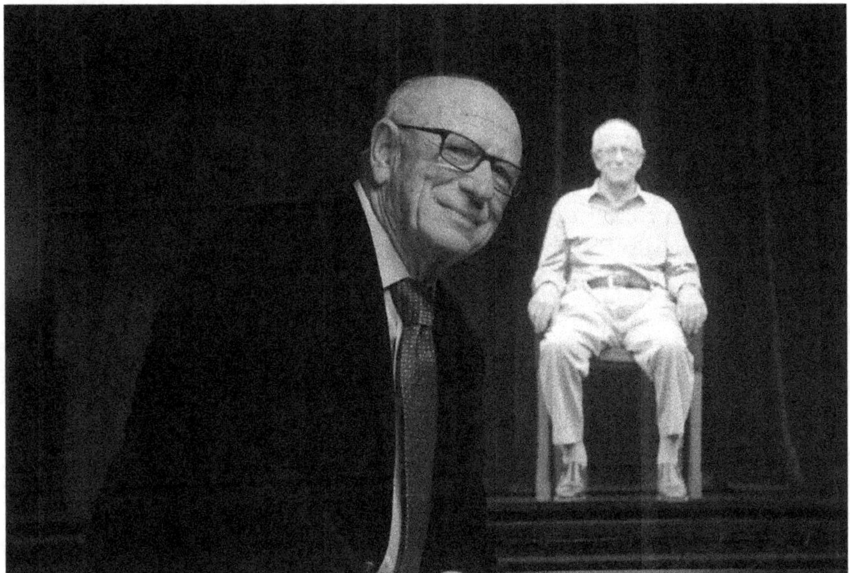

FIGURE 5.3. Holocaust survivor Sam Harris with his hologram in the Survivor Stories Experience at the Illinois Holocaust Museum, featuring *Dimensions in Testimony*, developed by the USC Shoah Foundation in association with the Illinois Holocaust Museum. Image by Ron Gould Studios.

curiosity drives learning. Gutter's above affirmation that every time he speaks, part of him becomes embedded in the visitor reflects this sense of potentially eliminating the psychological distance and becoming one with the survivor, an ultimate definition of empathy: stepping into someone else's shoes.

The reasons these experiences feel so real and powerful and for which museums opt for this technique over the overt display of death merit further discussion. From Gutter's example, it seems that it is not just the access to the personal and authentic voice of the survivor that is of importance but also the potential of the hologram to become someone – rather than something – who looks at, responds to and speaks back at the viewer. The level and degree of the interaction creates the illusion that we are actually looked at, talked back to, considered; it makes us feel more present at the moment of engagement. This fabricated sense of being looked at creates the conditions of a gaze that makes us more aware of our own sense of presence. Nicholas Mirzoeff (1999) refers to Jean-Paul Sartre's description of a similar situation in which one may look through a keyhole without any awareness of the self, until the moment footsteps are heard in the hall. Awareness of the self is gained through the realisation that one is gazed at, because – according to Sartre – the gaze of the other is what validates one's existence. According to Mirzoeff (1999), in an era when human experience is more visual than ever, while also increasingly visualised through interactive technologies, seeing becomes more than believing. And in this case, it is about seeing one's self and one's own position in the holographic narratives. Returning to the above discussion about the ease with which people can refute, deny or remain detached from the trauma of others, placing them in a direct position of being looked at forces them to become part of that trauma and unable to refuse their own position in the particular narrative. They are locked in the gaze of the holograms of the survivors and their testimonies.

Certainly, the degree to which technology's virtual materiality is able to trigger emotional and visceral responses is difficult to assess. It does however confirm that the museum's approach to curatorship acknowledges the significance of proximity to the 'original' object/experience/personal account. Essentially, *Dimensions in Testimony* serves here as an example of how the deployment of emerging technologies could revise curatorial storytelling, as well as the authorial voice, by challenging existing narrative devices, negotiating collectivity through affect and transforming exhibitions into spaces of political agency. However, if seeing is more than believing, then one needs to also question the responsibility of such visual mediation of human experience, trauma and conflicted histories. On the one hand, in the case of *Dimensions in Testimony*, technology seems to have the potential to trigger visitors' empathy and possible agency and critical involvement with the histories it narrates, as well as to broaden the museum's existing narratives about the Holocaust. On the other, technology is in danger of becoming another means of exploitation and excessive mediation of trauma caused by survivors' personal accounts.

Holography, Testimony and Curatorial Approaches

While recognising the significance of safeguarding testimony and the personal account to allow the opening up of processes of history making and a more inclusive bottom-up approach to record keeping, one cannot but also identify an equally relevant risk for the commercialisation and spectacularisation of trauma in ways that not only revictimise the survivors but also shy away from an honest and critical engagement with the past. Huyssen argues that the challenge with Holocaust memory remains the same: 'ideological exploitation, saturation on the one hand, evasion, indifference on the other' (Ganito and Agostinho 2013: 5). So the question, then, is whether emerging technologies, and holographic technologies in particular, can offer an alternative solution to the above ethical dilemma embedded in the politics of testimony or whether they simply perpetuate it.

As Andrea Witcomb (2013) suggests, giving testimony is not a simple process because it has a dual function. It is a psychological process of providing evidence and overcoming the absence of the dead. It is also a process of addressing the observers, the perpetrators, the bystanders who are thus held accountable, as well as other survivors and present-day audiences who, as listeners, can offer the victims their sense of being human and whole again (Witcomb 2013). However, as the experience of the Holocaust historically 'represents the loss of faith in the possibility of empathy' (Witcomb 2013: 261), one can assume that if the survivors' testimonies are unable to reach audiences in the intended way – as a means of making them whole again – then a real risk of reliving the trauma (by reliving a lack of empathy) is prominent.

Other theorists suggest that reliving the trauma in the present is inherent to the process of testimony, because trauma remains '"owned" and unshareable even once it is communicated' (Bennett 2005: 6). Survivors are invited to recall experiences and memories of a past event, which continue to have an impact on their lives up until the moment of their testimonies. Thus, as technologies of mediation, museums must consider the ways in which individual and collective memory can be communicated through holograms such as the ones used in *Dimensions in Testimony* and the implications of such mediation. This is especially so, as the narrative structures shaped by the personal account seem to be less based on a cognitive, detached engagement and are directed more by what Sharon Macdonald (2013) calls an embodied mode of engagement with the past, linked to debates about the relationship between history and emotions.

Similarly, audiences to *Dimensions in Testimony* are not detached from the widespread mediation of the trauma of the Holocaust in other media. Marianne Hirsch's work on postmemory has defined how memory about the Holocaust has been transmitted to the next generation through the recollections and personal stories of the survivors, achieved in a deeply affective and unconscious manner (Hirsch 2012). In more recent years, it has also been recognised that postmemory can be attained through more than personal accounts; it can also be mediated through other popular sources, such as social media, YouTube videos, photographs, online news channels and movies. In the museum, the personal testimony has been used parallel to and in close connection with other forms of 'evidence', such as photographs or personal objects (i.e. passports, shoes, clothes, etc.) – all additional technologies of mediation aiming to trigger an emotional response through identification.

Thus, for audiences, narratives such as the ones experienced in *Dimensions in Testimony* are likely to have varying effects. In the best-case scenario, the audience finds a way to connect with the survivors and their testimonies. After all, 'witnesses can "see" better into, or listen more effectively to, themselves; and viewers, similarly, respond to that intimacy' (Hartman 2001: 118), which leads to a sense of empathy. Empathy can nevertheless be a complicated emotion that might conceal feelings of guilt and shame. The rupture with the image of Western civilisation as the bastion of elevated values can lead to feelings of resentment (Bennett

2005; LaCapra 1998). Alternatively, testimonies about the Holocaust (or any other traumatic event), enhanced by the event's concurrent visualisation in our oversaturated media societies, can cause a secondary traumatisation: the immediacy of the narration in combination with the visual immediacy of the images can be particularly painful. Finally, survivors' stories can sometimes fail altogether to resonate with audiences, falling short of the desired critical engagement.

Andrea Witcomb (2016) gives the example of the 'Shrine of Remembrance' at the Australian War Memorial to argue that an extreme approach to evoke emotion in presenting and exhibiting history often leads to uncritical sentimentality. At the same time, though, the use of narrative and storytelling – as a way of shaping our perception of ourselves and our position in the world – is 'a means of creating empathetic links between the subjects and audiences of museum displays' (Hans, Hale, and MacLeod 2012: xxii). Nevertheless, narrative as the result of an embodied experience with the past (Macdonald 2013) and as an acknowledged human construct becomes a process of inclusions, exclusions, editing, incompletion and biases; the museum needs to remain alert of all relevant dangers and inconsistencies. As Hans et al. argue, 'In creating a coherent story to tell, contested narratives and dissonant voices are quieted, and the heterogeneous and ultimately unknowable truth is left behind' (2012: xxii). History has tended to be overtly criticised as a human construct, linked to elitist institutional practices that aimed at organising the past based on interests and biases, yet masked as value-free facts, while memory has instead been increasingly seen as providing a true and unviolated account (Macdonald 2013).

As a result, many museums today embrace and adopt the bottom-up approach to storytelling – already discussed in this chapter – opting for multiple personal stories over the authoritative voice of an expert curator. This approach can, however, romanticise memory as real and authentic, overlooking memory's equally problematic and hugely subjective nature. Survivors' testimonies are narrated in the first person. They are the subjective recollections of what happened and are very specific to each survivor's own experiences. But, as Geoffrey Hartman argues, 'the past cannot be confined to the past' (2001: 117),[13] and when it comes to Holocaust survivors, the past has continued to shape the lives and the memories they are called to unearth and share as testimony. These testimonies are also more than about bearing witness to something that happened; indeed, they are about speaking in the place of those who did not survive, testifying to that which cannot be witnessed – their deaths.

Considering the above, how can one evaluate the degree – if any at all – to which affect through technology is a positive and desired curatorial approach, or whether the use of holograms ends up spectacularising and commercialising trauma to such a degree that it diverts from the possibility of critical engagement with the history to which they testify? In other words, does the use of holograms – with their potential to create a sense of proximity and to activate a level of enthusiasm due to their quality of the magical – offer a viable alternative to the exhibition of difficult and/or traumatic histories? Or does testimony documented and presented through holograms of survivors simply risk romanticising the past and its narration? While all these are valid questions that museums need to consider in their curatorial decisions, the use of holographic technologies itself adds to the issues at hand. While technologies can be fascinating and fun, as they engage the senses and incite curiosity, they can be easily bypassed by visitors. And although the creators of *Dimensions in Testimony* claim that this project was not about technology, visitors can quickly and easily think and feel otherwise. Often associated with the fear of dumbing down an exhibition, reducing the museum experience to one of 'edutainment' at the expense of scholarship and solemnity, or bearing the weight of imminent obsoleteness (Newell 2012) and, more currently, contributing to fake news, the use of technologies is not as straightforward as initially thought.

Conclusion: Why Holography Then?

The Holocaust is among the many historical events that have had a tremendous impact on both personal and collective memories, shaping history and its narration in very specific ways that are influenced by both memory and trauma. This is especially true considering that 'the passing of time results in inevitable erasures, and conscious or unconscious forms of denial, evasion, and forgetting make questions about the past in the present extremely difficult to answer' (Huyssen in Eser 2018: n.p.). The idea that it is mainly through the acute representations of death that museums can sustain memory and secure remembering of the past in the present has been increasingly challenged and gradually replaced by the personal narrative. In this chapter, *Dimensions in Testimony* was used as a case study to argue about the use of interactive holographic technologies in the museum as a way of supporting the individual voice and storytelling that in effect can lead to a critical dialogue with history and the past. Despite the acknowledged risks of exploitation and spectacularisation of trauma, as well as the sensitisation of memory in displays of personal testimonies, holographic technologies can offer two things that are distinctive and useful.

For one, they can resolve Bennett's question on how 'the staging of shock can become more than an aesthetic conceit or a kind of metaphoric appropriation of trauma' (2005: 11). Holographic technologies – especially those without headsets – provide a temporal and spatial distinction from the viewer: the viewer cannot touch them; holograms and viewers inhabit a different position in the experienced environment; the viewer bears witness to gestures and movements of the hologram that might momentarily distract from the story being told; and holograms still exist even if the viewer walks away from the display. While the sense of immersion and the argument about emerging technology's success is based on a desired proximity between the viewer and the hologram, I argue here that a certain degree of 'failure' of proximity is essential if critical engagement is the aim.

While seen by many as a disadvantage and a failure of technology that needs to be resolved, maintaining distance (which runs counter to the philosophy of VR and AR immersive technologies) is actually necessary in order to achieve empathy and critical engagement with difficult and/or traumatic histories. Empathy is indeed achieved when psychological distance is eliminated, but not to the point that you become the other (Bennett 2005), as Pinchas Gutter seems to believe. What Bennett calls an empathy grounded in affinity – '*feeling for* another as insofar as we can imagine *being* that other' (2005: 10, emphasis in original) – is, I argue here, a condition where all the feelings of secondary trauma, guilt or resentment discussed above can be made manifest. Instead, what museums should do is create the conditions for an encounter that will allow empathy grounded on a *feeling for* another, who remains irreducible and different (Bennett 2005: 10) by being temporally and spatially distanced from the viewer. In other words, experiencing the holograms of survivors as another – not as something – allows for enough psychological proximity while at the same time maintaining enough distance to feel empathy grounded on *a feeling for* rather than *being* another.

The second contribution of holographic technologies paradoxically rests on their problematic nature of phantasmagoria and the magical, which is directly linked to fears around the spectacularisation of trauma. However, it is because of this quality that audiences are attracted to holographic technologies like the ones used in *Dimensions in Testimony* to an extent that it could potentially contribute to politics of testimony: transforming trauma from a psychological condition or state of being to a political argument (Fassin 2008). As Fassin argues, trauma is not just a psychological condition but 'also the political expression of a state of the world' (2008: 533). In his analysis, he affirms that to speak of *political subjectification* is to speak of a subject and of subjectivities within a framework of social interaction. In other words, the subject needs to be able not just to be present but also to present himself/herself (Fassin 2008). Holograms of survivors not only represent the story of the Holocaust but also become subjects that represent themselves and engage with visitors in a simulated environment of social interaction. Their stories thus become about more than a personal trauma, the experience of violence or testifying for those who did not survive, which would demote survivors to the category of trauma victim or to the condition of victimisation. Reimaging the survivors as holograms offers both survivors and viewers the opportunity to interpret violence not merely through the lens of trauma or the explicit representation of death through secondary sources in the museum but through conversation. The upholding of a sense of agency inherent in a situation where the viewer guides the discussion allows the viewer to exist politically, because he/she bears first-hand witness to Holocaust testimonies. Viewers become witnesses of affect: that which is produced by testimony – *feeling for* the other during the interaction with the holograms – but also 'that which testifies (the suffering of the people)' (Fassin 2008: 539). In effect, contemporary visitors are going to be the future survivors, able to testify their experience with these holograms and sustain Holocaust memory through the politics of affect and testimony.

Elena Stylianou is Associate Professor in Art and Art History at European University Cyprus and Director of the Nicosia Municipal Arts Center (NiMAC), associated with the Pierides Foundation. Her research and curatorial work focus on photography, modern and contemporary art, and museum and curatorial practices. She has curated numerous exhibitions in Cyprus and published widely in journals and edited volumes. She co-edited *Contemporary Art from Cyprus: Politics, Identities and Cultures Across Borders* (Bloomsbury, 2021) and *Museums and Photography: Displaying Death* (Routledge, 2018). She holds a doctorate from Teachers College, Columbia University, and has received several awards, including a Fulbright Scholarship and a Getty–CAA grant. She previously held a postdoctoral position at UCL and is involved in multiple EU-funded projects, including AccessibleEU.

Notes

1. From the Illinois Holocaust Museum and Education Center Facebook page, Facebook post on 9 April 2021, relating to Museum CEO Susan Abrams's talk at TEDxWilmette about how museums can use interactive technologies to give visitors the opportunity to engage with history. Retrieved 19 July 2021 from https://www.facebook.com/IHMEC.
2. Augmented reality (AR) and mixed reality (MR) are often used interchangeably, even by companies within the emerging technology industry. Some theorists argue that MR is an umbrella definition that refers to the blending of real and virtual environments (Kassahun et al. 2018; Sieburg 2019). Others argue that AR is an umbrella term that includes all other subcategories (including MR) and covers any technology that puts a digital overlay on the real world (Frayne 2019). For the purposes of this chapter, I have adopted the first definition of MR as a technology that covers various forms of AR, including those that use holographic technologies for the creation of 3D holographic images/objects/people with which the user can engage (constituting a virtual environment) and which are then overlaid on real-world environments.
3. Maria Shehade and Theopisti Stylianou-Lambert (2000) in research that explores the experiences of museum professionals with VR, mention that one of the limitations of VR in museums is its high cost of maintenance. This, along with a lack of staff expertise and the need to keep up with newly released software versions, are among the reasons VR technologies tend to be limited for use in temporary exhibitions. The same applies for other emerging technologies such as holograms. Sean Johnston (2009) also identifies the

cost of maintenance as one of the major reasons these technologies are often only used in temporary museum exhibitions.

4. Maimone et al. mention that, despite digital holography's powerful features, the technology was often associated with noise, low contrast, high-bandwidth requirements and expensive computations, among others things, 'relegating it to the status of a perpetually "future" technology' (2017: 2).

5. Since its inception in the 1960s, holography was variously termed as 'holoscopy', 'wave front reconstruction', and 'diffraction microscopy' (Johnston 2005). Over the years, terms, categories and manifestations have continued to vary. Defining the range of categories of holographic technology is beyond the scope of this chapter, but some recent examples of its different manifestations, such as holographic pyramids, holographic smokescreens, volumetric images (considered to be the closest to an actual 3D hologram as we'd recognize from sci-fi movies), can be found on company websites and blogs by optical engineers and physicists. See Kerrigan 2018; Merali 2010; Neverovich 2019; Sieburg 2019. Also, the HoloCenter: Center for the Holographic Arts website at http://holocenter.org/ and various company websites, such as Microsoft at https://www.microsoft.com/en-us/hololens.

6. Microsoft's HoloLens was developed in 2015 and is a headset with transparent lenses that create holographic projections that are displayed in the real world and which only the wearer can see and interact with (Sieburg 2019). Microsoft refers to these three-dimensional projections as mixed reality holograms. See https://www.microsoft.com/en-us/hololens.

7. Microsoft's Mixed Reality Capture Studio in San Francisco used 106 cameras to record the hologram of Dr Jemison (Richardson 2019).

8. From the Atlanta History Center website: https://www.atlantahistorycenter.com/explore/exhibitions/cyclorama-the-big-picture.

9. As stated by Kia Meredith-Caballero, a producer at Cortina Productions who worked on the restoration of the cyclorama. See https://www.cortinaproductions.com/battle-of-atlanta/.

10. In an email correspondence with Dr Martha Stroud (29 October 2020), associate director and senior research officer at the USC Shoah Foundation, she explained that *Dimensions in Testimony* is, in fact, constituted of a two-dimensional display of video clips and that, institutionally, the Shoah Foundation avoids the use of the term 'hologram'. The USC Shoah Foundation has worked with leaders in the field of three-dimensional video capture, referred to as volumetric capture, to ensure that the *Dimensions in Testimony* interviews can be projected as holograms when that technology is available. As she further explained in our correspondence, the USC Shoah Foundation developed and built one of the first-ever mobile volumetric capture filming rigs, with twenty-three 4K cameras circling the interviewee in 360 degrees. Some of the *Dimensions in Testimony* museum partners have installed a holographic Pepper's Ghost theatre for their visitors to interact with. Pepper's Ghost displays, as already described above, are visual illusions that use lighting, specialized glass and high-definition projection to give the appearance of depth to two-dimensional videos, making it seem like a three-dimensional hologram. Dr Stroud further emphasized that the most significant aspect of the project is the innovative interactivity provided by *Dimensions in Testimony*, calling it a collection of interactive biographies. This aspect is essential, and it is further analyzed in this chapter.

11. Also, for an extensive discussion on Holocaust deniers, pseudohistory and debates about the extent to which this falls within freedom of speech, see Shermer and Grobman (2000).

12. From the website of the USC Shoah Foundation: https://sfi.usc.edu/dit.

13. Geoffrey Hartman (2001) discusses recording survivor testimonies for an oral histories project conducted at Yale University. The project started in 1979, and by 1981 it was able to create the first video archive of Holocaust testimonies, which in many ways is reminiscent of *Dimensions in Testimony*. In this chapter, Hartman raises several issues relevant to ethics, the power of the camera, voyeurism and the politics of testimony.

References

Adorno, Theodor. 1973. *Negative Dialectics*. New York: Continuum.

Alexander, Jeffrey C. 2004. 'Towards a Theory of Cultural Trauma', in Jeffrey C. Alexander et al. (eds), *Cultural Trauma and Collective Identity*. Berkeley: University of California Press, pp. 1–30.

Bennett, Jill. 2005. *Empathic Vision: Affect, Trauma and Contemporary Art*. Stanford, CA: Stanford University Press.

Corning, Anne. 2019. 'Seeing in 3D: Advancements in Holographic Display Technology'. Radiant Vision Systems website. Retrieved 16 June 2020 from https://www.radiantvision systems.com/blog/seeing-3d-advancements-holographic-display-technology.

Dodge, Ryan. 2016. 'Technology – Are Museums Keeping Pace?' *MUSE: The Voice of Canada's Museum Community* 35(1): 40–45.

Eser, Patrick. 2018. 'State of the Art in Memory Studies: An Interview with Andreas Huyssen'. Politika website. Retrieved 28 February 2020 from https://www.politika.io/en/notice/state-of-the-art-in-memory-studies-an-interview-with-andreas-huyssen.

Fassin, Didier. 2008. 'The Humanitarian Politics of Testimony: Subjectification through Trauma in the Israeli–Palestinian Conflict', *Cultural Anthropology* 23(3): 531–58.

Frayne, Shawn. 2019. 'Holograms, VR, AR & the Future of Reality'. Looking Glass Blog. Retrieved 14 June 2020 from https://blog.lookingglassfactory.com/announcements/holograms-vr-ar-the-future-of-reality/.

Ganito, Tânia, and Daniela Agostinho. 2013. 'On Memory and the Yet to Come: Interview with Andreas Huyssen', *Diffractions: Graduate Journal for the Study of Culture* 1: 1–7.

Goode, Lauren. 2017. 'Are Holograms the Future of How We Capture Memories?' The Verge website. Retrieved 10 February 2020 from https://www.theverge.com/2017/11/7/16613234/next-level-ar-vr-memories-holograms-8i-actress-shoah-foundation.

Grau, Oliver. 2003. *Virtual Art: From Illusion to Immersion*. Cambridge, MA: MIT Press.

Greenberg, Reesa. 2007. 'Mirroring Evil, Evil Mirrored: Timing, Trauma, and Temporary Exhibitions', in Griselda Pollock and Joyce Zemans (eds), *Museums after Modernism: Strategies of Engagement*. Malden, Oxford and Victoria: Blackwell Publishing, pp. 104–18.

Hans, L. H, J. Hale and S. MacLeod. 2012. 'Introduction: Museum Making – The Place of Narrative', in S. MacLeod et al. (eds), *Museum Making: Narratives, Architectures, Exhibitions*. New York: Routledge, pp. xx–xxiii.

Hansen, Jeff. 'Mixed Reality Museum in Kyoto: A unique insight into centuries-old Japanese artwork'. Microsoft / Features. Retrieved 19 July 2021 from https://news.microsoft.com/apac/features/mixed-reality-museum-kyoto-unique-insight-centuries-old-japanese-artwork/.

Hartman, Geoffrey. 2001. 'Tele-suffering and Testimony in the Dot Com Era', in Barbie Zelizer (ed.), *Visual Culture and the Holocaust*. New Brunswick, NJ: Rutgers University Press, pp. 111–26.

Hirsch, Marianne. 2012. *The Generation of Postmemory: Writing and Visual Culture after the Holocaust*. New York: Columbia University Press.

Huyssen, Andreas. 2000. 'Present Past: Politics, Media, Amnesia', *Public Culture* 12(1): 21–38.

Johnston, Sean. 2005. 'Shifting Perspectives: Holography and the Emergence of Technical Communities', *Technology and Culture* 4(1): 77–103.

———. 2009. 'Representing Holography in Museum Collections', in P. Morris and Klaus Staubermann (eds), *Illuminating Instruments*. Washington, DC: Smithsonian University Press, pp. 97–116.

———. 2017. 'Holograms: The Story of a Word and Its Cultural Uses', *Leonardo* 50(5): 493–99.

Kassahun, M. B., et al. 2018. 'A Survey of Augmented, Virtual, and Mixed Reality for Cultural Heritage', *ACM Journal of Computing and Cultural Heritage* 11(2): 1–36.

Katsaridou, Iro. 2017. 'Honoring the Dead: Photography and the Display of the Jewish Necropolis at the Jewish Museum of Thessaloniki', in Elena Stylianou and Theopisti Stylianou-Lambert (eds), *Museums and Photography: Displaying Death*. New York: Routledge, pp. 40–61.

Kerrigan, Saoirse. 2018. '13 Hologram Projections around the World That Are More than Just a Pretty Display'. Interesting Engineering website. Retrieved 14 June 2020 from https://interestingengineering.com/13-hologram-projections-around-the-world-that-are-more-than-just-a-pretty-display.

Kristeva, Julia. 1982. *Powers of Horror: An Essay on Abjection*. New York: Columbia University Press.

LaCapra, Dominick. 1998. *History and Memory after Auschwitz*. Ithaca, NY: Cornell University Press.

Macdonald, Sharon. 2013. *Memorylands: Heritage and Identity in Europe Today*. New York: Routledge.

Maimone, A., et al. 2017. 'Holographic Near-Eye Displays for Virtual and Augmented Reality', *ACM Transactions on Graphics* 36(4): 1–16.

McMullan, Thomas. 2016. 'The Virtual Holocaust Survivor: How History Gained New Dimensions', The Guardian. Retrieved 19 July 2021 from https://www.theguardian.com/technology/2016/jun/18/holocaust-survivor-hologram-pinchas-gutter-new-dimensions-history.

Merali, Zeeya. 2010. 'Star Wars–Style Holograms: A New Hope?' Nature website. Retrieved 16 June 2020 from https://www.nature.com/news/2010/101103/full/news.2010.579.html.

Mirzoeff, Nicholas. 1999. *Introduction to Visual Culture*. New York: Routledge.

Murphy, Adrian. 2015. 'Technology in Museums: Making the Latest Advances Work for Our Cultural Institutions'. Museums + Heritage Advisor website. Retrieved 14 June 2020 from https://advisor.museumsandheritage.com/features/technology-in-museums-making-the-latest-advances-work-for-our-cultural-institutions/.

Neverovich, Maria-Isabella. 2019. 'How Does Holographic Projection Work?' Hypervsn website. Retrieved 16 June 2020 from https://hypervsn.com/blog/How-Does-Holographic-Projection-Work.html.

Newell, Jenny. 2012. 'Old Objects, New Media: Historical Collections, Digitization and Affect', *Journal of Material Culture* 17(3): 287–306.

O'Brien, Sara Ashley. 2017. 'Shoah Foundation Is Using Technology to Preserve Holocaust Survivor Stories'. CNN Business website. Retrieved 3 February 2020 from https://money.cnn.com/2017/04/24/technology/shoah-foundation-holocaust-remembrance-day/index.html.

Pardes, Arielle. 2018. 'For Museums, Augmented Reality Is the Next Frontier'. Wired website. Retrieved 20 February 2020 from https://www.wired.com/story/museums-augmented-reality-next-frontier/.

Perry, Rachel E. 2017. 'Remediating Death at Yad Vashem's Holocaust History Museum', in Elena Stylianou and Theopisti Stylianou-Lambert (eds), *Museums and Photography: Displaying Death*. New York: Routledge, pp. 216–37.

Pietroni, E., et al. 2019. 'Bringing the Illusion of Reality Inside Museums – A Methodological Proposal for an Advance Museology Using Holographic Showcases', *Informatics* 6(2): 1–43.

Popescu, Adam. 2018. 'Stephen Spielberg on Storytelling's Power to Fight Hate', Art & Design, *New York Times*. Retrieved 3 February 2020 from https://www.nytimes.com/2018/12/18/arts/design/steven-spielberg-shoah-foundation-schindlers-list.html.

Richardson, Jim. 2019. 'How Are Museums Using HoloLens?' MuseumNext website. Retrieved 20 June 2020 from https://www.museumnext.com/article/museums-and-hololens/.

Shehade, Maria, and Theopisti Stylianou-Lambert. 2020. 'Virtual Reality in Museums: Exploring the Experiences of Museum Professional', *Applied Sciences* 10(11): 4031.

Shermer, Michael, and Alex Grobman. 2000. *Denying History: Who Says the Holocaust Never Happened and Why Do They Say It?* Berkeley: University of California Press.

Sieburg, Karl. 2019. 'Creating Holograms with the Microsoft HoloLens'. Codeburst.io blog on Medium website. Retrieved 20 June 2020 from https://codeburst.io/creating-holograms-with-the-microsoft-hololens-6f06fe46893e.

Stylianou, Elena. 2019. 'Affect and Trauma in Museums: An Interpretive Framework for Understanding the *Real Thing* and Its Political Potential', *Museum Management and Curatorship* 34(3): 306–22.

Witcomb, Andrea. 2010. 'Remembering the Dead by Affecting the Living: The Case of Miniature Model of Treblinka', in Sandra H. Dudley (ed.) *Museum Materialities: Objects, Engagements, Interpretations*. New York: Routledge, pp. 39–52.

———. 2013. 'Testimony, Memory, and Art at the Jewish Holocaust Museum, Melbourne, Australia', in Viv Golding and Wayne Modest (eds), *Museums and Communities: Curators, Collections and Collaboration*. New York: Bloomsbury, pp. 260–74.

———. 2016. 'Beyond Sentimentality and Glorification: Using a History of Emotions to Deal with the Horror of War', in Danielle Drozdzewski, Sarah De Nardi and Emma Waterton (eds), *Memory, Place and Identity: Commemoration and Remembrance of War and Conflict*. New York: Routledge, pp. 205–20.

Witcomb, Andrea, and Alexandra Bounia. 2019. 'The Restorative Museum: Understanding the Work of Memory at the Museum of Refugee Memory in Skala Loutron, Lesvos, Greece', in Sarah De Nardi et al. (eds), *The Routledge Handbook of Memory and Place*. New York: Routledge, pp. 13–21.

Chapter 6

'WE CAN'T FIX THE FUTURE IF THEY DON'T RECOGNISE OUR PAST'

The Uses of Immersive Technologies for a Child Sexual Abuse Museum in Australia

Lily Hibberd

Introduction

When Australian prime minister Scott Morrison announced on Monday, 22 October 2018, that he would, as part of his national apology to survivors and victims of child sexual abuse, 'commit to establishing a national museum, a place of truth and commemoration, to raise awareness and understanding of the impacts of child sexual abuse' (Morrison 2018), it came as a surprise. Made in response to the Royal Commission into Institutional Responses to Child Sexual Abuse (Australian Government 2014b), Morrison's apology not only spanned 3,489 separate establishments (state-run, religious and cultural organisations), it also implicated thousands of victims with different experiences of abuse.[1] A year later, Morrison (2019) provided an update on the progress of the promises; however, the child sexual abuse museum was not mentioned. The only recent reference appears on the second to last page of a progress report stating there will be 'updates about further work on the museum' (Australian Government 2019a: 100).

Given the challenges of creating such a museum from ethical, practical and aesthetic perspectives, let alone the expense, it seems unlikely that this promise will be realised. Despite this impasse, the proposal raises important questions about the role of contemporary museums in addressing what has been defined as 'difficult heritage' (Logan and Reeves 2009; Macdonald 2009).[2] For instance, how can historic child sexual abuse be represented in a public place? What sort of materials, archives, evidence or scenography would be appropriate, ethical and safe? How can this be done without glossing over the evidence and the traumatic reality? How can a museum adequately represent the diverse experiences of so many different victims? And, finally, who would this museum serve: the victims, the state or the public, adults or children?

According to the Australian Institute of Family Studies (Quadara 2013: n.p.), child sexual abuse is a 'profoundly hidden form of harm – due to secrecy, shame, embarrassment, and disbelief'. The public, too, share in the perceived taboo of child sexual abuse. Truth-telling and open accounts of the legacies of child sexual abuse are crucial not only for survivors but also for strengthening general understanding and developing prevention strategies. Creative arts is a powerful means to both open up difficult topics and translate raw trauma in ways that the public can cope with and apprehend. Truth-telling of child sexual abuse has yet to harness the possibilities of experimental immersive technologies, which could be used to generate the novel documentation of historic child sexual abuse and to provide the means for its inclusion in museums. In this chapter, I take up the challenges implicated in the Australian government pledge as an occasion to examine this potential from three perspectives.

First, I consider the unique ways that survivors themselves have forged new tropes of immersion and novel museological approaches. This is based on insights that I gained during the creation of the 3D 360-degree film *Parragirls Past, Present: Unlocking Memories of Institutional 'Care'* (2017), which explores the experiences of abuse that took place at Parramatta Girls Home, a former Australian child welfare institution, in the 1960s and early 1970s. Second, I offer a brief overview of how children's interests and childhood are currently represented in museums to illustrate the lack of suitable approaches to date for a child sexual abuse museum. Third, innovations arising from *Parragirls Past, Present* are highlighted to outline the applicability of immersive media for this purpose. As the proposed Australian national memorial museum is intended to be dedicated to child sexual abuse that occurred in numerous Australian public and private organisations responsible for the education and/or care of children, I am not suggesting that the single instance of *Parragirls* is suitable for this larger history.[3] Instead, I draw on our novel approaches and knowledge to delineate what might be appropriate and ethical for the museum's subject matter while also being viable and empowering for survivors, as well as what might better serve the need for deeper public understanding of this difficult heritage.

The Genesis of *Parragirls Past, Present*

The immersive film *Parragirls Past, Present*, coauthored with media artists Alex Davies and Volker Kuchelmeister and five former residents of Parramatta Girls

Home, developed from many years of groundwork and collaboration. In 2006, three former residents of the girls home – Bonney Djuric, Lynette Aitken and Christina Green – formed an advocacy group to support other adult survivors. Self-named 'Parragirls', these women had been teenage inmates of the Parramatta Girls Home, a child welfare institution on the correctional or reformatory model that operated in Western Sydney from 1887 to 1974. It was Bonney Djuric, herself an artist and writer, who invited me in 2012 to establish Parragirls Memory Project as a collaboration with Parragirls at the nexus of contemporary art and social history.

The project was crucially located on the site of the institution where the abuse had taken place, a site that had been closed to almost all former residents since the day of their release. In most cases, this meant that more than forty years had elapsed since they had set foot on the premises. The memory project provided the unique opportunity to retrieve or reform autobiographical memories through direct contact with the girls home, sometimes involuntarily triggering or forming episodic memories, as part of the identifying traces after many decades (Berntsen and Hall 2004; Mace 2007).[4]

As a result of three years of creative experimentation and several curated exhibitions, all taking place on site from 2012 to 2014, it emerged that the women's testimonies were inextricably tied to traces of memory embedded in that place (Hibberd and Djuric 2019; PFFP n.d.). The site itself provoked vital forms of institutional witnessing through experimental creative documentation, including performance, digital media, sound art and installation art in direct relation to and in physical interaction with the site (Hibberd 2014).

At the outset, our intention was to generate new ways for Parragirls' marginalised memories to be included in the Australian narrative, memories they had independently given form to through painting, printmaking, quilting and creative writing. The process, however, of working at the site with Parragirls led to a range of innovations that prompted us to explore digital media as the means to tackle the complexity of this difficult heritage for both documentary and museological posterity. There were several other circumstances that additionally influenced this progress, and these are important to briefly provide as background.

When we began collaborating in 2012, there were few precedents to follow, as the medical model dominated the majority of art projects we examined. Most of these centred on creativity as a therapeutic tool or relegated victims' creative work as naïve or as the product of mentally ill or defective minds. Parragirls were highly aware that such approaches reinforced their status as stigmatised victims, unable to speak for themselves, in contrast to the autonomous creative practices and historical authorship they had already established.

Moreover, during this period, a number of Parragirls working on the memory project were involved in the Royal Commission into Institutional Responses to Child Sexual Abuse (Australian Government 2014a), either by offering public testimony or by giving private evidence, as two hundred women did; others were part of compensation cases against the New South Wales state government welfare department (now named Family and Community Services, or FaCS). This process heightened the awareness that Parragirls' contemporary artworks were needed not only to contribute to the public record but also to act as a counter or alternate history from a survivor's perspective.

In addition, public inquiries had led to intense legal and media scrutiny on Parragirls. Demands were made for sensationalist news stories (rapes, beatings, escapes, riots), and their testimony was used for public justice without any personal (let alone financial) redress or empowerment as authors of that testimony. As such, there was a need to generate new accounts and forms to bridge the divide between survivors' memories and the sometimes distorted representation of child sexual abuse in journalism and in government and judicial documentation, as well as between survivors and in wider public memory.

Finally, questions of ownership over historical recordings were sharply underscored for many of the Parragirls, whose childhoods (and arguably also their adult lives) had been entirely controlled by the state welfare department. For most Parragirls, the only photographs, texts or records of their childhood are 'official' ones produced by the welfare department (admissions, medical or punishment registers, or psychological reports); as they later found out, these were frequently untruthful or concealed facts. As for many other records of children who had been in Australian state care, the Parragirls' records remained largely inaccessible until state welfare agencies began to open them up under the spotlight of the Royal Commission (see the Final Report, Commonwealth of Australia 2017: 10). *Parragirls Past, Present* was generated in the context of lifelong, large-scale and perpetuated trauma that prompted a yearning for public reckoning and memorialisation, for which no appropriate documentary witnessing yet existed.

Parragirls Past, Present: Immersive Media and the Remaking of Traumatic Memory

A range of practical, aesthetic, conceptual and artistic innovations came about as part of producing an immersive film with Parragirls. Surveying these innovations offers a basis for reflecting on their relevance to a museum devoted to commemorating historic child sexual abuse.

When the *Parragirls Past, Present* project was commissioned in 2016 for the Big Anxiety festival in Sydney, it was decided that it would inaugurate the Expanded Perception and Interaction Centre (EPICentre), a new medical visualisation laboratory at the University of New South Wales. As it was designed specifically for EPICentre's 360-degree 3D cylinder environment, the film was destined for a predetermined format: on the highest resolution cylindrical screen in the world at 120 million pixels in 3D. The 360-degree panoramic projection cylinder measures 3.2 metres in diameter, with a height of 2.98 metres. Its rear-projection display screens operate in active stereoscopic 3D and full HD, and its 36 speakers and surround-sound audio system are designed to generate and play spatialised ambisonic sound.

At the start, there seemed to be a vast distance between this computational possibility and the challenging reality of working on the site, such as being denied access to certain buildings under state government control or not being able to enter others because they were simply too terrifying for Parragirls to confront. It was, however, direct interaction with Parragirls at the Parramatta Girls Home – a place where former occupants were still uncovering and trying to understand the past for themselves – that shaped the creation of the work. Over several months, we met frequently with two Parragirls in particular, Bonney Djuric and Jenny McNally, whose integral role as cowriters of the script was ultimately fundamental to the film project. The women continued the work they had been doing for several years: walking around the precinct, seeking traces, telling stories, trying to verify memories. Repeated visits, tours and recordings exposed the need for a richer aesthetic to allow for the multiplicities of memory and time, and the uncertainty of knowing if any of their recollections were real. The question of the authenticity of digitally reconstructed places and experience in immersive technologies was important, and we felt that we could not proceed without Bonney and Jenny's insights into the implications of a 360-degree 3D virtual reality (VR) for this reconstruction.

EPICentre was due to be completed a month before the launch of the film, so Jenny, Volker and I visited UNSW's iCinema research centre, which has a fully interactive 360-degree 3D cylinder, where we experienced a range of narrative, immersive and experimental artworks. Jenny was very quick to recognise the aptitude of this platform for representing memories of Parramatta Girls Home, as she found that total immersion in a virtual environment was similar to her recollection of institutional isolation and that it resonated with some of the impacts that childhood abuse has on memory. As a result of this and many other dialogues, the work turned to focus on an experience that would convey what is like it is to remember trauma, to try to recreate what is like to have to remake such memories. Parragirls' directions, as described below, were pivotal to restructuring conventional narrative and the optical aspects of the 3D 360-degree environment for the film, specifically to place viewers of this work within the fraught embodied reality of reliving trauma in the present.

The opportunity to create a dynamic, fully interactive encounter in the EPICentre system was significant; however, a number of features of VR and heritage visualisation presented problems for Parragirls. Three main contradictions arose that required specific conceptual and technical innovations: one, traumatic memory versus realism; two, different degrees of freedom for trauma victims versus users of VR; three, empowered creative authorship versus the notion of virtual empathy. As I will discuss, the solutions we developed to overcome these contradictions are important for understanding the larger question of what role immersive technologies might have in a museum devoted to child sexual abuse.

Authenticity and Traumatic Memory in Immersive Media

The first of these contradictions centres on differing ideals about heritage and memorialisation. The reconstruction of traumatic memory produces painful effects for survivors of childhood abuse, which conflicts with nostalgic notions of the past. This problem is compounded by assumptions that digital heritage is an authentic reconstruction and that only photographic realism can truthfully convey historical events. In contrast, Parragirls describe coming back to the girls home fifty years later as part of a continuous re-creation of the past that is never complete. This is because many years had passed, so that when they interacted with spaces that they could barely recall, they had to fill in many lacunae in recollection. And, though immersion in a 3D environment tends to promote a sense of being present in a place, Parragirls were remembering a past that was no longer evident because the contemporary site was undergoing major renovation.

Trauma adds another level to the difficulty of immersion in memory, in which blankness, voids, dissociation and fragmentation are prominent features, which Parragirls often compare to Alice falling down the rabbit hole into Wonderland (Carroll 1865). The process of walking the site and recording stories, videos and digital audio over one year, however, allowed Parragirls to create a platform for missing or episodic memories, which, according to Tulving (2002: 5), permits 'mental time travel through subjective time, from the present to the past'. Narratives for the film script took shape in the same manner as these memories: as a jigsaw puzzle with lots of missing pieces. This disjunction of temporalities, nonetheless, prompted us to explore the abstraction of traumatic memory in a digitally constructed immersive world, as we juxtaposed contrasting forms of visual documentation within the 3D world to find a way to overcome photographic realism. We briefly considered archival images, but they emulated the look of a township museum, with 2D images oddly suspended in the 3D space. More crucially, the only existing historic photos of the site were those created by the welfare department, which presented a sanitised history (and blacked out, if identifiable, the girls' faces).

After several months of experimentation with different forms of immersive documentation (including 360-degree video, aerial and spatial scanning and panoramic photography), visualisation artist Volker Kuchelmeister suggested we try a method called point cloud. We all agreed that this aesthetic, featuring broken fields of vision, black voids and image fragmentation, was ideal to render the

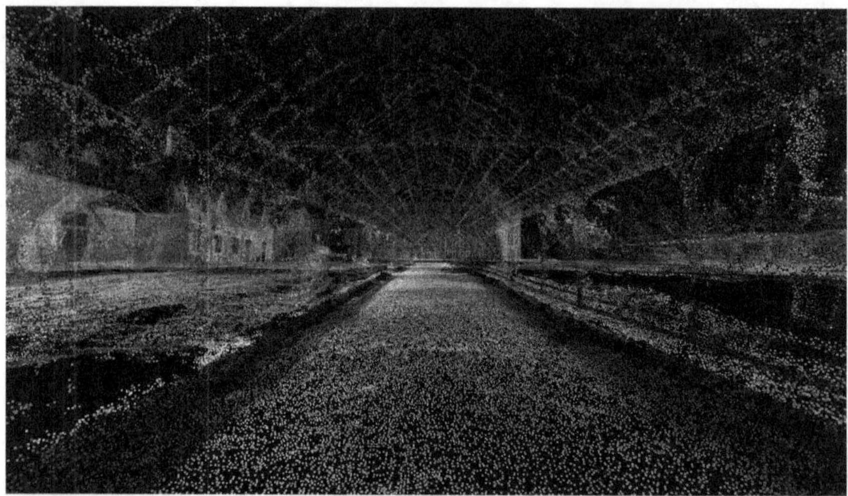

FIGURE 6.1. *Parragirls Past, Present: Unlocking Memories of Institutional 'Care'*, 2017. Still from immersive 3D 360-degree film (23 minutes). Created by Volker Kuchelmeister, Alex Davies and Lily Hibberd, with (Parragirls) Bonney Djuric, Gypsie Hayes, Jenny McNally, Tony Nicholas and Lynne Paskovski. Image courtesy of the artists.

complexities of traumatic memory and its intangible dimensions. Furthermore, for spectators in the EPICentre experience, the visual scape would form and re-form over time during their interaction, again behaving like human memory in generating new bits and pieces to fill the gaps.

Three-dimensional photogrammetric scans of the outside spaces of Parramatta Girls Home provided the basis for the point cloud representation (figure 6.1). In order to build a point cloud, a large number of discrete data 'points' or elements are required, each with information about their position (in 3D) and their nominal colour.[5] Specialised software then ingests all of these points and redistributes them in a 3D space, while a photogrammetry algorithm estimates the parameters for a camera (i.e. first-person) point of view, which produces visuals or footage of the 3D scene. The point cloud was also critical as a means to underscore the incongruity of conventional realism for the historiography of Parramatta Girls Home and the kaleidoscopic nature of witnessing trauma. In *Parragirls Past, Present*, the point cloud creates a tacit visual dissolution as the scattered particles hang over a film of light punctuated with black holes, which are in fact large areas of missing data (inaccessible areas) in the original site survey.

Other strategies conceived to produce disorientation in the work, based on conversations with Parragirls, included sound design, which we quickly realised was pivotal for the polyvocal narratives of Parragirls, as well as shifting temporalities and mnemonic gaps. A process of deep mapping and more than fifty hours of recording site walks exposed that these recollections were generally nonlinear.[6]

As such, Alex Davies and I developed several experimental modes that built on Parragirls' recurrent paths through the site. The architecture of the main external corridor, known as the 'covered way', where twice-daily line-ups and scrubbing punishments took place (figure 1) became a central motif for the temporality of remembering, standing for 'something else', as Bonney describes in the film, something 'between a past and a present'.

Yet, in decoupling the story from its referenced location, we were able to destabilise storytelling conventions that tend towards nostalgia. The experimental ambisonic design was also crafted with nonlinear temporalities in mind. We developed, for example, a unique dynamic that displaced sound effects around the 3D environment (thirty-six speakers in EPICentre). In our experiments with spatialised acoustics, we aimed to engage audiences in a dissonant realm of 'dialectical sonority', in which sound becomes tacit material that resonates with a concrete sense of historical experience that Hall (2010: 86) claims holds 'a revolutionary energy that can be actualised for later cultural-political use. Sound, thus, inaugurates a listening gaze that moves from melancholic remembrance to utopian redemption'.[7] At certain points in *Parragirls Past, Present*, sounds seem to emanate from beyond the visible realm of the 3D scene, resonating with acousmatic and nondiegetic techniques developed in opera and cinema (see Chion 1994). Parragirls' voices, however, remain firmly present, right beside us through the use of binaural recording (see chapter 10 for more details on the work's embodied acoustic effects), except for a brief cacophonous moment early in the film, in which all of Parragirls' voices and dozens of narratives are interleaved.[8]

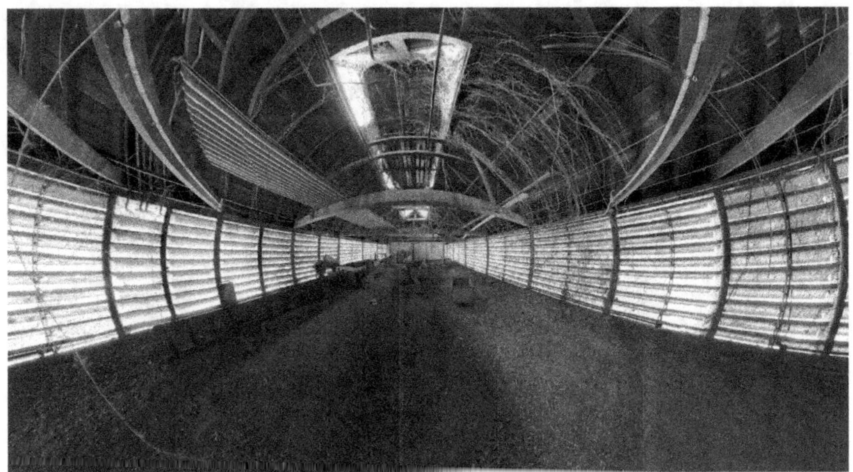

FIGURE 6.2. *Parragirls Past, Present: Unlocking Memories of Institutional 'Care'*, 2017. Panoramic production still of the loft. 3D 360-degree immersive film (23 minutes). Image courtesy of the artists.

In parallel, Parragirls approached their visits to the girls home with forensic eyes, as a means to overcome the fissures and idiosyncrasies of memory. Most were looking for traces, such as graffiti they had left behind when in solitary confinement (they refer to these as 'scratchings'). Four interior spaces were particularly important in this context as the key sites of solitary confinement where most of this abuse took place: the basement dungeon, the isolation block (demolished), segregation in the Bethel building, and the loft (figure 6.2). Bonney, among others, had also been working with Royal Commission detectives, who we knew had adopted 3D imaging to record certain spaces as supporting evidence to prosecute two former superintendents of the girls home. When the first stereoscopic panoramic photographs Volker created of these spaces were presented to Parragirls, the panoramas prompted them to further describe what could not be seen: memories of beatings and sexual assault that were also very difficult to verbalise. As such, the panoramas became an instrument of narrative witnessing beyond present-day sight in the film. When juxtaposed with the textured 3D mesh point cloud model, these panoramas produced a dialectic between the dissolute exterior world and the photogenic realism of the interior scenes. The transition between these two visual formats was achieved with an effect that appeared to penetrate the skin of their distinct aesthetic realms (see Kuchelmeister, Hibberd and Davies 2018).

Different Degrees of Freedom: Victims and VR Spectators

The second significant issue we faced during production was the paradox of differing degrees of freedom between the institutional experience and the liberties promoted in fully immersive VR – the power to look and liberty of movement. The first of these, the gaze, was deployed by guards in Parramatta Girls Home, who used direct visual surveillance to control all physical movement, day and night. Girls were also not allowed to look around or speak during mealtimes, during muster or while doing (futile) punishments, including scrubbing brick walls, floors and open-air concrete paths. The power of omnipresent vision is well known thanks to the work of Michel Foucault on the panoptic prison design (1991), through which he advanced the notion that disciplinary institutions (schools, prisons, child reformatories, psychiatric hospitals) deploy the assumption that subjects will apply this surveillance to discipline themselves.[9]

In contrast, mainstream VR promotes a notional freedom to look all around at whatever or whomever you want to. Although there are plenty of collective forms of immersive interaction, I contend that first-person, user-oriented VR replicates structural power relations of panoptic surveillance.[10] To illustrate, when you enter as a first-person viewer into a 360-degree panoramic scene, the landscape opens itself up to you as the viewer at the centre of the experience – a visual orientation that upholds the one-way power to look that is central to sur-veillance. When a viewer is empowered with this optical privilege in the context of power imbalance, it reinforces the lack of control that a victim has over the way that perpetrators scrutinise them (at the girls home, there were strip searches and no doors on toilets or showers). For sexual abuse survivors, the twofold ex-posure and lack of right to determine the representation of their bodies in their remediation (in media and courtroom documentation) compounds victimhood and shame. Parragirls Bonney and Jenny, coauthors of the film script, recognised instantly that placing a user at the optical centre of a vicarious surveillance expe-rience emulated the optics they had experienced at Parramatta Girls Home. The solution we developed in *Parragirls Past, Present* was to displace the first-person point of view, instead positioning the spectator alongside Parragirls (whom we don't see) via binaural audio that situates their voices next to our ears.

The second main freedom generally provided to users in a VR experience is the freedom to move through and explore an environment, mostly reliant on gaming conventions. After experiencing a number of interactive media works and navigating through virtual scenarios, Jenny and Bonney protested that they could never allow the spectators to wander freely through the virtual spaces of the girls home. Although branching narratives and interactive overlays – as fea-tures of mixed reality – could have been interesting to explore, for Parragirls a game-like interaction was incompatible with their experience of memory re-trieval. This was not a playground.

Deciding how people would move through the 3D digital reconstruction required a lot of thought, but we ultimately decided that, instead of allowing viewers to drive the experience, we would force movement on them. This was done by generating 360-degree virtual camera shots that slowly tracked through the site. The sensation this produced was uneasy, like being dragged through the girls home, which is at times even more unsettling because the ground seems to dissolve and walls and trees pass right through you, as though you too are frag-mented and unbodied (for more on embodied aspects of the work, see chapter 9 in this volume). This effect was also apparently visceral for reviewer Kit Mac-Farlane (2019: 133), who remarked that the 'slow, powerless drift – almost like being wheeled around unwillingly – suggests the impetus of an ominous dream, an aesthetic that effectively paints the home as a nightmarish site of trauma from the not-so-distant past'.

Empowered Authorship or Empathic Virtual Reality?

The third challenge we confronted was how to avoid reiterating the stereotype of Parragirls as exotic (sex or trauma victim) subjects, which appears contradictory but is inherent to the popular notion of virtual reality as an 'empathy machine'

(Milk 2015). Exhorting the spectatorship of suffering (see Sontag 2003), this latest VR trope builds on the 'thanatouristic' gaze of dark tourism (Lennon and Foley 2000; Seaton 1996). It also reinforces the established libidinal and gendered pleasures inherent to the cinematic gaze that Laura Mulvey (1975: 59) calls 'scopophilia', or the pleasure of 'taking other people as objects' on screen. Media theorist Lisa Nakamura (2020: 51) has also criticised this aspect of VR, stating that its 'empathic feeling[s] are founded on the concept of toxic [white] re-embodiment: occupying the body of another who might not even own their own body'. The preponderance of VR experiences focused on racialised and gendered minorities being represented as victims of poverty, displacement or abuse supports Nakamura's claim, notable in a series of 360-degree films produced by United Nations Virtual Reality (UNVR), including *Clouds over Sidra* (2015), which follows a Syrian girl's daily life in a refugee camp (see chapter 4 in this volume), and *Waves of Grace* (2015), in which a woman seeks to heal the Ebola virus through faith.

Parragirls Past, Present defies tropes of victimhood, scopophilia and dark tourism quite simply because Parragirls were aware that they had the means to document Parramatta Girls Home in their own way and that they were the authors of the artwork. For this reason, they automatically wanted to foreground their stories and the sensory world of trauma instead of being visually depicted. They had no desire to be 'in the frame' or to become the subject of the gaze of others. Because of this aversion, we never see a human figure in *Parragirls Past, Present*, and yet they seem to be all the more tangibly close to us – and we seem to be closer to them. The Parragirls invite us to enter into their space of memory, to walk with them and hear the crimes perpetrated against children, so that we feel co-present in both place and time. We are also 'there', sharing the experience and their pain with them and seeing Parramatta Girls Home from within rather than as outsiders looking in, pretending to inhabit the Parragirls' bodies or (as the VR cliché goes) 'stepping into their shoes'.

Museums, Children and Trauma Memorialisation

Examining how museums address traumatic histories involving children reveals the difficulties of such projects and the lack of research into new technologies that might support the representation of child trauma in public spaces. The reorientation of public institutions towards their constituent citizens, which occurred in the wake of critical postcolonial and heritage studies, has produced a civic turn (see Bennett 2006). While struggling to wrest itself from its 'disciplinary' foundations (Hooper-Greenhill 1992: 198), the museum has been remodelled as participatory or inclusive and tasked to engage a wider public as well as marginalised members of society (Coleman 2018; Janes and Sandell 2019; McSweeney and Kavanagh 2016).[11] Museums have additionally experimented with new technological forms and formats to enhance public engagement, a trajectory that digital museology has spearheaded for more than a decade (Eriksson, Stage and Valtysson 2019; Cameron and Kenderdine 2007). Yet, the presumption of total access in today's participatory museums is that positive or hopeful narratives about human rights can overcome oppression (Wodtke 2015: 206), that *through* the museum we can emerge from the dark past to enlightenment. Nonetheless, a notable reshaping of digital museum scenography has occurred, in tandem with immersive and interactive media (see Parry and Sawyer 2005).

In parallel with these developments, museums have sought to create more accessible experiences for children (Wells 2009) and, in catering to their needs and capacity for learning, to make encounters 'hands-on' and playful (Mayfield 2005). Yet, the two main genres of museums either representing childhood or being aimed at children have thus far tended to privilege nostalgic or positivist narratives that avoid difficult or traumatic topics (Hamer 2019; Roberts 2006). As such, the inclusion of children in museum design and programming has rarely extended to questions of trauma.

The exceptions to this trend are several memorial museums that commemorate violations committed against children. The Children's Room at Rwanda's Kigali Genocide Memorial, for example, features several rooms filled with portraits in lightboxes of dozens of massacred children (Sodaro 2018: 169). Yad Vashem, the World Holocaust Remembrance Center in Jerusalem, Israel, also has a memorial dedicated to the 1.5 million Jewish children murdered during the Holocaust, set in a pitch-black space filled with images of children lit by candles (see Yad Vashem 2019). As they adopt the aesthetics of installation art, these two memorials are reminiscent of the work of artists Christian Boltanski and Alfredo Jaar, as well as, more specifically, pieces produced about genocide that combine photographs in immersive installations (such as Boltanski's *Réserve des Suisses Morts*, 1990, and Jaar's *The Silence of Nduwayezu*, 1997).

Another approach is found in the Canadian Museum for Human Rights (CMHR),[12] which exemplifies the contemporary museological shift to promoting transformative justice in addition to memorialising atrocity. *The Witness Blanket* exhibit, for instance, contends with the challenging Canadian history of Indian residential schools: hundreds of thousands of First Nations children were forcibly removed, institutionalised and often neglected or systematically abused in government or church-run establishments. Taking the form of a large quilt-style assemblage of items collected from residential schools and other sites, the work allows viewers to touch the objects secured to the wall, making the tactility of the installation its most potent aspect.

These last three examples notably eschew child participation. Child witnesses are also absent from these installations, which ultimately present the experience from an adult's point of view (Fingerson 2009). Although there is not scope in this chapter to expand on such a complex ethical topic, some of the ways we developed *Parragirls Past, Present* could possibly be applied to gathering and bringing children's direct testimony of sexual abuse into the public domain. This proposition is not, however, made lightly given the many serious ethical issues that would need to be addressed, including the likelihood that children would not be able to fully consent to their experiences being made public, the risk of such material being traumatic for children, how to assure the concerned child's privacy, and how to prevent the content from being misused once in the public domain, to name a few. The fact remains, nonetheless, that children are also excluded from having a role in shaping the public narrative of child sexual abuse, and there is a gap in research in this respect. Regardless, the representation of child sexual abuse is one of the more unlikely topics to be found in today's museums. One of the key strategies to amend this oversight, I would suggest, is to give survivors a central place in the conception and design process for a museum of child sexual abuse, taking up creative collaboration using new immersive and interactive technologies, in conjunction with knowledge sets across children's and memorial museums, which I will now delineate.

The Uses of Immersive Media for a Memorial Museum of Child Sexual Abuse

No precedent exists yet for a museum devoted to child sexual abuse. For this reason alone, it is apparent that the Australian government's proposal requires new and sophisticated methods to represent such trauma in an ethical and inclusive way. In this final section I review how *Parragirls Past, Present* might inform this impasse. Taking into consideration the complexity of immersing viewers in the traumatic memories of others, alongside the optics and ethics of spectatorship in the context of suffering, I delineate how mediating technologies could do justice to the subject matter of child sexual abuse while being viable for survivors and serving the public need for deeper understanding of this difficult heritage. Four paradigms emerging at the juncture of immersive media and social justice agendas are, I suggest, crucial to realising these perplexing objectives: (1) how inclusive and collaborative design and curation of immersive media installations can be used to overcome documentary conventions that privilege 'looking at' others, instead permitting audiences to engage with survivors as empowered and living witnesses of that traumatic content; (2) centralising survivors as authors and creators of the narratives, concept design, visualisation and sound design of immersive media installations; (3) conveying traumatic events without graphic illustration or sensationalising victims; and (4) embracing experimental methods in digital place documentation to circumvent tropes of heritage authenticity and nostalgic memorialisation.

More specifically, *Parragirls Past, Present* offers new approaches to the representation of trauma that museums are not largely designed to display, as I have detailed throughout this chapter. First, it shows how the incongruity of conventional realism and traumatic memory can be reimagined in an aesthetics of 'dissonance', as disjunction of temporalities and flows between dialectical and divergent memory, images, sounds and experience. Further, the structure of the immersive film destabilises storytelling conventions that tend toward nostalgia. Instead of linear modes that constrain notions of recollection to a contained past time, the application to the museum's design of some of the multidimensional and layered temporalities apparent in the film's spatial and sound design, such as plural narratives, binaural recording and the juxtaposition of contrasting visualisation formats, could be a powerful way to include the polyvocal and diverse experiences of child sexual abuse.

Second, it reveals that while museums are expected to be contextually specific and based on hard evidence and artefacts, there is a dearth of materials from the perspective of the survivors of child sexual abuse; the only images available are those that are created by the state or that depict abandoned former establishments. As such, the proposed museum has very little appropriate documentary material to display. *Parragirls* was fabricated from traces of memory regained and reconstructed from embodied and collective processes for which immersive VR provided a heritage architecture. This dynamic, living archive is a powerful record of an intangible yet pervasive experience, since child sexual abuse is widespread yet has no single or collective site of memory.

Third, while interactivity has become increasingly ubiquitous in digital museums, and incorporated into experience-centred visitor design, the design of interfaces needs to be carefully considered in the context of lived trauma. Instead of presuming that visitors will be given free rein to explore the spaces and experiences of child sexual abuse (past or present), Parragirls is an example of reflexive dynamic in which visitors interact in a dialogical way with active subjects and grasp events from a survivor's perspective (as distinct from experiencing empathy). *Parragirls Past, Present* is an example of this reflexive mode because it situates us *with* survivors and offers the palpable sense of being co-present as we engage anew with the girls home, becoming co-witnesses and cohabiting or sharing the experience rather than looking onto the spectacle from a distance. It is also a crucial example of how to ensure that child sexual abuse victims are not depicted or objectified as being powerless. As I outlined earlier, there is a need to thwart the tendency of VR to gaze 'upon' another. And there is plenty of scope for further innovation as technologies of immersion span interactive panoramas to multifaceted, omnispatial, omnidirectional and multitemporal methods that are able to situate visitors in an adaptive reality.

Other simple strategies include shifting the camera lens away from the eye of the filmmaker as a first-person viewer (as the proxy for the eventual spectator's) or handing the camera over to survivors. Such approaches can radically alter how a work is conceived at the outset, as occurred in the groundwork for *Parragirls Past, Present*. For instance, Parragirls prompted a range of countervisual and contested representations, including shifting, discordant or uncertain optical positions, and acoustics that problematise issues of spectatorship in immersive media while harnessing the power of presence. While our work was limited in the scope of interaction, different degrees of freedom could be carefully developed in the proposed museum to get the balance right between witnessing and exploiting trauma, and to avoid opening up difficult experiences for voyeurism.

Fourth, while it is highly risky to re-expose victims to accounts of childhood sexual abuse, Parragirls demonstrates that survivors are able to generate and curate their own public testimony and decide what is appropriate to share with different audiences and age groups. Anyone viewing *Parragirls Past, Present* will note the equilibrium between clear, direct testimony about abuse and the absence of explicitly shocking revelations. During production, Parragirls guided the editing process based on several contingencies to draw the distinction between what they needed to divulge and what might be unsafe for others. It remained important to convey the truth of the violence they were subjected to, on one hand, while also being wary of memories of sexual abuse being transmitted to others (especially to children) and affecting other victims for whom re-traumatisation was a real and serious risk. And they made these distinctions, even when they could not withstand hearing the testimony themselves, while being adamant that they did not want the public to feel sorry for them. It is thus vital that survivors of child sexual abuse have a central role in authoring narratives, generating concepts for visualisations and immersive media installations and designing museums.

Finally, the film was in fact imagined as a museum itself – a living memorial museum in which Parragirls' memories and their lived experiences could be preserved within a digital reconstruction of Parramatta Girls Home. Likewise, a museum devoted to representing child sexual abuse would also need to attend to the significance of place for survivors of childhood abuse. Even though they cannot be homogenised and are primarily located in the bodies of survivors, memories of abuse may also tied to the homes, institutions or schools where the crimes happened. In terms of validating memory, digital visualisation of place can be vital to the public and survivors themselves: to the public's belief in victim testimony, and to unlock or support traumatic memories that survivors themselves struggle to put back together. Such a museum could be a total experience, made up of unbroken immersive VR installations – an immersive account that imparts otherwise incomprehensible aspects, namely the tacit material of traumatic embodied memory (see chapter 9 in this volume on embodied historiography).

While the Royal Commission investigated specific sites of child sexual abuse, the proposed museum is intended to be situated in the Australian capital city of Canberra. Advanced technologies of place and heritage documentation, such as those employed in the making of *Parragirls Past, Present*, could provide a solution to the Australian government's greatest dilemma: how could such a museum represent locations and sites that are widely dispersed and not otherwise accessible? *Parragirls* is a work that represents how collaborative approaches could support the reconstruction and recording of plural, difficult childhood memories, utilising new aesthetic strategies where immersive media *is* the museum.

Conclusion

This chapter has highlighted the need to develop new approaches to the representation of childhood trauma, revealing some of the main obstacles for designing an Australian memorial museum devoted to child sexual abuse. When it comes to difficult heritage, Australian museums tend to rely on modes of place representation that swing between expectations of authenticity, historical objectivity and nostalgic chronicling. None of these are appropriate to convey the visceral yet contested nature of memory associated with childhood trauma.

In *Parragirls Past, Present*, we sought to avoid these tropes. Instead, we deployed dissonant and deep-mapping methods to create nonlinear and polyvocal encounters akin to traumatic memory itself, which also created strong and real emotions for the viewer. The film demonstrates that the subject of sexual abuse can be represented without graphic illustration or sensationalised narratives, an approach that is fundamental for the reiterating to victims that their testimony is credible without an horrific account. It also shows that the effective witnessing can take place without victims' bodies being exposed to the gaze of others. Nonetheless it remained crucial for Parragirls in making an immersive reconstruction that people would know and feel the visceral sense of fear that Parramatta Girls Home still fosters in them fifty years later. It was vital that the full force of the crimes committed against them be known, with the ultimate hope that this might help prevent these crimes from ever being repeated.

The Australian national museum of child sexual abuse must be a place for victims' self-authored stories, where official, authorised narratives are eschewed, especially in the context where organisations responsible for the abuse are involved or control the outcomes (e.g. the welfare department; see Hibberd and Djuric 2019). The answers to the challenges I have outlined here also require a lot more serious interdisciplinary work. Taken alone, *Parragirls Past, Present* does not offer answers for the problem of how to design a museum devoted to child sexual abuse. But it could contribute to the museological and historiographic landscape to make a space for emerging approaches to difficult histories and the role of immersive media in documenting memories of abuse. As a collaborative project, the *Parragirls* film demonstrates that supporting victims of childhood abuse to generate their own works results in powerful first-hand testimony for the public. Finally, reimagining the museum in terms of this film could support the conception of unique aesthetics and approaches for the representation of child sexual abuse. The knowledge we gained could additionally assist heritage, museum, judicial, welfare and immersive media sectors, and all those seeking a form for the difficult vision of a 'place of truth and commemoration, to raise awareness and understanding of the impacts of child sexual abuse' (Morrison 2018: n.p.). Fulfilling this promise, above all, would address the gap that Parragirl Jenny McNally identified in her final words in *Parragirls Past, Present*: 'We can't fix the future if they don't recognise our past'.

Acknowledgements

Parragirls Past, Present is an outcome of an Australian Research Council Discovery Early Career Researcher Award, number DE160100142.

Lily Hibberd is a multidisciplinary artist, researcher and writer whose practice spans performance, moving image, installation, and archival research. Her work frequently interrogates the intersection of historical memory, science, and technology and has been presented in more than fifty international exhibitions and festivals, including the 22nd Biennale of Sydney (NIRIN), the Perth International Arts Festival, and the Edinburgh International Science Festival. Hibberd has a PhD from Monash University, and a frequent author and co-author of academic and artistic publications. She is founding editor of un Magazine, co-founder of Parragirls Memory Project, and currently a researcher at Université Paris Cité, lecturer at Parsons Paris, and Adjunct Lecturer at UNSW Sydney.

Notes

1. This figure is cited in the Australian Government's Royal Commission into Institutional Responses to Child Sexual Abuse, 'Final Information Update', Australian Government, 2019b. Also noteworthy is the scope of the commission, which was limited to investigating a timeframe of about seventy years because it relied on witness accounts.
2. For more comprehensive background on this term, see the introduction to chapter 9, coauthored by Hibberd and Kenderdine, in this volume. The author also wishes to acknowledge the contribution of Bonney Djuric, Volker Kuchelmeister and Alex Davies in the creation of *Parragirls Past, Present* and the shared knowledge we generated therein.
3. See Australian Government, Royal Commission, 'Terms of Reference', 2014.
4. For a comprehensive account of Parragirls Memory Project, see Hibberd and Djuric 2019.

5. With enough photogrammetric images, a full 3D mesh can be created by correlating multiple photographs from many points of view, using a photogrammetry algorithm to generate a 3D model of the entire scene.

6. Deep mapping is a recent concept based on the combination of geospatial technologies with new notions of narrative (Bodenhamer, Corrigan and Harris 2013). The concept has also been taken up in visualisation and immersive media practice, where new tools such as photogrammetry, geolocation and panoramic imaging permit forms of storytelling that map multiple aspects and dimensions of place, narrative and time – all of which we applied in collaboration with Parragirls during the making of the film.

7. Hall specifically expands on Walter Benjamin's writings in which, according to Hall (2010: 84), he 'develops a concept of sound that is equivalent – in its epistemological and metaphysical presuppositions – to the constitutive properties of the dialectical image'.

8. The final output of the film is 23:05 minutes, formatted as 360-degree equirectangular, stereoscopic 3D, 4k, with spatial audio (Ambisonic B-format), while the terrestrial photogrammetry dataset for the 1.5-hectare site comprised 24M points.

9. Critical criminologist Michelle Brown argues (2017) that 'penal optics' persist in normalised visual practices.

10. Interestingly, quite a few virtual reality projects have been created to demonstrate what it is like to be in prison (i.e. *6 x 9: A Virtual Experience of Solitary Confinement*, and Project Empathy). See *6 x 9*: https://www.theguardian.com/world/ng-interactive/2016/apr/27/6x9-a-virtual-experience-of-solitary-confinement; Project Empathy: https://www.projectempathyvr.com/the-series.

11. Pervasive critique has also been levelled at cultural heritage organisations safeguarding human rights (and UNESCO at large) in relation to universalism (Barrett 2015) and the homogenisation of diverse experiences under a unifying, largely Western neoliberal agenda (Milne 2015).

12. At the time of writing (June 2020), the CMHR was making headlines with public outcry over homophobic, racist and sexual harassment claims against its staff and systemic issues with organisation as a whole. In August 2020, an interim report issued as part of an internal investigation of the allegations stated that 'racism within the Canadian Museum for Human Rights is pervasive and systemic' (Harris 2020: 1).

References

Australian Government. 2014a. *Report of Case Study No 7: Child Sexual Abuse at the Parramatta Training School for Girls and the Institution for Girls in Hay*. Royal Commission into Institutional Responses to Child Sexual Abuse. Retrieved 18 December 2019 from www.childabuseroyalcommission.gov.au/case-studies/case-study-07-parramatta-training-school-girls.

———. 2014b. 'Terms of Reference'. Royal Commission into Institutional Responses to Child Sexual Abuse. Retrieved 20 August 2020 from https://www.childabuseroyalcommission.gov.au/terms-reference.

———. 2019a. *Annual Progress Report: Implementation of Recommendations from the Final Report of the Royal Commission into Institutional Responses to Child Sexual Abuse*. Canberra: Australian Government. Retrieved 11 June 2020 from https://www.childabuseroyalcommissionresponse.gov.au/sites/default/files/2019-12/annual_progress_report_2019.pdf.

———. 2019b. Royal Commission into Institutional Responses to Child Sexual Abuse, 'Final Information Update'. Retrieved 18 August 2020 from https://www.royalcommission.gov .au/sites/default/files/2019-01/carc-final-information-update.pdf.

Barrett, Jennifer. 2015. 'Museums, Human Rights, and Universalism Reconsidered', in Andrea Witcomb and Kylie Message (eds), *Museum Theory*, vol. 1 of *The International Handbooks of Museum Studies*. New York: Wiley-Blackwell, pp. 93–116.

Bennett, Tony. 2006. 'Civic Seeing: Museums and the Organisation of Vision', in Sharon Macdonald (ed.), *Companion to Museum Studies*. Oxford: Blackwell, pp. 263–81.

Berntsen, Dorthe, and Nicoline Marie Hall. 2004. 'The Episodic Nature of Involuntary Autobiographical Memories', *Memory and Cognition* 32(5): 789–803.

Bodenhamer, David J., John Corrigan and Trevor M. Harris. 2013. 'Deep Mapping and the Spatial Humanities', *International Journal of Humanities and Arts Computing* 7(1–2): 170–75.

Brown, Michelle. 2017. 'Penal Optics and the Struggle for the Right to Look: Visuality and Prison Tourism in the Carceral Era', in Sarah Hodgkinson et al. (eds), *Palgrave Handbook of Prison Tourism*. Basingstoke: Palgrave Macmillan, pp. 153–67.

Cameron, Fiona, and Sarah Kenderdine (eds). 2007. *Digital Cultural Heritage: A Critical Discourse*. Cambridge, MA: MIT Press.

Carroll, Lewis. 1865. *Alice's Adventures in Wonderland*. London: Macmillan.

Chion, Michel. 1994. *Audio-Vision: Sound on Screen*, trans. and ed. Claudia Gorbman. New York: Columbia University Press.

Coleman, Laura-Edythe. 2018. *Understanding and Implementing Inclusion in Museums*. Lanham, MD: Rowman & Littlefield.

Commonwealth of Australia. 2017. *Final Report: Recordkeeping and Information-Sharing*, vol. 8. Royal Commission into Institutional Responses to Child Sexual Abuse. Retrieved 10 September 2020 from https://www.childabuseroyalcommission.gov.au/recordkeeping-and-information-sharing

Eriksson, Birgit, Carsten Stage and Bjarki Valtysson. 2019. *Cultures of Participation: Arts, Digital Media and Cultural Institutions*. London: Routledge.

Fingerson, Laura. 2009. 'Children's Bodies'. In Jens Qvortrup, William Corsaro and Michael-Sebastian Honig (eds), *The Palgrave Handbook of Childhood Studies*. Basingstoke: Palgrave Macmillan, pp. 217–27.

Foucault, Michel. 1991. *Discipline and Punish: The Birth of the Prison*, trans. A. M. Sheridan Smith. London: Penguin.

Hall, Mirko. 2010. 'Dialectical Sonority: Walter Benjamin's Acoustics of Profane Illumination', *Telos* 152: 83–102.

Hamer, Naomi. 2019. 'The Hybrid Exhibits of the Story Museum: The Child as Creative Artist and the Limits to Hands-on Participation', *Museum and Society* 17(3): 390–403.

Harris, Laurelle A. 2020. 'Phase One Report: Rebuilding the Foundation; External Review into Systemic Racism and Oppression at the Canadian Museum for Human Rights'. Winnipeg: Harris Law Corporation. Retrieved 10 September 2020 from https://humanrights .ca/sites/prod/files/2020-08/A-FullReport_EN.pdf.

Hibberd, Lily. 2014. 'Making Future Memory', in Paul Ashton and Jacqueline Z. Wilson (eds), *Silent System: Forgotten Australians and the Institutionalisation of Women and Children*. Melbourne: Australian Scholarly Publishing, pp. 103–15.

Hibberd, Lily, with Bonney Djuric. 2019. *Parragirls: Reimagining Parramatta Girls Home*. Sydney: NewSouth Publishing.

Hooper-Greenhill, Eileen. 1992. *Museums and the Shaping of Knowledge*. New York: Routledge.

Janes, Robert, and Richard Sandell (eds). 2019. *Museum Activism*. New York: Routledge.

'Kigali Genocide Memorial'. n.d. Retrieved 10 January 2020 from https://www.kgm.rw/memorial/.

Kuchelmeister, Volker, Lily Hibberd and Alex Davies. 2018. 'Affect and Place Representation in Immersive Media: The "Parragirls Past, Present" Project'. Conference proceeding, Electronic Visualisation in the Arts (EVA), London, 2018.

Lennon, John, and Malcom Foley (eds). 2000. *Dark Tourism: The Attraction of Death and Disaster*. London: Continuum.

Logan, William, and Kier Reeves. 2009. 'Introduction', in William Logan and Kier Reeves (eds), *Places of Pain and Shame: Dealing with 'Difficult Heritage'*. New York: Routledge, pp. 1–14.

Macdonald, Sharon. 2009. *Difficult Heritage: Negotiating the Nazi Past in Nuremberg and Beyond*. London: Routledge.

Mace, John. 2007. 'Involuntary Memory: Concept and Theory', in John Mace (ed.), *New Perspectives in Cognitive Psychology: Involuntary Memory*. Malden, MA: Blackwell, pp. 1–19.

MacFarlane, Kit. 2019. 'Cinema for Claustrophiles: Virtual Reality at the Adelaide Film Festival and Beyond', *Metro: Media and Education Magazine* 200: 128–35.

Mayfield, Margie. 2005. 'Children's Museums: Purposes, Practices and Play?' *Early Child Development and Care* 175(2): 179–92.

McNally, Jenny. 2017. *Parragirls Past, Present*. Parragirls and UNSW media artists. 3D 360-degree film (23 minutes). Retrieved 31 January 2020 from https://www.parragirlsmovie.com/.

McSweeney, Kayte, and Jen Kavanagh (eds). 2016. *Museum Participation: New Directions for Audience Collaboration*. Edinburgh: MuseumsEtc.

Milk, Chris. 2015. 'How Virtual Reality Can Create the Ultimate Empathy Machine'. TED Talk. Retrieved 10 September 2020 from https://www.ted.com/talks/chris_milk_how_virtual_reality_can_create_the_ultimate_empathy_machine?language=en.

Milne, Heather. 2015. 'Human Rights and/or Market Logic: Neoliberalism, Difficult Knowledge and the Canadian Museum for Human Rights', *Review of Education, Pedagogy, and Cultural Studies* 37: 106–24.

Morrison, Scott. 2018. 'Scott Morrison's National Apology to Australian Survivors and Victims of Child Sexual Abuse – Full Speech', *The Guardian*, 22 October. Retrieved 7 January 2020 from https://www.theguardian.com/australia-news/2018/oct/22/scott-morrisons-national-apology-to-australian-survivors-and-victims-of-child-sexual-abuse-full-speech.

———. 2019. 'Address, Anniversary of National Apology to Victims and Survivors of Institutional Sexual Abuse', 22 October. Retrieved 10 December 2019 from https://www.pm.gov.au/media/address-anniversary-national-apology-victims-and-survivors-institutional-sexual-abuse.

Mulvey, Laura. 1975. 'Visual Pleasure and Narrative Cinema', *Screen* 16(3): 6–18.

Nakamura, Lisa. 2020. 'Feeling Good about Feeling Bad: Virtuous Virtual Reality and the Automation of Racial Empathy', *Journal of Visual Culture*, 19(1): 47–64.

Parry, Ross, and Andrew Sawyer. 2005. 'Space and the Machine: Adaptive Museums, Pervasive Technology and the New Gallery Environment', in Suzanne MacLeod (ed.), *Reshaping Museum Space: Architecture, Design, Exhibitions*. London: Routledge, pp. 39–52.

PFFP (Paramatta Female Factory Precinct). n.d. Parramatta Female Factory Precinct Memory Project. Retrieved 11 June 2020 from https://www.pffpmemory.org.au/.

Quadara, Antonia. 2013. 'Child Sexual Abuse: Summary of Adult Survivors' Therapeutic Needs'. Canberra: Australian Institute of Family Studies.

Roberts, Sharon. 2006. 'Minor Concerns: Representations of Children and Childhood in British Museums', *Museum and Society* 4(3): 152–65.

Seaton, Tony. 1996. 'Guided by the Dark: From Thanatopsis to Thanatourism', *International Journal of Heritage Studies* 2(4): 234–44.
Sodaro, Amy. 2018. *Exhibiting Atrocity: Memorial Museums and the Politics of Past Violence.* New Brunswick, NJ: Rutgers University Press.
Sontag, Susan. 2003. *Regarding the Pain of Others.* New York: Farrar, Straus and Giroux.
Tulving, Endel. 2002. 'Episodic Memory: From Mind to Brain', *Annual Review of Psychology* 53: 5– 25.
Wells, Karen. 2009. *Childhood in a Global Perspective.* Cambridge: Polity Press.
Wodtke, Larissa. 2015. 'A Lovely Building for Difficult Knowledge: The Architecture of the Canadian Museum for Human Rights', *Review of Education, Pedagogy, and Cultural Studies* 37: 207–26.
'Yad Vashem: World Holocaust Remembrance Center'. 2019. Retrieved 10 January 2020 from https://www.yadvashem.org/remembrance/commemorative-sites/children-memorial.html.

Chapter 7

Experiencing the Anthropocene

The Contested Heritage of Climate Breakdown

Colin Sterling

Introduction

This chapter draws together two significant trends in recent heritage discourse and practice that have yet to be considered simultaneously in any great depth. The first concerns the rapid upsurge in artistic, museological and heritage-led engagements with issues related to global warming, extinction, the Anthropocene and the broader 'climate emergency' that contains and underpins all of these. While debates on this topic have been ongoing across the sector for some time now (see Cameron, Hodge and Salazar 2013; Harvey and Perry 2015; L'Internationale 2016), recent years have seen a significant shift in the urgency and prominence of various declarations, cultural programmes, manifestos and future strategies linking the work of museums, galleries, conservation bodies and heritage organisations to the question of climate change. In particular, initiatives such as Culture Declares Emergency and the Climate Heritage Network have sought to shift the discussion away from concerns over endangerment and loss to explore the different ways in which heritage, broadly defined, might support wider strategies of 'climate action' (e.g. ICOMOS 2019). This chapter contributes to these debates through the lens of critical heritage thinking and practice (Harrison 2013; Winter 2013; Sterling 2020a), which allows for a more nuanced understanding of the relationship between heritage and climate change to emerge.

The second strand I pick up on here relates directly to the overarching aims of the volume and concerns a widespread move towards immersive and experiential forms of entertainment, storytelling and interpretation across the cultural sector (Griffiths 2008; Jackson and Kidd 2011; Kidd 2018). Again, this should be seen as an evolution rather than a sudden rupture, as questions of 'experience' and 'immersion' have been a consistent feature of discourse in museums and heritage since at least the 1980s (Vergo 1989; Dicks 2003; Holtorf 2005, 2009). What has changed in recent years, however, is the sheer diversity and sophistication of immersive approaches to gallery design, exhibition staging and audience engagement. Partly this has been driven by major developments in virtual, augmented, mixed and extended reality environments, but we should not limit discussions of immersion to this technological angle. As Jenny Kidd (2018: n.p.) writes, 'Immersive heritage practice has a number of key defining characteristics; it is story-led, audience and participation centered, multimodal, multisensory and attuned to its environment'. Drawing on wider engagements with 'the immersive' in theatre studies (Dinesh 2016; Warren 2017; Machon 2013), education (Liu et al. 2017), and VR and games design (Bucher 2017), Kidd (2018: n.p.) goes on to define immersive heritage encounters as 'bounded experience[s] at the nexus of a story, the body and the senses'. Crucially for my purposes, there is also a growing interest in the *critical* potential of such experiences, which are seen to offer new ways of opening up the narratives, epistemologies and practices of heritage to renewed scrutiny (Gröppel-Wegener and Kidd 2019; Sterling 2019). Running against the overtly consumerist model of the 'experience economy' (Pine and Gilmore 1999), work in this vein typically aims to unsettle and subvert the production of heritage meaning through dissonance, active questioning and the prioritisation of affect over didactic forms of interpretation.

My interest in bringing these two strands together stems from the oft-repeated claim that the consequences of climate change and the Anthropocene need to be *experienced* to be understood and therefore addressed in any meaningful way. As curator Marnie Benney suggests in her *Field Guide to Mobilizing Climate Action*, 'One of the most difficult problems is how to connect invisible atmospheric changes to the felt experience of daily life. How can people not just intellectually understand, but viscerally feel and internalise the issues in a way that inspires action?' (Benney 2019: n.p.). Notably, when the Palais de Tokyo staged *Exit* in 2015 – a vast 360-degree video installation bringing the raw statistics of global warming to life – one of the scientists involved in the project described the display as a 'planetarium of the Anthropocene', arguing that 'one of the key problems of climate change discussions today is that people cannot directly relate to them . . . they cannot experience them; the time scale of planetary change does not match the human experience' (Gemenne in Ellis-Petersen 2015: n.p.). More recently, Markus Reymann – director and cofounder of Ocean Space, a new venue fusing art and science in Venice – made clear that 'experiences – not facts or data – are more likely to challenge and change our behaviour. . . . Hard facts are important but what matters most, in terms of effecting change, is what moves us on a personal level' (in Judah 2019: n.p.). This message is now so commonplace that it has become something of a cliché, emphasising a gap between the supposedly distant scenarios of climate science and the tangible, felt experience of environmental collapse.

Current crises force us to question this logic. As I write this chapter, wildfires in Australia have killed dozens of people and untold numbers of nonhuman kin. Images of smoke-filled skies fill social media and online news channels. And this visceral experience of a world on fire is but one example of the lived realities of climate change now confronted by many communities around the globe. The idea of 'immersing' museum visitors in such traumatic experiences seems deeply insensitive, and yet the logic of displaced experience continues to underpin the moral and aesthetic work of much climate change interpretation. As the above quotes demonstrate, this political and ethical project is rightly focused on inspiring action and effecting change, but there is a lack of clear direction around how exactly different forms of climate 'experience' might provoke the social, economic and subjective transformations required to address this emergency.

Rather than attempt a comprehensive overview of artistic and museological approaches to climate change and the Anthropocene in this chapter (see Miles 2010; Davis and Turpin 2015), I want to think critically about the meaning of experiential forms of interpretation when it comes to these subjects. To do this I first look at two exhibitions held recently in London – Olafur Eliasson's *In Real Life* (Tate Modern, 11 July 2019–5 January 2020) and *The Great Animal Orchestra* (The Store X 180 The Strand, 2 October–8 December 2019), a collaboration between sound ecologist Bernie Krause and immersive specialists United Visual Artists. Reading these projects through Timothy Morton's definition of the hyperobject (2013), I ask to what extent the emphasis placed on experience in both exhibitions carries the potential for the kinds of radical systemic change demanded by the climate emergency. Looking across various approaches to climate engagement and critical immersive design, I then consider what it might mean to 'experience' the Anthropocene as a site of *contested* heritage. Does this framing allow for the experiential to also become a space of radical change? What forms of heritage experience may be required to inspire future action on climate breakdown? Building on the work of historian Joan Scott (1991: 777), the tentative thoughts sketched out here recognise that we need to look beyond subjective experience as 'an originary point of explanation' and focus instead on the processes through which experience itself is produced, articulated and contested. Against the backdrop of the Anthropocene and rapid global warming, this approach seems all the more necessary for any museum mediation that might attempt to develop alternative futures through heritage practice.

Estranged Bodies

In 2005 environmentalist Bill McKibben argued that global warming – 'the biggest thing that's happened since human civilization emerged' – had so far failed to register 'in our gut' – 'though we know about it, we don't *know* about it,' suggested McKibben (2005: n.p., original emphasis) – 'it isn't part of our culture'. It would be difficult to make the same argument in 2022. Recent years have seen a vast profusion of novels, exhibitions, installations, plays and other cultural interventions focused on global warming, from Richard Powers's *The Overstory* to the 2019 Venice Biennale, where the issue of climate change was front and centre in many pavilions. This shift cannot be traced to a particular message or moment, but rather emerges from a convergence of scientific evidence, global protests and social experience: the Fridays for Future school strike movement; the funeral processions of Extinction Rebellion; the dire warning of the UN's Intergovernmental Panel on Climate Change that we have until 2030 to keep global warming to 1.5 degrees Celsius above preindustrial levels. Against a backdrop of unprecedented wildfires, rising sea levels, melting permafrost and extreme droughts, climate change *is* now part of our culture, and it may be understood and analysed as a cultural and historical problem as well as an environmental phenomenon (Chakrabarty 2009).

While climate change and the Anthropocene are not interchangeable terms, the recognition that human activity has so profoundly altered the Earth System that we may now be entering a new geological epoch has further galvanised critical and creative responses to the ecological crisis (Davis and Turpin 2015; Lewis and Maslin 2018). Partly this is because the very status of a geological epoch seems to capture the spatial and temporal magnitude of the catastrophe in a way that 'global warming' and 'climate change' struggle to achieve, but it is also because the very concept of 'the Anthropocene' is rife with paradox: a fertile breeding ground for creative mediation. As Anna Tsing (2015: 19) writes, 'Although some interpreters see the name as implying the triumph of humans, the opposite seems more accurate: without planning or intention, humans have made a mess of our planet'. This mess is not the result of some 'species biology,' however. As Tsing continues, 'The most convincing Anthropocene time line begins . . . with the advent of modern capitalism, which has directed long-distance destruction of landscapes and ecologies' (2015: 19). This has led some to claim that 'Capitalocene' may be a more accurate label for the new era (Moore 2017, 2018), a designation that 'demands systemic change located in flesh-and-blood, situated, complex histories' (Haraway 2016a: 238). According to this perspective, the crisis of climate change 'owes not simply to a substance like oil or coal, or to a chemical element like carbon . . . but to complex socio-economic, political, and material operations, involving classes and commodities, imperialisms and empress, and biotechnology and militarism' (Demos 2017: 86). Here we begin to see overlaps with many themes familiar to scholars of contested or dissonant heritage: a convergence that underpins my own interest in what might be termed critical Anthropocene studies (Sterling 2020b).

In 2003 Danish-Icelandic artist Olafur Eliasson installed *The Weather Project* in the Turbine Hall at Tate Modern. Using the relatively lo-fi technology of mirrors, two hundred monofrequency lights, a large semicircular screen and artificial mist, this site-specific work created the illusion of an indoor sun. Enraptured by the eerie light of this vast immersive installation, many visitors spent hours inside the hall, lying on the floor, dancing, chatting, taking pictures, or otherwise occupying the space – a collective performance reflected back into the room by a huge mirror suspended from the ceiling. As Charlotte Klonk (2009: 194) writes in her book *Spaces of Experience*, Eliasson's work 'tapped into a new need at the beginning of the twenty-first century' – a need for 'deeply sensual and immersive' experiences that might simultaneously allow participants to 'escape into another realm'. By *re*-presenting the everyday experience of sunlight and atmosphere, *The Weather Project* did more than simply 'bring the outside in', however – it sought to enact alternative modes of mediating and *being in* the world. It is this form of affective and highly immersive museological displacement that interests me in this chapter and, I think, can tell us much about the promises and limitations of experiential design to address the contested heritage of climate breakdown.

Eliasson has emerged as a particularly prominent voice around creative responses to the climate crisis. His installations, exhibitions and sculptures are regularly shown alongside major climate conferences, and he now serves as chair of the Design and Content Committee for the UN Live Museum, which is developing new programmes around climate action at different scales (see below). At the same time, Eliasson's work is particularly concerned with a highly experiential mode of audience engagement, as described in a lavish publication of the studio's work gathered under the title *Experience* (Eliasson 2018). This approach is not simply about designing spaces of entertainment and consumption but is rather addressed specifically to the problem of shifting perspectives on the place of humans within the world. As Caroline Jones (2016: 29) has argued, Eliasson's work 'plunges the visitor into disorienting environments that aim to shift the human *Umwelt*, sensitizing us to the cosmos'. It is in this sense that we might see his work as explicitly seeking to understand how experience, as a 'concept and question', can model future action (Jones 2016: 29).

The exhibition *In Real Life*, a retrospective of Eliasson's career spanning forty works and almost thirty years, underlined this strategic imperative. Across sculptural installations, immersive environments, light-based media and photographic studies, the exhibition sought to communicate the need for action 'by communicating crises in imaginative ways' (Godfrey 2019: 33). As with all Eliasson's work, this ecological attunement specifically aimed to challenge normative readings of space, time and nature. *Big Bang Fountain* (2014), for example, is made up of little more than a small fountain in the middle of a pitch-black room illuminated by a strobe light, which catches short bursts of water at 'the apex of their trajectory, freezing them in the frenzied and globular form they take at the instant before they are pulled down by gravity' (Eliasson 2014: n.p). In the early work *Moss Wall* (1994), meanwhile, a huge vertical expanse of lichen is allowed to shrink and fade as it dries. The installation is then watered, and the moss expands to fill the space with its fragrance. These carefully orchestrated (and precisely engineered) installations seem to confront a widespread feeling that nature and culture have been falsely separated in the postindustrial world – an ongoing theme in Eliasson's work and symptomatic of a wider philosophical turn towards the non-anthropocentric (Braidotti 2013; Grusin 2015; Sterling 2020a).

To address this divide, Eliasson returns time and again to the body itself – to the radical *presence* of being in the world. This strategy evokes the kind of 'affective belonging' that Rosi Braidotti and Maria Hlavajova (2018: 13) describe in the *Posthuman Glossary*, where affect is understood to combine 'emotions usually held as opposites: nostalgia with the passion for utopian vision; the politics of life itself with the spectre of mass extinction; melancholia with anticipation; mourning for the past with a brutalist passion for the not-yet'. Caught between the enclosed, ritualistic nature of the exhibition space and the urgent need to transform behaviours outside, *in the real world*, Eliasson creates spaces and environments that subvert traditional renderings of human subjectivity. *Din blinde passager* from 2010, for example, fills a long narrow corridor with brightly illuminated fog, severely reducing the capacity for sight and amplifying the other senses (figure 7.1). By re-modelling experience in this way Eliasson seeks to disorient the visitor, but to what end? Stumbling from the fog, where are we headed now?

A partial response to this question could be found in the final room of the exhibition – an 'Expanded Studio' documenting the many projects Eliasson has worked on outside the familiar structures of the art world, from writing a cookbook and designing the facade of a concert venue to producing a low-energy light for rural communities. Along one side of the studio a room-length pinboard of books, articles and concepts explored numerous 'key terms' underpinning this broader practice, including Atmosphere, Journey, Data and – somewhere around the middle – Experience. Here the visitor was asked a simple yet profound question: *If we can only know reality through our experience, then how should we understand the production of experience itself?* In the context of global warming and the Anthropocene, this question takes on a renewed urgency, as the 'reality' of such phenomena often escapes human comprehension. Eliasson models and *reproduces* experience precisely as a means of 'knowing' this reality otherwise. While the nature of experience always exceeds what is planned and anticipated, this epistemological and ontological project is thus chiefly concerned with shaping future thought and action.

We can expand on this analysis with reference to Timothy Morton's influential notion of 'the hyperobject' (2013), which explicitly seeks to name those entities

FIGURE 7.1. Olafur Eliasson, *Din blinde passager* (Your blind passenger), 2010. Fluorescent lamps, monofrequency lamps, fog machine, ventilator, wood, aluminium, steel, fabric, plastic sheet. Dimensions variable. Installation view: Tate Modern, London, 2019. Image by Anders Sune Berg. Courtesy of the artist; neugerriemschneider, Berlin; Tanya Bonakdar Gallery, New York / Los Angeles. © 2010 Olafur Eliasson.

and phenomena that are so distributed in space and time that they exceed human understanding. In many ways this theorisation rehearses McKibben's (2005: n.p.) earlier belief that global warming is difficult to understand and therefore to address precisely because 'when something is happening everywhere all at once, it threatens constantly to become backdrop, context, instead of event'. For Morton however there is neither a background nor a foreground to climate change: it fully envelops us and yet always escapes direct apprehension. This radically undermines the Kantian idea of a 'privileged transcendental sphere' of human thought and action, where reality is knowable only through scientific observation and 'human' (read Western, male, heterosexual, able-bodied) subjectivity (Morton 2013: 18). As Morton (2013: 99) contends – and as Eliasson's artworks evoke – the loss of background and foreground is undermining the 'fragile aesthetic effect' we call the world: 'True planetary awareness is the creeping realisation not that "We Are the World," but that we aren't'.

Labelling climate change as a hyperobject also means attending to its deep historical causes and future effects in new ways. This is because hyperobjects for Morton (2013: 138) 'do not quite exist in a present, since they scoop the standard reference points from the idea of a present time'. For me this is precisely what Eliasson's experiential approach seeks to model.[1] Ecological awareness here ultimately depends on a 'sense of intimacy . . . a sense of being close, even too close, to other lifeforms, of having them under one's skin' (2013: 139). What troubles me with this tactic however is that while Eliasson's immersive installations bring the problem of climate change close through sensual, affective techniques, they also gloss over certain complexities and injustices (both historic and unfolding) in the service of an almost spiritual (re)awakening. 'Experience' in this reading transcends all, standing in for a deeper historical consciousness or indeed any radical project of systemic change. From this perspective – and to borrow from Fredric Jameson (2015: 120) – the 'reduction to the body' that Eliasson's work evokes may be seen as symptomatic of 'our current political paralysis and inability to imagine, let alone organise, the future and future change'.

We can explore this further in relation to *The Great Animal Orchestra*, an immersive digital installation created by London-based arts practice United Visual Artists (UVA) in response to an archive of some fifteen thousand animal noises collected by sound ecologist Bernie Krause since the 1960s. Perhaps best known for their installation work bringing together light, sound and movement to create temporal events in specific locations, UVA explicitly aims to 'create instruments that manipulate our perception and expose the relativity of our experience' (UVA 2018). This approach is manifest in *The Great Animal Orchestra*, which communicates the meticulous archival and scientific work carried out by Krause through an immersive environment that 'three-dimensionalises sound' (UVA 2019: 17). To achieve this, UVA developed a software algorithm that translates sonic data into light, creating a live spectrogram[2] that seems to inscribe various animal sounds onto the walls of the physical space – a pitch-black room surrounded on three sides by a shallow pool of water (figure 7.2).

For Krause (2019: 20), soundscapes are 'incomparable, now quite rare, and priceless' – a kind of intangible more-than-human inheritance that is all too often devalued over other sensory 'treasures'. This sense of scarcity and endangerment is registered in the fact that over 50 percent of the sites at which Krause (2019: 32) carried out his recordings are now 'completely silent or so radically altered that the biophonies and geophonies can no longer be heard in any of their original form – mostly as a result of human endeavour'. Dramatically evoking Rachel Carson's *Silent Spring* (1962 [1991]), the soundscapes documented by Krause thus evidence a rapid decline in biodiversity over the past five decades: one of the key markers of the Anthropocene for geologists looking to date this new epoch (Lewis and Maslin 2018).

First shown in 2016 at the Fondation Cartier pour l'art contemporain in Paris, *The Great Animal Orchestra* lasts just over an hour, with numerous animal soundscapes recorded at different times and in different parts of the world projected into the space. In the words of UVA founder Matthew Clark (2019: 19), this approach 'visualises the sound that the audience hears in the installation in real time, which embodies a sense of the here and now, something happening immediately, and feels alive'. Going further, Clark (2019: 21) has referred to the orchestra as a 'performative space' in which 'the architecture, the people, and the

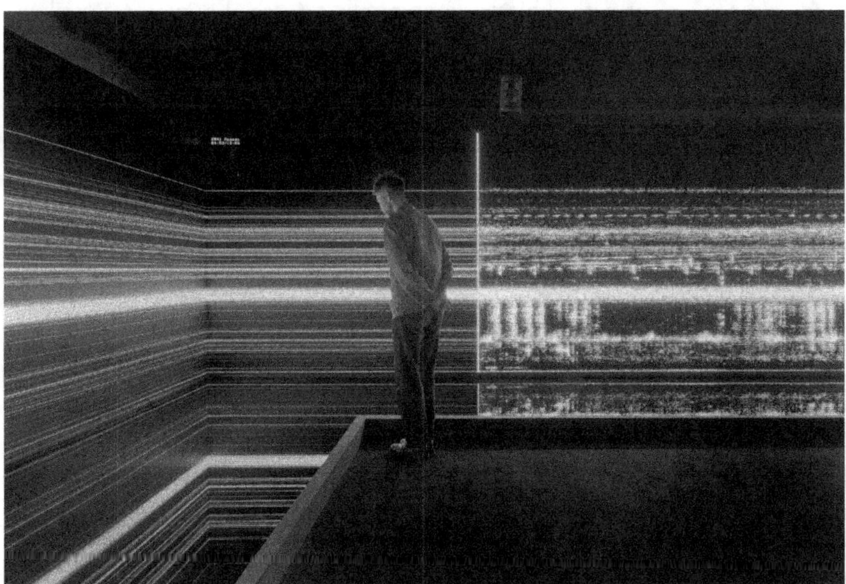

FIGURE 7.2. United Visual Artists, *The Great Animal Orchestra* (2019). Installation view, The Store X 180 The Strand. Image by Jack Hems.

work coexist to create the experience together'. As with Eliasson's work, this experience is deeply affective, driving home the *closeness* of the hyperobject:

> The fabric of these sounds, sensations of vibrant domains of living organisms, leave an impression of humidity on the surface of your skin – a sense that typifies the presence of tropical rainforests; the varying intensities and pitches of Arctic wind will send a chill through your body; while other sounds will suggest the piquant aromas given off by the soil and vegetation; and, if you listen carefully, they will evoke in your mind's eye an image of the landscape through the expression of the acoustic textures. (Krause 2019: 34)

This notion of *experiencing* the extinction crisis as it unfolds is vital to the project. There is a tension here, however, as the dark and contemplative environment designed by UVA seems at odds with the activist imperative Krause (2019: 31) imagines for his work, which specifically aims to contribute towards 'the myriad tactics we might engage with in order to navigate the tricky prognoses of our future'. The irony in this case is that the very aesthetic qualities of *The Great Animal Orchestra* rely on a sense of dislocation that is in many ways alienating from the outside it seeks to communicate. As Krause (2019: 86) himself admits, 'nothing virtual will ever supplant the marvels that you will personally discover in wild habitats'. What does it mean to submit ourselves to the digital *experience* of biodiversity loss in the Anthropocene? What strategic actions or future tactics does this chamber of ecologies compel? UVA's installation exemplifies a certain mode of engagement with subjects that typically transcend human comprehension (in this case, the hyperobject of anthropogenic extinction), but the experience it relies on is more of a fatalistic lament rather than a call to action. As T. J. Demos (2019: n.p.) has recently argued in an insightful critique of Extinction Rebellion's approach to the climate emergency, 'While there's real mourning to be done – for lost species, for historical and ongoing climate violence, for structural injustice – militancy is more than ever necessary, meaning a diversity of tactics dedicated to structural change, but grounded in careful political analysis and organizing'.

The two short case studies I have introduced here sit outside the traditional framework of the museum, and yet I find them useful for thinking through where the broad field of 'museum mediation' may be heading. As immersive and experiential approaches to art and storytelling increase in popularity and sophistication, we need to ensure that the important strides made in critical heritage interpretation over the past two decades are not discarded in the service of a depoliticised aesthetic experience. Here we would do well to remember Scott's (1991: 797) comment that 'what counts as experience is neither self-evident nor straightforward; it is always contested, and always therefore political'. The interconnected concerns of climate change, the Anthropocene and extinction challenge familiar approaches to interpretation and mediation, but we need to critically interrogate the ease with which immersion and experience are deployed to convey these issues.

Critical Climate Experiences

Despite their immersive, multisensorial character, the experiences I have discussed so far in this chapter are defined by a certain level of passivity. In bringing the Anthropocene close, they rely on a contemplative and embodied sense of absorption. Experience in this reading is more about the felt qualities of a particular event, history or subject rather than any active engagement in an unfolding narrative. Such experiences run the risk of smoothing over the complexities and contradictions of climate change and the Anthropocene as interconnected and highly contested phenomena.

As Sara Perry (2019: 359) notes in her insightful paper on the 'enchantment' of the archaeological record, numerous studies have shown that people are 'receptive to the possibility of cultural sites calling into question how they think about things'. Borrowing from political theorist Jane Bennett (2001), 'enchantment' in this context builds on precisely the kinds of emotive engagement seen in the work of Eliasson and UVA, only with the added imperative of bringing about 'ethically minded action on the world' (Perry 2019: 360). While Perry's (2019: 363) work focuses primarily on digital heritage interpretation, her suggestion that 'uncanny distance, sensory agitation, or surprise' might inspire action can, I think, be applied more broadly to the kinds of experiences I am interested in here. Indeed, *critical* climate experiences may be defined by this sense of potential change, brought about through alternative encounters with global warming as an historical, social, political *and* environmental concern. To borrow from Perry (2019: 362), such a potentiality 'needs to be trained, it requires attention, it demands a capacity to imagine and manoeuvre through sometimes complex, sometimes mundane narratives'.

My interest in the relationship between critical heritage and climate breakdown builds on various critiques of the Anthropocene developed across the arts, humanities and social sciences in recent years (e.g. Haraway 2016b; Chakrabarty 2016; Demos 2017; Farrier 2019; Yusoff 2018; Harrison and Sterling 2020). At the core of this work is a desire to acknowledge and unravel the injustices inscribed in the very concept of the Anthropocene, which flattens historical responsibilities in a new 'universal' narrative of human-induced environmental degradation. As Christophe Bonneuil and Jean-Baptiste Fressoz (2016: 71–72) write in a passage that is worth quoting at length:

The challenges of the Anthropocene demand a differentiated view of humanity, not just for the sake of historical truth, or to assess the responsibilities of the past, but also to pursue future policies that are more effective and more just; to construct a common world in which ordinary people will not be blamed for everything while the ecological crimes of the big corporations are left unpunished. . . . The wealth of humanity and its capacity for future adaptation come from the diversity of its cultures, which are so many experiments in ways of worthily inhabiting the Earth.

Demos (2019: n.p.) reiterates this stance when he notes that by focusing on global warming as a near-future scenario, it is 'as if the disaster hasn't already occurred – in past invasions, slaveries, genocides, all perpetuated in ongoing land grabs, displacements, and extractivism.' The highly politicised emergence of climate change and the Anthropocene is crucial to both these critiques. As Andreas Malm (2018: 5) contends, 'Global warming is the result of actions in the past . . . the storm of climate change draws its force from countless acts of combustion over, to be exact, the past two centuries'. Crucially, however, these 'acts of combustion' should always be located socially and politically: Great Britain and the United States, for example, contributed around 60 percent of the cumulative total emissions of greenhouse gases before 1900 and still made up almost 50 percent in 1980 (Bonneuil and Fressoz 2016: 116). This state-level accountability (which is also a story of colonialism, globalisation and rampant consumerism) can be distilled further when we consider that just 'ninety corporations are responsible for 63 per cent of the cumulative emissions of carbon dioxide and methane between 1850 and today' (Bonneuil and Fressoz 2016: 68; also see Demos 2017).

Heritage practice has a key role to play in documenting and communicating the systemic roots and ongoing injustices of climate change, but this work must also acknowledge that many of the fundamental logics of the heritage field emerged alongside and in conjunction with nationalism, colonialism, globalisation and the consumption patterns of modern capitalism: precisely those forces that are now seen to have contributed to the so-called climate emergency. Thus, the *critical* heritage of climate breakdown must combine a project of outward historical (re)interpretation with reflexivity about the practices, ontologies and epistemologies of heritage itself.

To explore this idea further, I want to address a question that comes at the very end of Bonneuil and Fressoz's (2016: 289) book *The Shock of the Anthropocene*, where they ask what histories we must write to 'learn to inhabit' this new geological epoch. Three main points can be picked up on here from their wider analysis. First, any history of the Anthropocene should engage critically with its 'grandiose time frame' and inner contradictions so as not to anaesthetise politics (2016: 80). Second, the current historical moment does not represent 'a threshold in the acquiring of environmental awareness' so much as a 'culminating point' registering a long history of destructions and occlusions (2016: 170). Third, telling this complex history can be an 'emancipatory experience' –

one that might free us from 'repressive institutions' and 'alienating' imaginaries (2016: 291). It hardly needs stating that there are many ways in which heritage and museums may contribute to this project. To open up this discussion, I would like to briefly discuss another recent immersive artwork that goes some way to showing how the contested heritage of climate breakdown might be addressed.

John Akomfrah's *Purple* is a multiscreen video installation commissioned by the Barbican and first shown in their Curve gallery space in 2017. Incorporating six large screens and lasting for just over one hour, *Purple* moves between archival footage and newly shot scenes filmed in apparently pristine landscapes that nevertheless bear the imprint of human life. It is a visual grammar Akomfrah has used previously to great effect, from his early collaborative work with the Black Audio Film Collective (Eshun and Sagar 2007), to *Nine Muses* in 2010 and, most recently, the ambitious *Vertigo Sea* (2016). With *Purple*, however, this approach is elevated to symphonic proportions, with distinct movements looped together and propelled forward by a hypnotic score from long-time collaborator Trevor Mathison.

Central to the work is the figure of the watcher, gazing intently at electricity pylons, forests, communication arrays, polluted lakes (figure 7.3). This is not a single observer, however, but a multitude of witnesses, dispatched to scenes of ecological degradation around the world. The diversity of these locations is

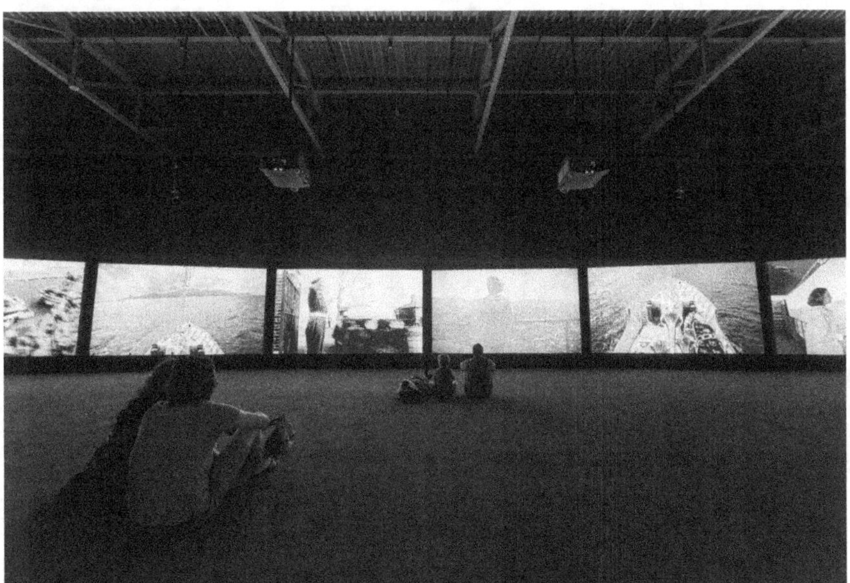

FIGURE 7.3. John Akomfrah, *Purple*, 2017. Six-channel HD video installation with 15.1 surround sound (colour, sound; 62 minutes). Installation view, ICA Watershed, Boston, 2019. Image by Meg Elkinton. Courtesy of Lisson Gallery. © Smoking Dog Films.

telling – the Isle of Skye, the coastlines of Alaska, the volcanic Marquesas Islands in the South Pacific. As the idea of the hyperobject conveys, the space of ruin now spreads to every corner of the planet; even and especially to those sites we might once have considered a refuge from human intervention. Here then Akomfrah seems to pose a question that resonates with Malm's rendering of the Anthropocene as a problem of the past and the future: how can we inject a sense of urgency into the act of historical witnessing when we always inevitably arrive too late at the crimes committed?

A common trope in creative work dealing with the Anthropocene is the historicisation of the present, as seen in Jan Zalasiewicz's 2008 book *The Earth after Us*, which asks what evidence extra-terrestrial explorers one hundred million years from now might find of our long-vanished human empire. Within this setting the human record is hard to distinguish from the nonhuman, suggesting an entanglement that radically undermines earlier anthropocentric narratives. As Zalasiewicz (2008: 224) admits, however, the geological record is 'skewed,' and the stories it contains 'need to be unravelled with a watchful and sceptical eye, one open to alternative possibilities'. *Purple* takes up this task in an immediate and quite profound way, and whilst the archives it leverages are visual rather than geological, the search for other histories and other imaginaries of the Anthropocene are central to Akomfrah's project.

The artist's filmic approach – typically disjointed, fragmented and multivocal – is well suited to this task. Most of the time the visual fragments that make up *Purple* speak to each other only in passing, but every now and then forgotten and surprising traces collide to open up new historical pathways. The birth of a child is juxtaposed with electricity pylons; high-speed car crashes intersect with a serene boating voyage. At certain junctures, multiple screens turn purple at once, displaying text that marks out six 'movements' in the score. There is a narrative of sorts on offer here, but it is circular and uneven. We see human life from cradle to grave, patterns of work and play, the rise of industry and methods of communication. Akomfrah has stated that this is his most autobiographical work, born out of a sudden recognition that much of his youth was spent in the shadow of a toxic power plant on the banks of the Thames. Poisonous clouds mixed with social frictions. Where Akomfrah has typically looked backwards and sideways to explore these tensions, now he also looks up and around: to mines and industry and fumes and – eventually – unforeseen material legacies (plastic, mineral, radioactive). Everyday life takes place within and against this surging immanence, evoked in *Purple* by the orchestral form of the multichannel work.

In many ways *Purple* builds on Akomfrah's previous work and its themes of race, migration, trade and colonial oppression in a relatively straightforward manner, most notably through the use of archival footage documenting the life of post-war migrants across the United Kingdom. *Purple* stretches this technique in significant ways, however, linking together well-known (though still vital) accounts of exploitation and alienation with contemporary views of environmental damage to forge new spaces of reflection and resistance. To this end, Akomfrah pays close attention to the textures of loss and change that constitute our sense of being in times of ecological crisis. Only now this subjectivity is inherently distributed – archived in stories, images, words and movements, and bound up with nonhuman forces that fluctuate between the mundane and the extraordinary. These 'records' stretch and disrupt the linear flow of time, upending already delicate processes of remembering and forgetting. Whatever we call it – climate change, global warming, the sixth mass extinction, the Anthropocene – there is a growing awareness of our entangled coevolution with an environment that is carefully balanced and increasingly volatile. As the idea of the hyperobject attests, there is no place of observation beyond the system. By reinforcing the interconnected pulse of a planet on the verge of ecological collapse, Akomfrah demonstrates the impossibility of subtracting *what has been* from *what will come*. The archive and the environment are intertwined in this immersive experience, not simply as historical artefacts or things to be remembered but as vital interlocutors in the main task of the present: charting alternative futures beyond the prison of so-called capitalist progress.

What forms of museum making and heritage experience are needed to convey the narrative complexities and transversal connections of the Anthropocene that *Purple* brings so vividly to life? A few brief examples may help to demonstrate the breadth of possible answers to this question.

At the start of 2019 the United Nations advertised for a number of curatorial positions as part of their development of UN Live, a new museum to be headquartered in Copenhagen and active around the world. Alongside a curator for 'people on the move' and a curator for youth engagement, this initial round of recruitment sought a curator for climate change – someone who might 'co-create in partnership with people in their local communities . . . to activate global audiences with their heads, hearts and hands' (UN Live 2019). Rather than a collection of objects, the museum we are told will be centred on 'stories and knowledge,' encouraging participants 'to be innovators and problem solvers' through 'experiential learning, collaboration, and play' (UN Live 2019). This objective is now being realised through the project 'My Mark: My City,' which aims to galvanise climate action at the local level, starting with urban communities as far apart as Anchorage and Kathmandu. Mobilising a new form of planetary museology, this distributed assemblage of workshops, exhibitions, newly commissioned artworks and community-led conversations evokes the kind of 'cosmopolitanism-from-below' outlined by Paul Gilroy (2004: 74), where 'being in the same present' means 'synchronizing difference' through agonistic encounters on the ground (see Jazeel 2011). This approach acknowledges that the shared yet differentiated experience of climate change now seems to dominate any global sense of *being in the same present* – a reformulation of the hyperobject that the UN's museological project both reflects and contributes towards.

Working at a very different scale, the artist group FICTILIS has developed *The Museum of Capitalism* as a way to imagine how we might educate current and future generations on the ideology, history and legacy of this particular world system. Responding directly to Moore's designation of the Capitalocene, this project – which held its inaugural exhibition in Oakland, California in 2017 – deploys the logics of the museum experience to provoke a form of ironic detachment that might provide the grounding for a critical reassessment of the present. As the curators ask in the accompanying catalogue: 'What better form than a museum to call progress into question, and how better to reorient ourselves in the present than with an institution we already use to orient ourselves toward the past?' (FICTILIS 2017: 14). The Brighton-based HIVE project is built around a similar premise, aiming to 'harness the power of art and imagination to reveal the hidden and constructed narratives and metaphors that limit our societies from seeing better ways' (HIVE 2019). To this end, their *Hidden Paths* exhibition (16–20 October 2019, ONCA Gallery, Brighton) included a virtual 'Museum of Futures' – a space in which to digitally 'archive' our current capitalist system and explore other ways of relating to the world.

These and many other emerging approaches to the design of museological experiences (digital and otherwise) point to the critical potentiality of the field when it comes to addressing the dissonant heritage of climate breakdown. Such experiences may be seen as 'testing grounds' for radical, systemic change, thus situating critical heritage thinking and practice as a vital interlocutor in shaping more just and equitable futures. Here we should remember that any specially designed experience will be generated and enacted through specific, embedded practices. As Kidd (2018) suggests, the immersive turn in museum and gallery design needs to be critiqued in relation to the framing, marketing and staging of such experiences, their potential impacts (social, economic and otherwise), and the significant resources that go into their production. 'Critical' heritage experiences do not begin and end with new narratives or modes of interpretation but rather gesture towards other forms of knowledge making, praxis and political engagement. The contested heritage of the Anthropocene presents a radical opportunity to develop precisely these kinds of multimodal experiences, which may respond to a growing sense of grief, rupture and accountability to unsettle familiar ways of doing and thinking heritage.

Conclusion

Museums are part of a broader cultural ecosystem through which the climate emergency is communicated, understood and experienced. While the various case studies I have introduced in this chapter underline the fact that no single type of 'experience' can capture the full complexity of this crisis, they also gesture towards new tactics of narrative, mediation and engagement that might begin to shift perspectives and model future action. In so doing they help to draw out some of the key characteristics that emerging digital technologies can adopt to deal with difficult heritage, from immersive encounters with the more-than-human to speculative modes of critical enquiry. We need the embodied spectacle of Eliasson's installations, the precise archival knowledge and sensory overload of *The Great Animal Orchestra*, the intricacy of Akomfrah's narrative symphony, the explorations of systemic injustice that animate the Museum of Capitalism, and the grounded cosmopolitanism of UN Live. We need all of this and more to convey the magnitude and urgency of climate breakdown as an historical, cultural and environmental phenomenon, and to imagine pathways out of the Anthropocene.

A narrow focus on the content and aesthetics of specially designed experiences – whether they be virtual, augmented, theatrical, filmic, digital, performative or any permutation of the above – may be unhelpful for this task. In trying to understand what it means to 'experience' the Anthropocene as a space of contested heritage, we also need to engage with the full implications of its status as a hyperobject. This means attending to the diverse ways in which heritage itself may be complicit with the forces and ideas that have led to widespread biodiversity loss and environmental breakdown. Put simply, in the context of museum mediation, we also 'experience' the Anthropocene in the marginalisation of certain voices, narratives and expressions within museological settings, in the perpetuation of colonial systems of meaning-making and display, in structural forms of aggression and violence, and in the acquiescence to unjust models of sponsorship, development and consumption. Future research in this area must focus on the production of immersive mediation within this broader ecology of experiences, where the potential for systemic change rests in the movements, flows and resistances of the experiential.

Colin Sterling is assistant professor of heritage, museums and the environment at the University of Amsterdam. He was previously a postdoctoral researcher and AHRC Early Career Leadership Fellow at UCL Institute of Archaeology. His research focuses on the political and ecological dimensions of heritage and museums in the past and the present. He is the author of *Heritage, Photography, and the Affective Past* (Routledge, 2020) and co-editor of *Deterritorializing the Future: Heritage in, of and after the Anthropocene* (Open Humanities Press, 2020). He is editor of the journal *Museums & Social Issues*.

Notes

1. Here it is worth noting that Morton appeared via a video recording in the Expanded Studio space of *In Real Life*, while Eliasson contributed to a recent radio show produced by Morton for the BBC, demonstrating a cross-fertilisation of ideas between the artist and philosopher
2. 'A spectrogram, or sonogram, is a graphic illustration of sound featuring time on one axis, frequency (expressed in Hertz) on another, and amplitude (sound intensity expressed in decibels) of each component represented by a different color' (Krause 2019: 26).

References

Bennett, Jane. 2001. *The Enchantment of Modern Life: Attachments, Crossings, and Ethics.* Princeton, NJ: Princeton University Press.

Benney, Marnie. 2019. 'The Climate Change Curator's Playbook: A Field Guide to Mobilizing Climate Action'. Retrieved 15 February 2020 from http://www.marniebenney.com/climate-change-curator-playbook.

Bonneuil, Christoph, and Jean-Baptiste Fressoz. 2016. *The Shock of the Anthropocene.* New York: Verso.

Braidotti, Rosi. 2013. *The Posthuman.* Cambridge: Polity.

Braidotti, Rosi, and Maria Hlavajova. 2018. 'Introduction', in Rosi Braidotti and Maria Hlavajova (eds), *The Posthuman Glossary.* London: Bloomsbury Academic, pp. 1–14.

Bucher, John. 2017. *Storytelling for Virtual Reality: Methods and Principles.* New York: Routledge.

Cameron, Fiona, Bob Hodge and Juan Francisco Salazar. 2013. 'Representing Climate Change in Museum Space and Places', *WIREs Climate Change* 4(1): 9–21.

Carson, Rachel. 1962 [1991]. *Silent Spring.* London: Penguin.

Chakrabarty, Dipesh. 2009. 'The Climate of History: Four Theses', *Critical Inquiry* 35: 197–222.

———. 2016. 'Humanities in the Anthropocene: The Crisis of an Enduring Kantian Fable', *New Literary History* 47(2/3): 377–97.

Clark, Matthew. 2019. 'Interview with Matthew Clark by Hans Ulrich Obrist', in Bernie Krause and United Visual Artists (eds), *The Great Animal Orchestra.* Paris: Fondation Cartier pour l'art contemporain, pp. 19–21.

Davis, Heather, and Etienne Turpin. 2015. *Art in the Anthropocene: Encounters among Aesthetics, Politics, Environments and Epistemologies.* Ann Arbor, MI: Open Humanities Press.

Demos, T. J. 2017. *Against the Anthropocene: Visual Culture and Environment Today.* Berlin: Sternberg.

———. 2019. 'Climate Control: From Emergency to Emergence', *e-flux journal* 104 (November). Retrieved 15 December 2019 from https://www.e-flux.com/journal/104/299286/climate-control-from-emergency-to-emergence/.

Dicks, Bella. 2003. *Culture on Display: The Production of Contemporary Visibility.* Berkshire: Open University Press.

Dinesh, Nandita. 2016. *Memos from a Theatre Lab: Exploring What Immersive Theatre 'Does'.* New York: Routledge.

Eliasson, Olafur. 2014. 'Big Bang Fountain'. Retrieved 15 February 2020 from https://olafu reliasson.net/archive/artwork/WEK109204/big-bang-fountain.

Eliasson, Ólafur. 2018. *Experience*. London: Phaidon.

Eshun, Kodwo, and A. Sagar. 2007. *The Ghosts of Songs: The Film Art of the Black Audio Film Collective*. Liverpool: Liverpool University Press.

Farrier, David. 2019. *Anthropocene Poetics: Deep Time, Sacrifice Zones, and Extinction*. Minneapolis: University of Minnesota Press.

FICTILIS (eds). 2017. *The Museum of Capitalism*. New York: Inventory Press.

Ellis-Petersen, Hannah. 2015. 'Global Panic: Art Show Exit Brings Climate Change to Shocking Life', *The Guardian*, 27 November 2015. Retrieved 27 September 2020 from https://www.theguardian.com/artanddesign/2015/nov/27/art-show-exit-climate-change-cop21-un-conference-paris.

Gilroy, Paul. 2004. *After Empire: Multiculture or Postcolonial Melancholia*. London: Routledge.

Godfrey, Mark (ed). 2019. *Olafur Eliasson: In Real Life*. London: Tate Publishing.

Griffiths, Alison. 2008. *Shivers Down Your Spine: Cinema, Museums and the Immersive View*. New York: Columbia University Press.

Gröppel-Wegener, Alice, and Jenny Kidd. 2019. *Critical Encounters with Immersive Storytelling: Genre, Narrative and Environments*. London: Routledge.

Grusin, Richard (ed.) 2015. *The Nonhuman Turn*. Minneapolis: University of Minnesota Press.

Haraway, Donna. 2016a. *Manifestly Haraway*. Minneapolis: University of Minnesota Press.

———. 2016b. *Staying with Trouble: Making Kin in the Chthulucene*. Durham, NC: Duke University Press.

Harrison, Rodney. 2013. *Heritage: Critical Approaches*. New York: Routledge.

Harrison, Rodney, and Colin Sterling. 2020. *Deterritorialising the Future: Heritage in, of and after the Anthropocene*. Ann Arbor, MI: Open Humanities Press.

Harvey, David C., and Jim Perry (eds). 2015. *The Future of Heritage as Climates Change: Loss, Adaptation and Creativity*. New York: Routledge.

HIVE. 2019. About the HIVE. Retrieved 15 February 2020 from https://systemchangehive.org/about/.

Holtorf, Cornelius. 2005. *From Stonehenge to Las Vegas: Archaeology as Popular Culture*. Walnut Creek, CA: Altamira Press.

Holtorf, Cornelius. 2009. 'Imagine This: Archaeology in the Experience Society', in Cornelius Holtorf and Angela Piccini (eds), *Contemporary Archaeologies: Excavating Now*. Bern: Peter Lang, pp. 47–64.

ICOMOS. 2019. *The Future of Our Pasts: Engaging Cultural Heritage in Climate Action*. Paris: ICOMOS.

Jackson, Anthony, and Jenny Kidd (eds.) 2011. *Performing Heritage: Research, Practice and Innovation in Museum Theatre and Live Interpretation*. Manchester: Manchester University Press.

Jameson, Fredric. 2015. 'The Aesthetics of Singularity', *New Left Review* 92 (March–April): 101–32.

Jazeel, Tariq. 2011. 'Spatializing Difference beyond Cosmopolitanism: Rethinking Planetary Futures', *Theory, Culture & Society* 28(5): 75–97.

Jones, Caroline. 2016. 'Modeling', in Caroline A. Jones, Rebecca Uchill and David Mather (eds). *Experience: Culture, Cognition and the Common Sense*. Cambridge, MA: MIT Press, pp. 13–33.

Judah, Hettie. 2019. 'There's a Flood of Climate Change-Related Art at the Venice Biennale. Can It Make a Difference – Or Is It Adding to the Problem?' *Artnet News*, 6 May 2019.

Retrieved 15 February 2020 from https://news.artnet.com/art-world/climate-change-ven ice-biennale-1532290.

Kidd, Jenny. 2018. '"Immersive" Heritage Encounters'. *The Museum Review* 3(1). Retrieved 13 November 2019 http://articles.themuseumreview.org/tmr_vol3no1_kidd.

Klonk, Charlotte. 2009. *Spaces of Experience: Art Gallery Interiors from 1800 to 2000*. New Haven, CT: Yale University Press.

Krause, Bernie. 2019. 'The Great Animal Orchestra: Voices from the Wild', in Bernie Krause and United Visual Artists, *The Great Animal Orchestra*. Paris: Fondation Cartier pour l'art contemporain, pp. 25–36.

Lewis, Simon L., and Mark A. Maslin. 2018. *The Human Planet: How We Created the Anthropocene*. London: Penguin.

L'Internationale (eds). 2016. *Ecologising Museums*. Paris: L'Internationale.

Liu, Dejian, Chris Dede, Ronghuai Huang and John Richards (eds). 2017. *Virtual, Augmented, and Mixed Realities in Education*. Singapore: Springer.

Machon, Josephine. 2013. *Immersive Theatres: Intimacy and Immediacy in Contemporary Performance*. New York: Palgrave Macmillan.

Malm, Andreas. 2018. *The Progress of This Storm: Nature and Society in a Warming World*. London: Verso.

McKibben, Bill. 2005. 'What the Warming World Needs Now Is Art, Sweet Art'. *Grist*, 22 April. Retrieved 15 February 2020 from https://grist.org/article/mckibben-imagine/.

Miles, Malcolm. 2010. 'Representing Nature: Art and Climate Change', *Cultural Geographies* 17(1): 19–35.

Moore, Jason W. 2017. 'The Capitalocene, Part I: On the Nature and Origins of Our Ecological Crisis', *Journal of Peasant Studies* 44(3): 594–630.

———. 2018. 'The Capitalocene Part II: Accumulation by Appropriation and the Centrality of Unpaid Work/Energy', *Journal of Peasant Studies* 45(2): 237–79.

Morton, T., 2013. *Hyperobjects: Philosophy and Ecology after the End of the World*. Minneapolis: University of Minnesota Press.

Perry, Sara. 2019. 'The Enchantment of the Archaeological Record', *European Journal of Archaeology* 22(3): 354–71.

Pine, B. Joseph, II, and James H. Gilmore. 2011. *The Experience Economy: Updated Edition*. Boston, MA: Harvard Business Review Press.

Scott, Joan. 1991. 'The Evidence of Experience', *Critical Inquiry* 17(4): 773–97.

Sterling, Colin. 2019. 'Designing "Critical" Heritage Experiences: Immersion, Enchantment and Autonomy'. *Archaeology International* 22(1): 100–113.

———. 2020a. 'Critical Heritage and the Posthumanities: Problems and Prospects'. *International Journal of Heritage Studies*. DOI: 10.1080/13527258.2020.1715464.

———. 2020b. 'Heritage as Critical Anthropocene Method', in Rodney Harrison and Colin Sterling (eds), *Deterritorializing the Future: Heritage in, of and after the Anthropocene*. London: Open Humanities Press, pp. 188–218.

Tsing, Anna Lowenhaupt. 2015. *The Mushroom at the End of the World: On the Possibility of Life in Capitalist Ruins*. Princeton, NJ: Princeton University Press.

UN Live. 2019. 'Job Description for "Curator of Climate Change"'. Advertisement, *Museum for the UN*, February. Retrieved 15 February 2020 from https://museumfortheun.org/.

UVA (United Visual Artists). 2018. 'About United Visual Artists'. Retrieved 15 February 2020 from https://www.uva.co.uk/about.

———. 2019. 'United Visual Artists', in Bernie Krause and United Visual Artists, *The Great Animal Orchestra*. Paris: Fondation Cartier pour l'art contemporain, p. 17.

Vergo, Peter (ed.). 1989. *The New Museology*. London: Reaktion.

Warren, Jason. 2017. *Creating Worlds: How to Make Immersive Theatre*. London: Nick Hern Books.

Winter, Tim. 2013. 'Clarifying the Critical in Critical Heritage Studies'. *International Journal of Heritage Studies* 19(6): 532–45.

Yusoff, Kathryn. 2018. *A Billion Black Anthropocenes or None*. Minneapolis: University of Minnesota Press.

Zalasiewicz, Jan. 2008. *The Earth after Us: What Legacy Will Humans Leave in the Rocks?* Oxford: Oxford University Press.

CREATING A SENSE OF PRESENCE, IMMERSION AND EMBODIMENT

Chapter 8

Designing Interactions

On the Use of Digital Technologies in the Musealisation of Difficult Built Heritage

Francesca Lanz and Elena Montanari

Introducing Difficult Built Heritage

The idea of 'difficult heritage' has been explored from different perspectives by several authors in the past decade, contributing to the establishment of a growing corpus of studies on the subject, and it is today quite widely deployed within and beyond discourses upon heritage and museum studies and practices. Mainly building on the work carried out by Sharon Macdonald (2009: 1), 'difficult heritage' is defined in relation to a 'past that is recognised as meaningful in the present, but that is also contested and awkward for public reconciliation with a positive and self-affirming identity.' As such, it may be 'troublesome because it threatens to break through into the present in disruptive ways' and raises questions about its 'public representation and reception,' as well as 'about practices of selection, preservation, cultural comparison and witnessing' (Macdonald 2009: 1).

Heritage of different kinds can be difficult in various ways. In this chapter, we focus on those cases where such a difficult nature is chiefly recalled by, is embedded in and results from heritage's built form. We will call it 'difficult *built* heritage'. By adding 'built' to 'difficult heritage', we intend to place the emphasis precisely on the actual or potential contribution of the physical and material features of some difficult heritage in determining its 'contentious' nature (Macdonald 2020). Indeed, difficult built heritage includes architectural assemblages at which different and nested levels of awkwardness converge and coalesce, resulting in a complex intertwinement of contentious meanings, painful stories and physical traces (Kusek and Purkla 2019; Pendlebury, Wang and Law 2018; Lanz 2018; Bassanelli and Postiglione 2013; Berger and Wong 2013; Logan and Reeves 2009; Macdonald 2009; Tunbridge and Ashworth 1996). These are buildings and other elements of the built environment onto which a great ideological load is and/or was placed, and that can be variously associated with difficult pasts and memories, possibly provoking distressing feelings still today, either at a local community level or on wider scales. What notably characterises difficult built heritage is that in the collective memory and imaginary, its built form and its specific architectural design and language iconically evoke its former uses, acting as a trigger for those memories and feelings. These are buildings that have been purposely conceived, designed and created to serve disputable, unpleasant or even obnoxious functions, as well as architectural complexes directly or indirectly connected with traumatic events, violence, segregation, oppression or abuse in their history of use. Examples include, but are not limited to, war infrastructures and remains; assets originally serving and representing disputed political ideologies, regimes or gangsterism; buildings related with colonialism and slavery, confinement, surveillance and control, past and present migration flows, and human trafficking or sweated labour.

In many cases, the architectural features of difficult built heritage make these buildings 'difficult' also from a design point of view. Many of them, indeed, fit with such a description of 'difficult built heritage' precisely because they have been purposely designed around a specific functional and symbolic programme. This is why their architectural typology and style inescapably and forthrightly link them to their history of uses and the associated difficult memories. This is also what often makes it very difficult to reuse them and adapt them to a new function without deeply altering their structure, spaces and layout (Hollis 2013) – let alone that such major transformations on the building fabric may not even be possible in the case of a listed heritage.

When dealing with difficult built heritage, matters of architectural design and preservation intertwine with questions of memorialisation, representation and communication of difficult stories and memories implying 'a political dimension (whether it is acknowledged or not) and, arguably, a profound responsibility in respect of the authenticity and ethics of representation' (Barton and Brown 2015: 238). Therefore, it stands to reason that whenever a reuse intervention becomes possible, needed or claimed, any intervention on this heritage is often rather troublesome. This type of reuse in fact 'demands not only a change of narrative . . . but a very particular negotiation with their architectural built form' (Pendlebury, Wang and Law 2018: 212), and it poses several dilemmas and hindrances concerning both design and preservation choices, and their impact on the meanings and memories associated with the building. In this chapter, by bringing to bear our backgrounds and expertise as architects, we outline the challenges and opportunities posed by the reuse of 'difficult built heritage' once it is reused as a museum, notably questioning the possible contribution – and drawbacks – of digital technologies in such a musealisation process and in defining the visitors' experience in these museums.

The Musealisation of Difficult Built Heritage

Various authors have already discussed the special challenges posed by the reuse of difficult built heritage for residential, leisure or third-sector use, highlighting the complexity of such a radical functional shift in the building use.[1] It requires a delicate negotiation with the past, the history of use and the architectural features of these buildings, which is often exposed to different interests and claims, and raises questions on 'strategic forgetting and selective remembrance' (Alun et al. 2013; Pendlebury et al. 2018) practices, heritage commodification and dark tourism. Musealisation however, is no less problematic. Indeed, it involves dealing with nested and intertwined issues pertaining to architectural preservation, museum design and collection display, ultimately regarding how the place, its material culture, stories and memories are narrated and experienced in these museums, and with which intents and effects. It is a matter of designing interactions in search of an equilibrium between the old and the new, spaces and display, material and immaterial tensions.

As for the adaptive reuse for any other function, the conversion into a museum firstly faces the design challenge of preserving the building's fabric and materiality while making it apt for hosting a new function, new users and all the necessary complementary functions. This notably means making the site suitable for the visiting public, providing the necessary technical systems and facilities of a contemporary museum, while meeting modern exhibition standards, as well as security and accessibility requirements. In the buildings included in 'difficult built heritage', these tasks are further complicated by the already mentioned often tight architectural features of such buildings.

At the same time, whenever a quite hard-line conservative approach to the pre-existing building fabric is adopted by the musealisation project—be it because of preservation regulations in force on-site and/or because of design choices—the exhibition designer may struggle to fit with it and the related constraints. On the one hand, the display apparatus, including cases, panels, labels and other elements, may collide or interfere aesthetically and physically with the original hosting spaces and their preservation. On the other hand, these pre-existing spaces with their highly iconic character and well-preserved material and immaterial features constitute an exhibition context that is definitively other than a neutral setting. Its visual strength and evocative power may interfere with the display by overpowering it – from a visual and aesthetic point of view – or competing with it in drawing visitors' attention. At the same time, these spaces, because of their peculiar and straightforward relationship with display itself and the objects exhibited, can end up overemphasising them, making their exhibition even more difficult also from a curatorial point of view.

Museums hosted at difficult built heritage locations in fact often hold collections related to their site history that constitute an important and foundational resource for these institutions but are a difficult heritage themselves, whose exhibition involves questions about what to display and how to transmit these collections to a broad public (Hamm and Schönberger 2021; Coleborne and MacKinnon 2011). The awkward or potentially disturbing nature of many of the items included in these collections may cause anxiety and discomfort, disagreement and dispute, misunderstanding, misuse and instrumentalisation. For this reason, these collections, more than others, must be properly contextualised and framed when publicly presented. At the same time, they often include a large number of historical records, pictures, letters, personal files and clinical cases, which may be difficult to display also from an exhibition design point of view. These are small items that can easily end up overlooked by visitors, especially when they are exhibited in such a particularly eye-catching context. Moreover, these records are often very fragile and sensitive, and they require an expert curator for handling them, which makes any handling by the visitors – e.g. browsing, reading or having a closer look – rather complicated. For these reasons, in many cases, it is rare, and most of these precious documents and their stories remain in the museum archives.

All the above makes the conversion of these sites into museums a delicate process, whose awkwardness, however, goes beyond architectural design considerations. Indeed, the musealisation of these buildings is a not only a moment of reuse involving a typological and functional shift for the building fabric, it is also a moment of public disclosure and representation of a difficult heritage, which is by definition quite complicated for what concerns its 'public representation and reception' (Macdonald 2009: 1). While working towards adaptive reuse in these sites, along with architectural issues and constraints, the designer has to deal with the difficult stories and memories embedded in their spaces and possibly support and enhance their 'meaningfulness' in the present. Especially within a musealisation project, the value of difficult built heritage is, in fact, related not only to its historical, architectural or artistic qualities, although often remarkable, but also to its potential – precisely because of the memories and stories it physically embeds – to act as a powerful place for fostering conscious and productive discourses on difficult yet meaningful pasts. In many aspects, museums at difficult built heritage sites can be regarded as 'sites of conscience' (Sevcenko 2011, 2010). As such, their actual and potential work is largely, yet not solely, based on the specific character of their site, which plays a crucial role in how messages are produced and conveyed by the museum and in how visitors themselves make meaning out of their own museum experience.

In the last twenty years, the number of musealisation projects of difficult heritage sites has been increasing. They variously deploy different curatorial strategies and design solutions aimed at overcoming at least some of the hurdles mentioned above, notably including an increase in the use of digital technologies into their exhibition design. It seems important thus to critically assess such a strategy, notably focusing on which contribution digital technologies may bring to the musealisation process, on what their use may allow to do in these sites, and on how their implementation can eventually support these museums in their work. To do so, we will draw on the comparison between two emblematic examples that sit at opposite extremes in the use of digital technologies in their museum and exhibition design: the former Horsens State Penitentiary (Denmark), today hosting the Fængselsmuseet, and the Museo di Storia della Psichiatria in Italy, at the former San Lazzaro Psychiatric Hospital in Reggio Emilia (Italy).

The Fængselsmuseet in Horsens

The Fængselsmuseet results from the reuse of the Horsens Statsfængsel (Horsens State Penitentiary), which was built between 1847 and 1853 as the first prison in Denmark designed on the basis of modern criminal law principles. It is thus considered the first modern prison of the state, implementing the progressist reformation of the prison system carried out by King Christian VIII (Scott and Flynn 2014). At the end of the nineteenth century, this was an innovative facility, with electricity and central heating, and was considered a progressive symbolic structure and a prominent urban landmark. It was composed of four-floor buildings organised around four wings and a middle wing, covering over 20,000 square metres, and was able to accommodate up to 500 detainees. In its 153-year-long function, it housed male prisoners from all over Denmark convicted of a penal crime and thus serving long prison sentences. Carceral life was organised according to the modern theories for internment and initially based on the adoption of the *Auburn system* (Randol 2014), which was gradually modified to improve the inmates' conditions.

Although some interventions were carried out over the decades, including renovations and expansions (Christiansen and Møller 1953; Nielsen and Vestergaard 2008), the prison has mainly retained its original form since 2006, when it was closed down. Because of its historical and architectural value as well as its solid imprint on the physical and social life of the city, after its decommission the former prison was identified as an architectural resource to be preserved and enhanced within a larger urban revitalisation process that was being started at that time. The whole site thus underwent an intense renovation project, funded with the help of the municipality.[2] This was mainly based on a 'conservative approach,' which was chiefly focused on the refurbishment of the buildings and involved a limited number of technical and spatial updates—the work that was needed to house a new functional program, and mostly related to creating museum facilities and improving the connections between the prison and the city. In 2012 the historic penitentiary reopened its doors as a multifunctional cultural centre. The complex, called Fængslet (i.e. the Danish word for 'prison'), gathers different cultural functions, among which is a prison museum aimed at narrating the history of this place.

The Fængselsmuseet is set within the four thousand square metres of the penitentiary's central building and occupies all four floors of the original building, including the common wards, the cells, the workshops, the kitchen, the medical ward, the chapel and the basement. The spaces of the old penitentiary have been set up to reproduce the same conditions they were in at the time of the prison closure, without involving any major architectural preservation or restoration interventions on the fabric of the building. This has been possible because this structure, unlikely many other decommissioned prisons, has not undergone any period of abandonment after its closure. The musealisation process could also benefit from the documentary support of a large number of historical records and objects documenting the site's history and which today constitute the core of a remarkable collection of material culture conserved by the museum.

Indeed, the institution owns more than fifteen thousand items, whose collection, preservation and display had already started before the closure of the penitentiary.[3] The collection mainly comprises prisoners' belongings, devices pertaining to the various activities carried out in prison (e.g. the workshops, the canteen and the nursery), medical reports, historical photos, audio and video interviews. Many of these objects, including personal effects left behind by the inmates, furniture such as beds, chairs, cupboards, telephones and old computer screens, are displayed at the museum today.

The exhibition is distributed over the different floors and spaces of the building and includes some 'thematic chapters', focusing on the Horsens prison's past framed within specific topics concerning justice and punishment from the mid-1800s to the present day. These are the 'last execution', 'prison tales', 'occupation and court cases behind bars' (examining the effect of the German occupation in 1940–45), 'children of prisoners', 'Lorentzen's tunnel' (documenting the story of the inmate who fled the penitentiary in 1949 by reconstructing the eighteen-metre-long tunnel and animating it by means of audio and video contributions) and the 'dark side' of the prison system (in the latest permanent exhibition, *Underworld*, opened on 11 October 2019, recounting the time when the basement was used for punishment, discipline and execution of the prisoners).

The site can be mainly defined as a museum of its own, meant to 'present history in a context' (Bjerrekaer 2017) and critically illustrating the story of the prison through an exhibition design aimed at creating a highly immersive experience. To do so, it taps into the evocative atmosphere of the place, exploits the collection's visual strength and hinges on the straightforward and direct link between the material culture on display and the exhibition context. As in other similar immersive displays, visitors are invited to 'step back in time' by walking within the former prison spaces as they were and variously interacting with the displayed items in their 'original' environments, by touching, sitting, opening drawers or playing table tennis, just as a detainee would have done.

In 2015, a major award-winning renovation was carried out at the museum to further enhance this immersive nature of the exhibition, chiefly by resorting to new technologies.[4] For this aim, the local studio specialising in digital technologies, Kvorning Design & Communication, in collaboration with AV-Huset, was entrusted with the design and implementation of innovative tools and devices. These include digital interfaces integrated into the museum spaces – e.g. touchscreens embedded in original cell tables – aimed at providing visitors with access to historical records, diaries and letters conserved in the archives. Along with this, the intervention implemented several technology-based installations that populated the museum spaces with some 'presences' animating the tour through projections, animations, lighting, video, audio and sensory settings. As they pass by the hallway, visitors catch a glimpse of faint figures moving along the walls, walking up the stairs or knocking on cell doors. Spaces resonate with voices and noises, such as tussles among prisoners on the gangways and the clanging of heavy cell doors. Odours emanate from here and there, such as the smoke in the wards or food odours from the kitchen.

The new design intervention also implemented some 'guiding figures' aimed at supporting the visit while also diversifying the tour and creating a reason for return visits. Although various types of guided and targeted group visits are offered (for tourists' groups, families, etc.), large numbers of people visit the museum without the support of a guide. In this case, at the beginning of their tour visitors can choose a virtual guide by selecting one ID card from among ten; the guides range from former inmates to guards or members of the support staff. The selected guide will thus accompany them along their tour by providing additional information on the prison's history and life based on his/her personal experience of it. Virtual guides feature actual former prison users who were living or working at the prison before its closure. When possible, they directly participated in the development and production of the contents associated with the virtual guide, which are staged mainly as site-specific audio-video installations. Their filmed contributions (short talks against a black background) are projected by means of fifty-six Panasonic Solid Shine™ laser projectors on the darkest walls of cells and offices. The character appears in the form of a life-size, moving figure, giving a speech directly addressing the visitor as if talking to him/her. Digital mapping is used to allow virtual images to interact with furnished spaces (e.g. in case the character needs to seem perched on top of an actual desk). In other cases, stories have been documented through archival research and then conveyed through different means, which do not involve the use of the videos (i.e. their physical appearance) but focus instead on their 'voices', delivered through oral and written contributions in their own words, as if they were addressing the visitors. These testimonies can be heard through an old telephone (re-enacted by a registered voice) or can be read as excerpts from diaries or letters projected onto walls or desktops; in some sites, historical pictures depicting the character or a related situation are projected, some of which are animated through short videos.

In order not to interfere either with the display or the museum spaces, and to enhance the immersive nature of the exhibition, most projectors are hidden in cupboards or placed vertically above entrance doors. This is made possible by the optical engine of the laser light source and by the fact that laser projectors can be rotated 360 degrees for installation at any angle; furthermore, they emit little heat and are virtually silent, and thus do not particularly intrude on exhibits even in confined spaces such as the cells. These contributions, moreover, are themselves activated through gestures by the visitors, thus allowing them to interact with spaces and objects that are connected with digital systems. For example, audio and video extracts start when visitors touch a bulletin board in the offices, answer the phone ringing in the ward, stand still on a precise place or sit down on a bed in the cells.

When the virtual guides come to life, they present moods, information or anecdotes, which always draw on their stories; they offer glimpses into carceral life and different perspectives on the penitentiary's past. These contributions may refer to dramatic and regretful memories, but they also reflect amusing and trivial ones, spanning from despised weekly fish day and the go-to guy for contraband to the use of illegal drugs in prison, from fights among the prisoners to the emotions felt for families and children.

Along with the above-mentioned reasons, museums also use such devices in an attempt to pursue a sort of 'inclusive integrity' (Wilson 2008: 58) by involving in the museum narrative multiple and possibly conflicting memories of different prison users, who may have experienced life in the prison in different ways and in different positions of power. In order to touch upon more current issues concerning carceral life and to spur visitors' involvement in such ongoing and potentially controversial debates (Bjerrekaer 2017), seven 'Discussion Rooms' have been included in the exhibition path. These are interactive stations, where visitors can expand their knowledge about current issues concerning prisons, punishment and penal systems, presented through a combination of historical records, experts' opinions, statistics and contents from recent newspapers and social media; furthermore, here people can contribute by participating in polls or leaving comments. The museum also includes another space dedicated to the creation of new content, the Insero mediaLab, which is composed of five contiguous rooms located in the heart of the building, furnished with a film and sound studio, a mini-cinema and a meeting room, where visitors can try media

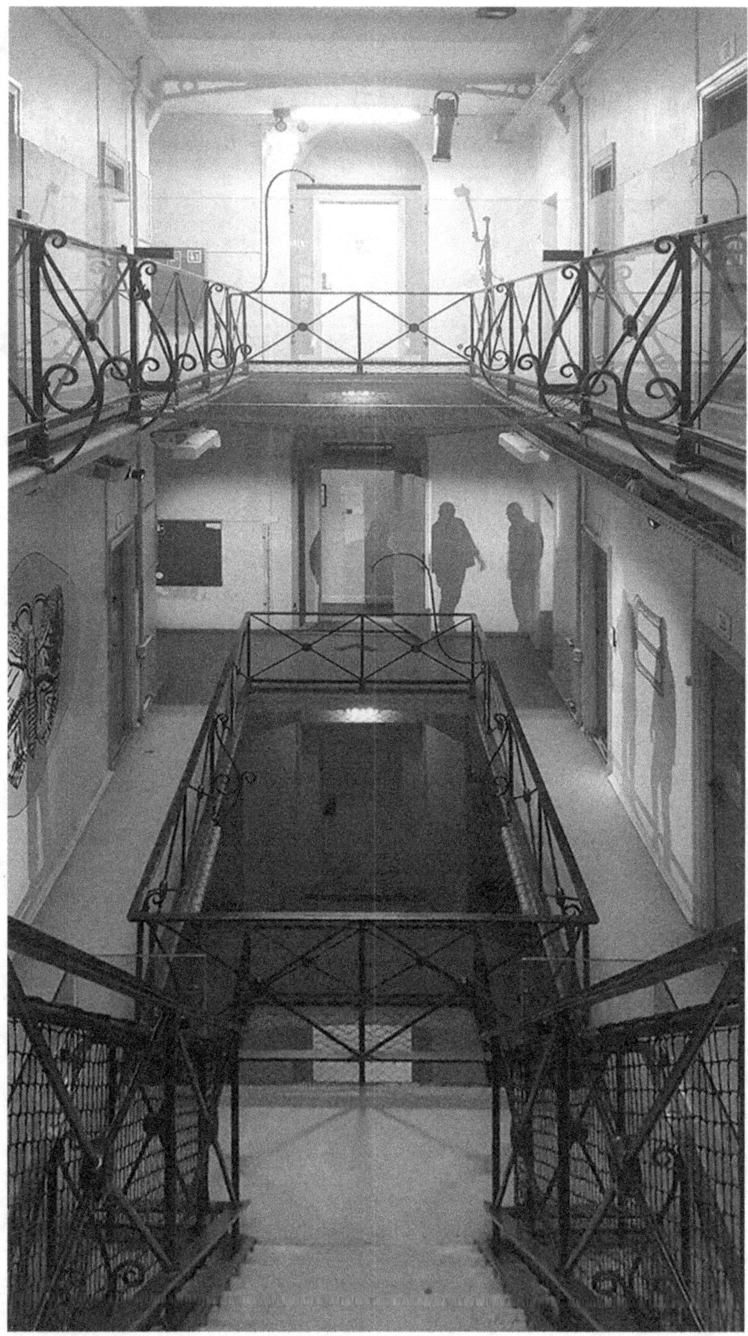

FIGURE 8.1. Fængsletmuseet (Prison Museum), Horsen, Denmark. The hallway. Image courtesy of the Fængsletmuseet.

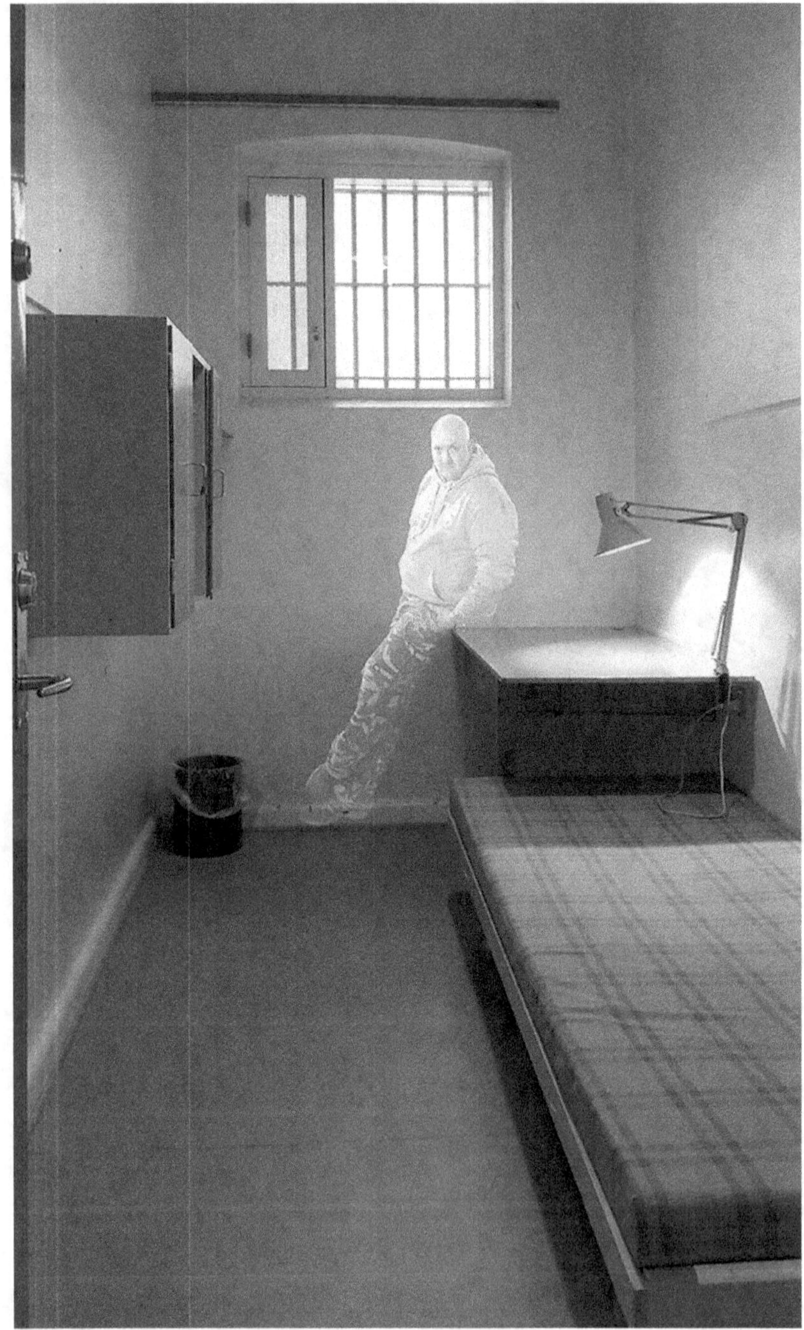

FIGURE 8.2. Fængsletmuseet (Prison Museum), Horsen, Denmark. A former cell. Image courtesy of the Fængsletmuseet.

production and storytelling. Visitors are also provided with the possibility to actively participate in the debates at home, before or after the tour (as they are given a personal code to access more information about their virtual guide). All the outcomes collected through these interaction and participation opportunities are then critically elaborated, processed and used by the curators for updating the museum's contents.

The example of the Fængselsmuseet demonstrates how in projects such as the one carried out at Horsen, which are characterised by distinctive tensions between exhibition design needs and architectural preservation instances, digital technologies can provide a number of solutions supporting the designer in his/her task. A widely recognised advantage of digital technologies, in fact, is their flexibility and light nature, which makes them an effective solution for integrating into the historical spaces different layers of narratives that relate to these spaces and the items on display but do not imply any major physical and aesthetic impact on the actual building fabric and materiality. As the Fængselsmuseet shows, although their implementation does involve some works (related to wiring, the installation of projectors and speakers, and the creation of suitable lighting conditions), if they are carefully designed, they can produce barely visible transformations and minimum physical alterations.

Many devices deploying either new or more conventional digital technologies, for example, differently from traditional wall-mounted panels and labels, offer the possibility to include in the display complementary information with nonobtrusive and potentially reversible interventions. These can span from small flat screens and touch screens up to interactive projection systems and virtual reality installations: most basic examples include digitalised information panels and labels that can substitute or complement the analogic ones, broadening their contents about specific topics and/or providing additional information on demand, as well allowing for an easy update whenever it may be needed, as for the devices used at Fængselsmuseet. Similarly, such devices can offer the possibility to expand content related to specific items on display as well as to some museum spaces and their architectural details, but they can also potentially create connections with other stories in space and time. At Fængselsmuseet, digital devices and installations provide the public with different kinds of information about the objects on display, connecting them with the witnesses' personal stories and memories, with the spaces in which they are exhibited and with contemporary issues and debates. Furthermore, as at Horsens, the use of digital terminals and the digitalisation of the collection can allow the inclusion of items in the display that could not be effectively exhibited in another way—such as personal letters, historical documents, pictures, clinical cases, inmates' files and oral histories. In this way, they contribute to providing access to collections and other precious materials that otherwise would have probably remained conserved in the archives despite their value and contribution to the museum work.

Overall, the intent beyond the digital project implemented at Fængselsmuseet was to ensure that visitors go through a 'guided visit' while being provided with a variety of information as they engage in an immersive experience hinged on the 'historical spaces' eloquence' (Heinich 2009: 66–67). The different digital devices and the audio-video installations implemented in the exhibition design are meant to expand and contextualise the museum's contents, not only serving as informative devices but also contributing to pluralising voices and perspectives and offering diverse interpretive frameworks (Hooper-Greenhill 2000: 51).

A similar rationale formed the basis of the exhibition project for the Museo di Storia della Psichiatria.

The Museo di Storia della Psichiatria in Reggio Emilia

The Museo di Storia della Psichiatria is hosted at the Lombroso Pavilion, one of the original buildings of the former San Lazzaro psychiatric hospital in Reggio Emilia. As with many other asylums in Europe and overseas, the hospital was established in the early nineteenth century within a positivist approach, in the belief that insanity should be 'treated' and could be cured and that the built environment could play a role in doing so (Ajroldi et al. 2013; Topp, Moran and Andrews 2007). After significant growth that made it a major site in Italy and Europe at the beginning of the twentieth century, it became a sort of small, self-sufficient town, which included more than twenty buildings organised in a cottage plan with about two thousand patients hospitalised every year. Shortly after that time, however, the hospital started a slow and regrettable decline, which characterised many other psychiatric institutions worldwide and eventually led to their closure, events spurred by the deinstitutionalisation process that started at the end of the 1960s.

The Lombroso Pavilion dates back to 1892. Originally named Casino Galloni, it hosted 'calm chronic patients' until 1911, when it was converted to the isolation of 'mad criminals' and thus enlarged with the addition of two lateral wings of cells. During its lifespan, the pavilion underwent minor changes until 1972, when it was considered obsolete and thus disused, falling into decay. In 2013 it was converted to host the Museo di Storia della Psichiatria, with the mission to serve as a place displaying the history of the former asylum and promoting knowledge and awareness about mental health care in the past and the present.

To do so, the museum counts on a rare, rich collection pertaining to the hospital's life and practices. The museum collection consists of several diverse items, including medical objects collected at the hospital since the 1870s[5]; about eight thousand artworks (paintings, drawings and potteries) created by the hospital patients from the 1970s onward; one hundred thousand case files of the former inmates, and one thousand boxes of other documents; a photographic collection with more than fifteen hundred pictures, the oldest dating back to nineteenth century, complemented by the library collection that holds about fifteen thousand volumes including historical books and new acquisitions.

The Museo di Storia della Psichiatria today grounds its work in this collection as well as in the evocative strength of its unique venue (Tagliabue 2013; Grassi, Farioli and Bombardieri 2013), i.e. the Lombroso Pavilion, restored to turn it into a museum that opened in 2013.[6] As Giorgia Lombardini, the municipality architect in charge for the reuse of the Lombroso, explains, the overall intervention was intended to preserve the spatial features of the building fabric, as well as its materiality, by following the guiding principle to 'integrate' what was missing not by replacing it but rather by evoking the same aesthetic impression to 'maintain intact the peculiar atmosphere of the place'.[7] Accurate surveys and archival research were carried out, with the contribution of Chiara Bombardieri, director of the library and future curator of the museum. Whenever structural interventions have been needed these were done by deploying original construction techniques and materials in the case of refurbishment, or as contemporary self-evident interventions in case of new additions. Interior wall finishing was restored, with specific attention paid to the conservation of the original nineteenth-century marmorino plasters and to some graffiti made by patients using spoons and soles. Other architectural elements, details and furniture were similarly restored, such as the cell doors, or tables and benches in the former dining room, which were originally fixed and distributed in the space according to security and surveillance rationales. Moreover, as part of the reuse intervention, the building containment wall, which was demolished in 1974, was rebuilt at the same size and in the same location as the original one, but as a wireframe structure in corten steel, with the twofold intention of symbolically evoking the former wall and serving as a support for temporary outdoor exhibitions.

The selection of the objects to be exhibited was a challenging process, which involved reflections on ethical issues, emotional impacts and the role and risks inherent in exhibiting such a difficult and possibly 'contentious' material culture (Grassi et al. 2013). With the key objective to design a museum able to foster informed critical reflections about mental health care and treatment in the past and today, the curators' team originally opted for a 'narrative' exhibition approach (Studio Azzurro 2011) and for extensive use of digital-based installations in the exhibition.[8] Aware of the strong evocative and emotional power of both the sites and the objects on display, their visual strength and their potential to open up to many stories, different possibly conflicting positions and complex discourses, the mandate given to exhibition design was to 'lessen the "emotional tone"' of the museum. The overarching design concept was thus to provide visitors with accurate information with the imperative objective to avoid clichés, instrumentalisations, and potential slips into voyeuristic drifts and dark tourism behaviours.

The studio Fuse*Factory, a firm based in Modena with expertise in the field of digital technologies and design, was in charge of designing the exhibition. The project was meant to extend throughout the two-storey building and include a visitable archive and a gallery for patients' artworks located at the upper level of the museum. A limited number of objects was to be displayed, accompanied by audio-visuals and multimedia installations. These installations and other interactive digital displays were aimed at providing visitors with different information about the San Lazzaro, the pavilion and the objects as well as access to selected clinical files, historical records and images from the hospital archive. It was also intended to enhance and expand some of the material elements of the building itself—in particular the graffiti in the former patients' cells. Touch screens were to be installed on the original wood tables on the ground floor: these were supposed to feature an interactive interface where information on the hospital's historical, cultural and social context was organised thematically and visualised with short texts and images from the archives. A selection of medical objects from the museum collection was to be displayed in the former cells, complemented by multimedia installations based on historical records and clinical cases. Along corridors, 'light boxes' (i.e. full-size backlit supports) were meant to display full-scale high-resolution printings of historical images of the pavilion interior spaces from the photographic archive. However, the 2008 global financial crisis led to cuts in public funds and impeded the creation of this exhibition design project.

Today the museum runs a wide range of different activities in collaboration with the Biblioteca Scientifica Carlo Livi, and it is extremely active in pursuing its mission. Nevertheless, the Lombroso Pavilion is open to the public only a few days a week, with free guided tours on Saturdays and for prearranged school visits on Wednesdays and Thursdays during school terms. Guided tours for the public and for schools adopt different models and protocols; nevertheless, they have some common elements. The visits—which usually last two hours for the public and three for schools—are led by both a museum guide and a 'cultural mediator'. The latter is an 'expert by experience', i.e. a person who experienced mental health problems, is now in the recovery phase and acts as a cultural mediator. He/she flanks the guide in the tour by reading aloud excerpts from historical clinical records and texts written by contemporary patients of the local mental health support services. For school visits, cultural mediators act as living witnesses, and usually appear together as a pair: during one-hour face-to-face onsite meetings, they recount their personal story, respond to students' questions and talk with them about mental health.

During the tour the guide narrates the story of the hospital, starting from its establishment, continuing to its closure and concluding with the current psychiatric system. Only a few objects are on display, and the museum lacks almost any supporting or complementary material, apart from two audio-visual programs based on historical inmates, created on the basis of archival material and pro-

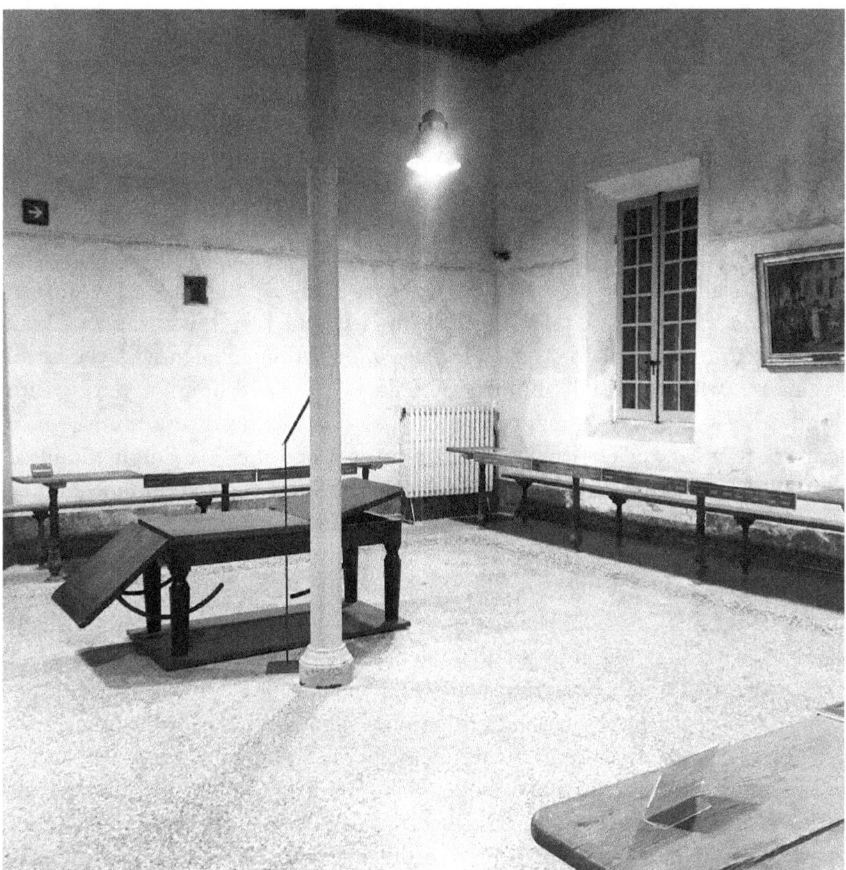

FIGURE 8.3. Museo di Storia della Psichiatria, Reggio Emilia, Italy. The former dining room. Image by Francesca Lanz.

jected by the guide onto two screens in one of the rooms on the ground floor. Quite interestingly, during the visit, the guide relies equally on objects on display as on the site itself. Medical objects and architectural elements of the site are used by the guides not only as means to illustrate their storytelling but also as clues to address possibly contentious topics and to trigger a discussion with and among the visitors.

The case of the Museo di Storia della Psichiatria is a perfect example of what might happen in an extreme case of disruptive malfunctioning in an ICT-based exhibition. The cost of a digital-based exhibition may be considerable, and, as we will learn from this case, not every institution can afford it. Along with the costs related to design and implementation, there are also regular and frequent expenses for maintenance and updates. The Fængselsmuseet has already undergone five renovations. Indeed, digital-based technological devices require constant maintenance; they may malfunction, and, considering the actual speed of advancement in the technological field, they may quickly become outdated. Moreover, when they play such a crucial role in the exhibition, any defect might have a detrimental effect on the display, to the extent that it may jeopardise the overall experience of the visit.

At Reggio Emilia, the impossibility of implementing such devices in the exhibition forced the designers and curator to devise a makeshift backup project with practically no budget, struggling—and partially failing—to deal with such a difficult context and the sensitive tasks it is assigned within such a museum. The need to provide visitors with adequate information collided with the issues of how and where to install informative analogue panels without interfering with or affecting the space's 'integrity'. Panels were thus reduced to a minimum in terms of number and information they provided, and they are simply mounted on walls or propped against pieces of furniture. Some of them are too hidden away to be noticed, while others are very difficult to read due to both graphic design issues (e.g. too much information for a written text) and ergonomic reading matters (e.g. being placed solely with regard for their aesthetic impact on the spaces). Information about the spaces of the pavilion is summarised in a single A4 take-away sheet found on standalone racks along the exhibition path; labels consist of small silver-grey metal plates that include the name and date of the items on display. The result is an exhibition design that is far from sufficient in providing visitors with the necessary information. The overall display lacks any informative means that would provide basic knowledge about the exhibited historical spaces and objects, about their original uses and purposes as well as their intended meaning within the display, to the extent that they may end up being overlooked, rendered meaningless or misinterpreted. At the same time, because many materials from the collection—notably historical images, documents and clinical records—are too fragile or difficult to display, it is impossible to exhibit them. For all these reasons, the museum warmly suggests visiting as part of a guided tour. Consequently, it is open only during limited times when guided tours are scheduled.

Conclusion: Interacting in, with and within Difficult Built Heritage

The Fængselsmuseet and the Museo di Storia della Psiachiatria emblematically exemplify the topics discussed in the introductory paragraphs about the challenges and potentialities of adaptively reusing difficult built heritage for museum purposes. Here in particular we build on them to highlight some possibilities and challenges in the use of digital technologies in exhibition design at these museums. In these conclusive remarks we draw the comparison between Fængselsmuseet and the Museo di Storia della Psiachiatria to bring forward some reflections, notably focusing on how digital technologies can interact and conjoin with the site materiality in creating a spatial context that may support the work these museums aim to do.

Both museums are the result of a reuse intervention based on a chiefly conservative approach to the pre-existing building fabric, backed up by a remarkable quality and conservation level of the spaces and the availability of significant documentation in archival and historical records. Fængselsmuseet and the Museo di Storia della Psichiatria are thus hosted in well-preserved historic spaces, where the original spatial features and materiality constitute an important resource deployed to offer a very specific experience and to eventually pursue the museums' missions. On the one hand, it consists of narrating and representing the history of their premise, i.e. a difficult heritage. On the other, similar to sites of conscience, these museums seek to unfold and problematise the past difficult memories and stories that are connected with their sites and link them with contemporary topics in order to foster awareness and productive debates about human rights and social issues.

To do so, both these institutions tap into their site deeply and intentionally to unfold the civic and pedagogical potential of these specific kinds of heritage sites (Golding 2008). Yet, in two very different ways their design critically exploits the 'darker' components of their heritage and the evocative environmental power of their spaces, contributing a special atmosphere at these museums with some specific implications and effects (Turner and Peters 2015). As already discussed by other authors, the peculiar 'atmospheres' at these memory sites are capable of engendering emotional responses within the public and prompting a certain empathy between the visitor and the presented stories, as well as personal reflection on them (Sumartojo and Pink 2019; Sumartojo 2019; Turner and Peters 2015; Edensor and Sumartojo 2015). The place atmosphere therefore has a crucial role in determining what the museum does, how it does it and what it allows to be done. As highlighted in recent works by Sumartojo and Pink (2019), atmosphere can be described as a quality, substantially defined in its feeling and meanings, depending on the physical, emotional, sensory and intellectual embodiment, attunement and engagement in the site, with the site and through the site. Understanding atmospheres as conditions, co-constituted and determined by a configuration of fixed and ever-changing material and immaterial elements within a site-specific experience, and resulting from the spatial, aesthetical, environmental and material characteristics of the context in which they arise, as well as from people's feeling, movement, memory, foreknowledge, expectations and interactions, we ask here which kind of atmosphere is emerging in these two museums in relation to the different use of digital and technological devices and installations in their exhibition design.

At the Museo di Storia della Psichiatria, visits are based on the interaction of visitors with a guide and with cultural mediators. As it emerges from our interviews with guides and from preliminary visitor studies, these encounters among people in the space create a very special atmosphere, one that varies every time. This atmosphere can materialise not only from dialogue but also from discussion and disagreement as well as intimacy and empathy. During our interviews with the museum's staff conducted between December and April 2020 as part of the institution's in-depth study, guides agreed about the lack of support for the exhibition design, its inefficiency in providing even basic essential information and its ineffectiveness in supporting them in their guided tours. When asked about which kind of tools they would like to have at their disposal, they regretted the lack of technological and digital devices and multimedia installations. However, when going further in our interviews, they increasingly became passionate about their work and began telling us about their professional but also personal experience of being a guide 'at the Lombroso' (the museum is named after the site, emblematically representing the strong embodied relationship between the museum and its venue). They told us about their engagement and that of their visitors, both with the space and among one another, which is chiefly based on informed dialogues spurred by the site materiality. Sometimes visitors feel so confident and involved that they recount their personal stories related to the hospital and mental health. When this happens, the guides afterwards delve deep into these testimonies through archival-based research: this enriches their knowledge of the site and informs their subsequent presentation to visitors, in the process of continuous learning for them and the evolution of the museum knowledge and narrative. At the same time, the experience of being involved in these tours is also vital for the mediators, for whom telling and retelling their stories is not only a work of raising awareness and dismantling bias about mental health but also a fundamental moment of their recovery process. Conversely, at Horsens, visits and interaction with the museum materiality, collection, stories and messages are mainly happening due to digital-based installations: voices, sounds, smells and figures interacting with the space aim to further foster visitors' engagement by providing an immersive and 'real' visit experience. However, the kind of interaction they offer is univocal and mostly singular and individual. The installations are meant to provide information and an immersive visit experience. Devices tell something *to* visitors, visitors act *on* them, thereby reducing technology to the role of informational providers and the supposed interaction to simple, one-way actions. Moreover, as we already highlighted in relation to other similar immersive exhibitions (Lanz 2016; Whitehead and Lanz 2020; Lanz and Whitehead 2019), such an approach risks embedding a certain level of gamification, which can result in a fair-like, sensation-heavy affective experience that leaves little space for personal and critical reflection, not least because immersion requires a kind of completeness or coherence in the imagination of place that is unambiguously definite and singular.

Both the museums' present situation shows pros and cons that exist in an opposition, seeming, for the moment, incapable of finding a point of encounter that may overcome all the problems and enhance the potentialities of these sites, leaving the choice to use these devices or not to the designer and/or the curators, or to contingent (e.g. economic) conditions. Is a convergence of the two experiences possible? Perhaps a potential future use of emerging digital technologies such as VR, AI or 3D modelling in difficult built heritages will enable to work further in this direction.

Acknowledgements

This chapter partially builds on the research activities carried out by Francesca Lanz within the research project ReMIND – Reactivating Neglected Heritages, Reweaving Unspoken Memories: A Study on the Adaptive Reuse of Former Asylums into 'Mind Museums', which has received funding from the European Union's Horizon 2020 research and innovation programme under the Marie Skłodowska-Curie grant agreement No. 841174.

Francesca Lanz, trained as an architect in Italy, formerly lecturer in interior architecture and exhibition design at Politecnico di Milano, is currently a Marie Skłodowska-Curie Fellow at Newcastle University and senior lecturer in interior architecture and design at Lincoln University. Her academic expertise lies at the intersection of different fields, ranging from interior architecture, museum and exhibition design to museum and heritage studies, with a particular interest on the potential intertwinements between different disciplinary approaches, theories and practices. Her research activity develops across these areas, and it notably revolves around the role of the built environment and museums in contemporary societies, with key attention to neglected heritages and difficult memories and stories. In the past years, she has contributed to several research programmes on these topics, including the EU-funded projects MeLa (2011–15) on museums and migrations, TRACES (2016–19) on contentious heritages, and ReMIND (2019–21) A Study on the Reuse of Former Psychiatric Asylums into 'Mind Museums'.

Elena Montanari is lecturer in interior architecture and exhibition design at the Department of Architecture and Urban Studies of Politecnico di Milano, where she has been contributing to national and international research projects – e.g. MeLa – European Museums in an Age of Migrations (2011–15), Transatlantic Transfers: The Italian Presence in Post-War America (2020–23), REC - Memorial Forms: Recordings in progress (RIBA 2021–22). Since 2016, she is responsible for numerous dissemination and research activities included in the programme of the UNESCO Chair in Preservation and Planning in World Heritage Cities, managed at the Mantova Campus. She is also variously committed to editorial activities: she is coordinator of the Bookseries Architectural Design and History (FrancoAngeli), and she serves as reviewer for several scientific journals. Her research work revolves around the interplay among interior architecture, museographic culture and heritage, with a particular focus on the adaptation of historical buildings into exhibition spaces, on the musealisation of 'difficult built heritage' and places of memory and on the rise of innovative theories and practices concerning exhibition design history and museographic heritage.

Notes

1. For example, as to the reuse of former asylums: Gibbeson 2018; Moon, Kearns and Alun 2015; Alun, Kearns, and Moon 2009; Alun, Kearns, and Moon 2013; Kearns, Alun and Moon 2010; Franklin 2002a, 2002b. As to the reuse of former prisons: Hodgkinson and Urquhart 2016; Barton and Brown 2015; Sharpley 2009; Wilson 2008; Lanz 2018.
2. The €4.5 million project was financed through the cooperation of Horsens Municipality, which acquired the prison from the Danish state, and the support from two major funds in Denmark.
3. Fifty years before the closure, a prison guard started to conserve old items, devices and records and organize and display them in the basement (placed inside simple cases or hung on the walls), where a small prison museum was already visible, forming the original core of the contemporary institution.
4. This update resulted in the assignment of the 2016 'Inavation Award' for best visitors' attraction and the 2016 'Museums + Heritage Award' for the best foreign (non-British) museum.
5. As in the case of Horsens's prison museum, the history of the museum at the former San Lazzaro hospital is as long as that of the whole asylum system and deeply intertwined with it. A preliminary form of exhibition already existed in the early stage of the structure's life; indeed, in line with the positivist approach of the time, several asylum directors had been collecting and displaying objects related to the material history of the site and of the medical practices employed back in time, with the purpose of showing advancements in the treatment of mental diseases. Even though interest in this exhibition decreased during the twentieth century – to the extent that after the First World War it had become a sort of storage facility – its existence contributed to the preservation of a large and quite unique collection.
6. The intervention was part of a larger urban rehabilitation plan for the area of the former San Lazzaro hospital; it started in February 2009, concluded in February 2011, cost a total amount of €3.1 million (€2,065,827.60 from the minister for cultural heritage and €1,034,172.40 from the Municipality of Reggio Emilia).
7. Interview with F. Lanz, May 2020.
8. The project was particularly inspired by Studio Azzurro's setting at the Museo Laboratorio della Mente in Rome (2008).

References

Ajroldi, Cesare, et al. (eds). 2013. *I Complessi Manicomiali in Italia tra Otto e Nocecento*. Milan: Electa.

Alun, Joseph, Robin Kearns and Graham Moon. 2009. 'Recycling Former Psychiatric Hospitals in New Zealand', *Health & Place*, 15(1): 79–87.

Alun, Joseph, Robin Kearns and Graham Moon. 2013. 'Re-imagining Psychiatric Asylum Spaces through Residential Redevelopment,' *Housing Studies* 28(1): 135–53.

Barton, Alana, and Alyson Brown. 2015. 'Show Me the Prison! The Development of Prison Tourism in the UK,' *Crime Media Culture*, 11(3): 237–58.

Bassanelli, Michela, and Gennaro Postiglione (eds). 2013. *Re-enacting the Past: Museography for Conflict Heritage*. Siracusa: LetteraVentidue.

Berger, Markus, and Liliane Wong (eds). 2013. *Difficult Memories: Reconciling Meaning – Int\AR Journal* 4.

Bjerrekaer, Anne. 2017. *Horsens Prison Museum: Recreating Life behind Bars*. The Best in Heritage 2017. Retrieved 21 January 2020 from https://presentations.thebestinheritage .com/2017/horsens-prison-museum.

Christiansen, Svend E., and Th. Møller. 1953. *Statsfængslet i Horsens: 1853–20. maj – 1953*. Copenhagen: Direktoratet for Fængselsvæsenet.

Coleborne, Catharine, MacKinnon, Dolly (eds). 2011. *Exhibiting Madness in Museums*. New York: Routledge.

Edensor, Tim, and Shanti Sumartojo. 2015. 'Designing Atmospheres: Introduction to Special Issue'. *Visual Communication* 14(3): 251–65.

Franklin, Bridget. 2002a. "Hospital–Heritage–Home: Reconstructing the Nineteenth Century Lunatic Asylum." *Housing, Theory and Society* 19(3–4): 170–84.

———. 2002b. "Monument to Madness: The Rehabilitation of the Victorian Lunatic Asylum." *Journal of Architectural Conservation* 8(3): 24–39.

Gibbeson, Carolyn Fay. 2018. 'After the Asylum: Place, Value and Heritage in the Redevelopment of Historic Former Asylums'. PhD thesis, University of Newcastle upon Tyne, School of Arts & Cultures.

Golding, Viv. 2008. 'Developing Pedagogies of Human Rights and Social Justice in the Prison Museum,' in Jacqueline Z. Wilson et al. (eds), *The Palgrave Handbook of Prison Tourism*. London: Palgrave, pp. 989–1010.

Grassi, Gaddomaria, Elisabetta Farioli and Chiara Bombardieri. 2013. "Perché parlare oggi di psichiatria e della sua storia." *Rivista Sperimentale di Freniatria* 87(2): 75–94.

Hamm, Marion, and Klaus Schönberger, eds. 2021. *Contentious Cultural Heritages and Arts*. Wieser Verlag, Založba Wieser: Klagenfurt/Celovec.

Heinich, Nathalie. 2009. *La fabrique du patrimoine*. Paris: Éditions de la Maison des Sciences de l'Homme.

Hodgkinson, Sarah, and Diane Urquhart. 2016. 'Prison Tourism,' in Glenn Hooper and John J. Lennon (eds), *Dark Tourism*. New York: Routledge, pp. 40–53.

Hollis, Edward. 2013. 'No Longer and No Yet', in Graham Cairns (ed.), *Reinventing Architecture and Interiors*. London: Libri Publishing, pp. 177–94.

Hooper-Greenhill, Eilean. 2000. *Museums and the Interpretation of Visual Culture*. New York: Routledge.

Kearns, Robin, Joseph Alun and Graham Moon. 2010. 'Memorialisation and Remembrance', *Social & Cultural Geography* 11(8): 731–49.

Kusek, Robert, and Jajek Purchla (eds). 2019. *Heritage and Society*. Krakow: International Cultural Centre.

Lanz, Francesca. 2016. 'Staging Migration (in) Museums', *Museum & Society* 14(1): 178–92.

Lanz, Francesca (ed.). 2018. *Patrimoni inattesi*. Siracusa: Letteraventidue.

Lanz, Francesca, and Chris Whitehead. 2019. 'Exhibiting Voids', in Burcu Dogramaci and Birgit Mersmann (eds), *Handbook of Art and Global Migration*. Berlin: de Gruyter, pp. 331–48.

Logan, William, and Keir Reeves. 2009. *Places of Pain and Shame: Dealing with 'Difficult Heritage'*. London: Routledge.

Luna, Raphael. 2013. 'Life of a Shell and the Collective Memory of a City'. *Int\AR Journal* 4, 30–35.

Macdonald, Sharon. 2009. *Difficult Heritage*. New York: Routledge.

———. 2020. 'Contentious Collections, Contentious Heritage', in Marion Hamm and Klaus Schönberger (eds), *Contentious Heritages and Arts: A Critical Companion*. Klagenfurt: Wieser Verlag.

Moon, Graham, Robin Kearns and Joseph Alun. 2015. *The Afterlives of the Psychiatric Asylums*. Burlington: Ashgate.

Nielsen, Mikkel, Kirkedahl Lysholm, and Anna Wowk Vestergaard. 2008. 'Horsens Statsfængsel 1853–2006', *Vejle Amts Historiske Samfund*: 48–76.

Pendlebury, John, Yi-Wen Wang and Andrew Law. 2018. 'Re-using Uncomfortable Heritage,' *International Journal of Heritage Studies* 24(3): 211–29.

Randol, Blake. 2014. 'Auburn System,' in Jay S. Albanese (ed.), *The Encyclopedia of Criminology and Criminal Justice*. Oxford: Wiley Blackwell, pp. 1–4.

Scott, David, and Nick Flynn. 2014. *Prison and Punishment*. London: Sage.

Sevcenko, Liz. 2010. 'Sites of Conscience: Heritage of and for Human Rights,' in Helmut K. Anheier and Yudhishthir Raj Isar (eds), *Cultures and Globalization*. London: SAGE, pp. 114–18.

———. 2011. 'Sites of Conscience: New Approaches to Conflicted Memory', *Museum International* 62(1–2): 20–25.

Sharpley, Richard. 2009. 'Shedding Light on Dark Tourism,' in Richard Sharpley and Jørgen Smidt-Jensen (eds). *1990. Tugt og Tremmer: Fængselsmuseet uden for murene*. Horsens: Horsens Museum.

Studio Azzuro. 2011. *Musei di Narrazione*. Milan: Silvana Editoriale.

Sumartojo, Shanti. 2019. 'Sensory Impact', in Danielle Drozdzewski and Carolyn Birdsall (eds), *Doing Memory Research*. Singapore: Palgrave Macmillan, pp. 21–37.

Sumartojo Shanti, and Sarah Pink. 2019. *Atmospheres and the Experiential Worlds*. London: Routledge.

Tagliabue, Luigi. 2013. 'Il valore di un Museo della Psichiatria a Reggio Emilia', *Rivista Sperimentale di Freniatria* 87(2): 95–111.

Topp, Leslie, James Moran and Jonothan Andrews (eds). 2007. *Madness, Architecture and the Built Environment*. London: Routledge.

Tunbridge, John E., and Gregory J. Ashworth. 1996. *Dissonant Heritage*. Chichester: Wiley.

Turner, Jennifer, and Kimberley Peters. 2015. 'Unlocking Carceral Atmospheres', *Visual Communication* 14(3): 309–30.

Whitehead, Chris, and Francesca Lanz. 2020. 'Only Connect,' in Mark O'Neill and Glenn Hooper (eds), *Connecting Museums*. New York: Routledge, pp. 186–202.

Wilson, Jacqueline Z. 2008. *Prison: Cultural Memory and Dark Tourism*. New York: Peter Lang Publishing.

Chapter 9

DARK MANOEUVRES

Digitally Reincorporating the Marginalised Body in the Museum

Lily Hibberd and Sarah Kenderdine

Introduction: Difficult Heritage in the Museum

Difficult heritage is a concept that only began to appear in museological discourse a decade after the first literature was published on the topic in the fields of cultural studies, critical heritage and anthropology (Logan and Reeves 2009; Macdonald 2009; Lehrer, Milton and Patterson 2011). The notion that heritage production itself might be difficult initially surfaced in the 1990s as part of wide-ranging critiques of historical interpretation and heritage practices as well as sociological, ethical and human rights questions about postcolonial and post-conflict societies (Giblin 2015). Prior to this, Tunbridge and Ashworth (1996), introduced the term 'dissonant heritage' to define how heritage might simultaneously create and contend with historical conflict, while Pitt and Britzman (2003) proposed that 'difficult knowledge' could offer new approaches to the pedagogy of trauma. The politics of heritage (Smith 2006, 2011) emerged as a novel concern following the 2003 ratification of the UNESCO Convention for the Safeguarding of the Intangible Heritage, alongside scepticism that this framework was being used to authorise new forms of nationalism and repression of extramarginal cultures (Aykan 2014).

Alivizatou (2006: 47) states that intangible cultural heritage (ICH) has an 'unconventional relationship' with museums. As the most visible and imposing purveyors of public history, however, museums share the propensity of ICH toward 'metacultural production', which reiterates prevailing cultural or dominant nation-state narratives (Kirshenblatt-Gimblett 2004: 61). In recent years, collecting institutions worldwide, including state archives, public galleries and libraries, have faced increasing demands for more inclusive, accessible and community-oriented or engaged civic structures (Bennett 2006; Schorch 2009; Zavala et al. 2017). Attention to problems of cultural colonialism, appropriation and exploitation, or 'dark tourism', in museums and at heritage sites has underpinned parallel critiques across public history, heritage, tourism, human rights, social justice and memory studies scholarship (Bennett 2004, 2018; Lennon and Foley 2000; Luke 2003; Sandell 2002, 2016).

Meanwhile, working outside official state channels, artists and activists such as Brook Andrew (Australia), Theaster Gates (United States), Doris Salcedo (Colombia) and Ai Weiwei (China) have, each in their own way, anthropologically excavated and exposed ongoing exclusion in museums of people due to racial or political discrimination, systemic erasure or oversight. The term 'difficult' may, as such, refer to an array of socio-political issues and heritage practices. Nonetheless, ensuring that heritage production does not reiterate past injustices for marginalised communities remains an enormous challenge for many societies and museums (Bennett 2018; Djuric, Hibberd and Steele 2018; Sandell 2016).

Although museums have begun to embrace and include more diverse audiences, a gap remains when it comes to 'difficult' bodies – which we contend entails bodies attached to specific individuals or communities for whom exclusion persists, either based on stereotypes of stigma about their bodies or due to marginalised corporeal practices. Two dimensions of the body are implicated here: first, the physical or living being that actively faces hardship due to stigma and the direct effects of systemic discrimination (e.g. against different cognitive, psychological or physical abilities, against minority groups and people of colour, or on the grounds of non-heterosexual orientation or non-binary gender identity); second, the embodied dimension of lived experience in which the body is a vessel or repertoire of knowledge that is vulnerable to being lost as a result of the displacement, disconnection or cultural oppression of socially transmitted practices (e.g. religious or ritual performance, a First Nations or minority cultural group and its customs).

Recent research in performance studies has promoted the concept of 'embodied historiography' to theorise forms of re-enactment and performative practice that enable the restoration, recollection and retelling of tacit knowledge (Johnson 2015). Other important performative work with trauma survivors has sought to engage and empower the body as a living document and form of testimony, as a repertoire through which otherwise inaccessible (repressed) knowledge can be unlocked (Branch and Hughes 2014; Hibberd 2014).

The vitality of performative archives as living repertoires of memory (Bal 2001; Bal, Crewe and Spitzer 1998; Taylor 2003; Trezise 2014) has also been advanced as a means of resistance to forms of oppression and normative or systemic violence (Butler 1999). In the museological domain, however, performance and performed practices are rarely regarded as an authentic means of historical account. The refusal to accept physical acts or corporeal reconstructions of the past as a legitimate heritage method means that many experiences (that cannot be conveyed otherwise) have no representation in museums, thus reinforcing their marginalisation. Arising from re-performed repertoires of memory (Taylor 2003, 2016), the notion of re-enacting the past importantly intersects with studies of embodied cognition that are fundamental to both immersive and interactive design (Kirsch 2013) – research that is central to the emergent domain we intend to delineate in this chapter, that of digital embodied historiography.

Bringing Difficult Bodies into the New Museum

Museums have been increasingly tasked to engage their public, not only through internal organisation, outlook and public appearance but also within the very fabric of the museum, by reinventing museum design and modalities of display and improving access to often vast and sometimes impenetrable holdings. New museology, which centres on the theorisation of museums as public-facing institutions (Hooper-Greenhill 1994; Vergo 1989), has been a central part of a wider transformation over the past two decades of the political and social landscape of heritage through critical approaches to exhibition and collection practice (Shelton 2013), as well as architectural design of museums and object displays (Gunn, Otto and Smith 2013).

What is additionally evident in the nascent turn in museums towards greater public or civic engagement is the orientation to the body (e.g. curatorial design that leads visitors on pathways, human-scale models, immersive video and sound installations, interactive touch or mobile screen interfaces). Yet this re-emphasis has introduced contradictions. While the new museum model permits different, more sensory entry points through more tactile and tacit encounters (Howes 2014; Falk and Dierking 2008; Kenderdine 2016), reconnecting collections to visitors' bodies has sometimes inadvertently opened artefacts to people who have not previously been acknowledged or given a place in the museum. For example, the 3D modelling of a First Nations tool or object never before displayed could prompt specific performative memories in its custodian community, who had not been previously given access, and to whom the object should be repatriated. Moreover, the interactive animation of archives connected to tacit knowledge is becoming increasingly prevalent in museums, but little attention is generally paid to the potentially negative or even traumatic impact of these developments on difficult bodies – on those for whom troubling memories are embedded in objects, or who find themselves misrepresented or altogether absent in the museum.

Critics of ICH have identified a similar gap, which they argue forms part of a neo-colonial, globalised heritage paradigm that promotes only those narratives that support authorised national accounts and political agendas – even narratives appearing under the auspices of human rights or social justice are susceptible to this paradoxical tendency (Collins 2011; Jacobs 2016; Munjeri 2004). Ultimately, although advances in digital museology would appear to be making museums more open and accessible, technological developments have been frequently overlaid on a flawed museological and epistemic foundation (Smith 2006).

Towards a Digital Embodied Historiography

In this chapter, we will focus on one overlooked aspect of this critique, specifically what the sensory possibilities of emergent immersive and engaged digital interfaces offer otherwise marginal embodied experiences. This gap will be examined both in terms of appropriate documentation as well as how the corporeal can be digitally reconfigured in museological contexts for distinct social, cultural and lived experiences. Our analysis will take place through the dual framework of digital cultural heritage and sensory museology (Cameron and Kenderdine 2007; Howes 2014) based on three recent projects – *Travelling Kungkarangkalpa*, *Parragirls Past, Present*, and the *Hong Kong Martial Arts Living Archive* – each developed in collaboration with respective local communities that have contended with marginalisation.

This examination will entail, first of all, an overview of the new forms of narrative immersive technology that support marginalised embodied knowledge. Secondly, we will explore the affordances of new interfaces that have been developed for the transmission of encoded embodied knowledge repertoires. Thirdly, to conclude, we will outline some of the new ground being broken for digital embodied historiography that might enable museums to create greater scope for the inclusion of difficult bodies and communities through these technologies in the future.

In this first section of our chapter, we discuss two major immersive media projects – *Travelling Kungkarangkalpa* and *Parragirls Past, Present* – in order to analyse some of the new immersive technologies being inaugurated to document, transcode and restage the unique temporalities and narratives of marginalised and difficult experiences that centre on the body.

New Narratives for Expansive Temporalities and Sacred Bodies: *Travelling Kungkarangkalpa*

Travelling Kungkarangkalpa is a two-part full-dome experience that was created in 2017 for the National Museum of Australia exhibition *Songlines: Tracking the*

Seven Sisters.[1] As an immersive dome-based or spherical video projection environment, similar to those seen in planetariums this immersive media work presents a First Nations narrative that spans Australia. In one of the oldest stories told on the continent, seven sisters are chased by Wati Nyiru or Yurlu, an evil spirit whose sexual pursuit drives the sisters eastward. Finally, they take flight into the night sky, and the sisters transform into the Pleiades star cluster. The second of the two immersive experiences created for *Travelling Kungkarangkalpa*, titled *Walinynga (Cave Hill) Experience*, provides particular insight into the challenge of bringing marginalised bodies into the museum. In this instance, restaging experiences of a physical site is difficult due to the sacred nature of the Aboriginal knowledge attached to it, knowledge that custodians must transmit in order to preserve while maintaining the secrecy of some aspects. It is not only an old story that is at stake in this situation but also *Tjukurpa*. Often simply translated as 'dreaming', *Tjukurpa* is both law and religion, as well as an entire epistemological and phenomenological system of knowing and being through the senses. Located in the remote Aṇangu, Pitjantjatjara and Yankunytjatjara (APY) lands of South Australia, Walinynga is the most extensive Australian rock art site to represent the Seven Sisters *Tjukurpa*, with the earliest paintings estimated to be thirty-four hundred years old (National Gallery of Australia n.d.).

Communities in this region also retain vivid memories of colonial violence: the forced removal of children under Stolen Generations policies (HREOC

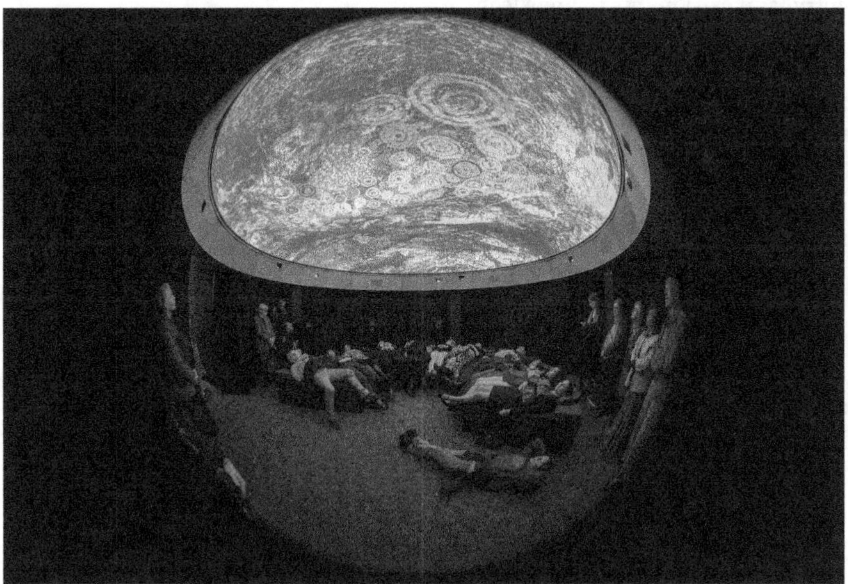

FIGURE 9.1. *Walinynga (Cave Hill) Experience, Travelling Kungkarangkalpa* installed in DomeLab for *Songlines: Tracking the Seven Sisters*, National Museum of Australia, 2017. Image by Sarah Kenderdine.

1997), British nuclear testing at Maralinga between 1956 and 1963 and the subsequent displacement of many of their people from the country (see Broinowski 2003). Yet another threat has loomed over this place: the absence of vessels for future memory due to dispossession and a lack of younger generations living on the land. These dangers led the Aṉangu elders to request the assistance of the National Museum and Australian National University to help them make a record of the cave. Moreover, according to the National Gallery's Songlines website (n.d.: n.p.), the community hoped this work might support 'a bid to gain protection as a national heritage site'.

The most profound aspects of Walinynga are embedded in practices based on ancient knowledge systems that require a wholly new approach. First and foremost, pictorial representations in Australian First Nations practices are not static or linear. As Nicholls (2017: n.p.) points out, 'Aboriginal art was the original and first form of "performance art", comprising visual art, dance, music and song, narrative and poetry'. The cave at Walinynga is thus experienced as part of a 'performing' multitude of temporalities, places, memories and dimensions. The cave provides the locus for a fully embodied, environmental narrative that folds tens of thousands of past stories into a narration that continuously evolves. If any Western conceptual rendition can approximate this phenomenon, it would be Deleuze and Guattari's *A Thousand Plateaus* (1987), which reconceives space and time as expansive, pluridimensional and rhizomatic – providing nonhierarchical entry (and exit) points to knowledge.

The vision of APY elders was crucial to the project. Their extended consultation with National Museum of Australia curators along with heritage consultants and a team of immersive visualisation specialists, led by Sarah Kenderdine, resulted in a full-dome work that heralds a new relationship between Australian First Nations peoples and public institutions. Nonetheless, translating thirty-four thousand years of Walinynga cultural heritage into a seven-minute experience involved finding new architectural and narrative forms for such vast and tacit knowledge.

First of all, Walinynga cave exists within a continuum of dome constructions, which throughout human history have been created as places of ritual, communion and transcendence. As found in Buddhist stupas, Jain temples, Islamic mosques and Christian cathedrals, arched enclosures have provided the ideal form for 'psycho-cosmological constructs' (McConville 2007: 1). Knowing that the Walinynga paintings were made to be seen by the light and liveness of fire supports the case for ancient caves as some of the earliest examples of embodied immersion (Lambert 2012). Designed to create a powerful sense of presence, or of 'being there' (Heeter 1992), Kenderdine's DomeLab is a modern multisensory sanctuary that shares common traits with its cave art predecessor. For instance, DomeLab's omnidirectional immersive environment was conceived to enhance cognitive engagement in a hemispheric gestalt (Kenderdine 2017, 2018; Kenderdine, Shaw and Gremmler 2012). Furthermore, because expanded spatio-temporalities are inherent to DomeLab's immersive architecture, it provides the ideal prosthetic architecture for the *Walinynga (Cave Hill) Experience* and its Anangu cosmologies and worldviews. As in the real Walinynga cave, our supine position under the dome allows us to focus on the vault enveloping our field of view. Being in this prone position, unusual in a public space, makes it easy to succumb to being transported into the remote desert and deep time of the Anangu Seven Sisters *Tjukurpa* (Kenderdine 2017).

Secondly, Walinynga's deeply embodied time required the novel amalgamation of a range of immersive strategies, including photogrammetric photography of the cave for a 3D model, allowing 3D animation for the full-dome visualisation, in combination with astrophotographic time-lapse sequences, 4k fisheye and panoramic imagery and aerial drone footage of the desert environment, in addition to ambisonic (spatialised) sound recordings. These different immersive forms coalesce within DomeLab to open the senses to a range of powerful simulacra that collectively emulate the real-life experience of Walinynga cave. The omnidirectional interactive DomeLab environment further enhances the cognitive exploration of the cave's unique attributes through patterns and layers of perception (Kenderdine, Shaw and Gremmler 2012), creating a sense of presence within the deep time of *Tjukurpa* and a 'knowledge system developed over 2000 generations that governs Aboriginal life' (Eccles 2018: n.p.).

In the *Walinynga (Cave Hill) Experience* Anangu elders allow us to lay down in the reconstructed cave just as their ancestors have done for many thousands of years, marking an extraordinary new form of museology in which the knowledge of the Seven Sisters *Tjukurpa* is passed on through the bodies of museum visitors. Allowing future generations to reimagine access to Walinynga through a virtual platform not only provides a means of transmitting past knowledge into the present but also offers scope for new ways to engage future generations to teach this knowledge and tell these stories through the body. The work, nonetheless, represents some of the contradictions facing the digitisation of First Nations' cultural heritage: to open up the cave is to open up bodies to the world, which in Australian Aboriginal lore and custom often contains sacred knowledge that needs to be kept secret. What this project means for the preservation of Walinynga *Tjukurpa* remains to be seen.

Parragirls Past, Present: Narrative Embodied Recollection through Immersive Technologies

The immersive film *Parragirls Past, Present: Unlocking Memories of Institutional 'Care'* (2017) pioneers a new approach to the mediated communication of trauma testimony as it represents childhood memories of past abuse suffered in a government welfare institution (further described in chapter 6 of this volume). In early 2016, five Parragirls – Bonney Djuric, Gypsie Hayes, Jenny McNally, Tony Nicholas and Lynne Paskovski – came together at Parramatta Girls Home to co-create this film with long-term collaborator Lily Hibberd and media artists Volker Kuchelmeister and Alex Davies.

Comparable to *Walinynga (Cave Hill) Experience*, the creation of *Parragirls Past, Present* was the result of long and committed cooperation with this marginalised community. Specifically, this involved more than seven years of groundwork and collaboration with Parragirls – a highly traumatised and dispersed group of people, whose memories have been buried under shame and public denial (as chronicled in Hibberd and Djuric 2019). All five collaborating Parragirls were involved in the major Australian judicial inquiry into child sexual abuse at the Parramatta Girls Home (Australian Government 2014). And the film was made in response to this process, particularly the adversity of renewed disclosure of childhood sexual abuse, as former residents were drawn into a legal and public exposition that regarded them as mere victims. Parragirl Lynne Paskovski refers to the effect of this process when she remarks in the first moments of the film: 'We walked out the gate fifty years ago and never thought anything more of it. You try to put it behind you, and then all of a sudden you have to start to remember things and that Pandora's Box is opened.' Few alternatives existed for Parragirls to author their own account of these experiences, apart from judicial transcripts or sensationalising news media. *Parragirls Past, Present* was created as a counterpoint designed to communicate physical, emotional and narrative experiences from their own perspective.

Moreover, in contrast to the state, media, heritage experts and historians, past occupants of Parramatta Girls Home had been powerless to create visual or textual records of their childhood. *Parragirls Past, Present* provided the means to convey the aftermath of abuse in direct contact with the site and to record an account of the effect of this on their lives, minds and bodies. What began to emerge over many months was a novel process of documentation through tacit, sensory and corporeal acts, or embodied historiography, which has been argued as a legitimate form of knowledge production (see Spatz 2015).

Beginning in 2012, when Parragirls first began working together on site as part of the memory project (see chapter 6 in this volume), they faced a disconnection or discord of the past and present that was distinctly located in their bodies – where the link to past abuse and trauma remained embedded. Retracing memory through the body involved firstly walking and describing memories of the girls home, but this rapidly evolved into re-enacting or re-situating themselves in significant spaces. Our collective concern was not the therapeutic aspects of these embodied performative acts, even though it seemed to be crucial for each person to undertake. There was a more fundamental impetus: to demonstrate that what they remembered was true because no one had ever believed it before. This trait defines the key difference between re-enactment for popular entertainment (i.e. war games) and that which sustains or restores embodied memory.

For Parragirls, the crux of the problem has been that the site cannot be divorced from their (abused) bodies. In legal and real terms, the possession and control of childhood bodies was total under the auspices of the state welfare department, lawyers and courts, the police, doctors (forced virginity testing), welfare officers, wardens (surveillance, deprivation, and physical, emotional and sexual abuse), priests (forced removal of children) and psychiatrists (psychotropic medication). As such, the most important issue for Parragirls has always been control: the power of others to determine how and when your body is seen, how it moves and what it looks like.

When the process of developing the script and concepts for *Parragirls Past, Present* began, the co-creators were already aware of the power of such corporeal testimony. A number of first-person-perspective artworks had been created using hand-held video (walking the site), as well as live art projects, such as the 2016 re-enactment performance *It's Time for Transparency* by Jenny McNally (see Hibberd and Djuric 2019). But it was the introduction of new tools and techniques of immersive digital documentation – using computational strategies – that enabled us to reorient the lens of embodied historiography away from the demonstrative performance of memory to the understanding that transmission might occur through being present in the place of witnessing with survivors. This insight allowed Parragirls to access a range of narratives and memories that would not otherwise have been available, some of which are described below.

Whereas in previous performative documentation Parragirls had used microphones and hand-held video cameras, in the first few months of filming for *Parragirls Past, Present*, the participants trialled a number of new ways to source material. One of these was a device called SenseCam, a small fisheye lens camera harnessed to the wearer that takes pictures based on sensory triggers (i.e. light, movement). The photos can be geolocated and eventually positioned in a reconstructed 3D spatial setting, mapped according to their original geographic coordinates. These images are known to function very well as memory cues, as they mirror cognitive aspects of embodied human memory. The idea was to include the resulting photographs as overlays in the 3D environment, representing Parragirls' subjective first-person and embodied memories. Bonney Djuric and Jenny McNally completed a number of walks on this basis; however, the quality of the images was poor, and they would have distracted from the powerful presence of the site itself that was taking shape as a 3D model (see chapter 6), which was intermittently shown to Parragirls as it progressed.

In one particularly fascinating viewing, Bonney Djuric and Jenny McNally observed that the virtual reality headset seemed to emulate their own brains, being akin to their sense of being swallowed up in an intensely illusory and sealed-off simulation of the real world – a comment that provided a new direction for the design of the work. The coevolution of immersive technology and perception has been extensively theorised, but this last lucid observation harkens to Jonathan Crary's notion of 'physiological optics' (1990: 16). Parragirls' insights revealed that there was something innate in virtual reality that could be exploited to learn about the expression of trauma through the mind and body, which Schroeter (2014: 131) describes as becoming 'acutely aware of the spatiality' of your own body through immersion in 3D images, in contrast to the being in the original physical space.

The impact of confronting memories of abuse in revisiting real spaces, for instance, had distinct impacts, including moments of confusion, blankness and dissociation. These nonlinear effects led to many debates about how bodies could act as a conduit for past memories in the present. Some of the most difficult scenes to realise were those that took place in the solitary cells, of which there were originally three at Parramatta Girls Home. Gypsie Hayes recounts being in the cell called 'Segregation': 'Yeah, Segregation. I spent nearly a month up there actually because that screw had given me such a flogging that he split my lip open. Both my eyes were blackened. I had bruises on me face. I had bruises over me body. Half me hair was pulled out.' For others it was impossible to re-enter these solitary confinement spaces, and because of this we had to consider whether they should be included in the film at all.

But then, during another session, Volker Kuchelmeister showed Jenny an extract of footage of the basement cell – a short clip that was also very dark. While

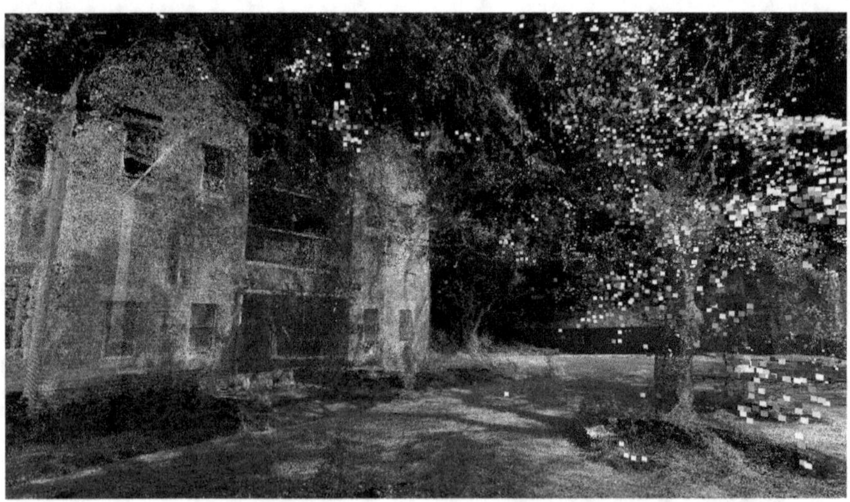

FIGURE 9.2. *Parragirls Past, Present: Unlocking Memories of Institutional 'Care'*, 2017. Still from immersive 3D 360-degree film, 23 minutes. Created by Volker Kuchelmeister, Alex Davies and Lily Hibberd, with (Parragirls) Bonney Djuric, Gypsie Hayes, Jenny McNally, Tony Nicholas and Lynne Paskovski. Image courtesy of the artists.

the screening affected her immensely, Jenny explained how it might be possible to make the representation of the space tolerable for victims by relying on testimony to convey what happened there to others instead of photographically depicting it. This led to a brief basement scene being included in the film that was quickly occluded so that we are left with only Gypsie's voiceover: 'It was just a cold place, a dark place . . .'

Further, as Parragirls specifically shaped the narrative of the work, they validated memories of abuse by using the immersive film to displace embodied experiences of Parramatta Girls Home, including punishments, isolation and the awareness of being under surveillance (see Hibberd 2014). Many hours of discussion with cowriters and narrators Bonney Djuric and Jenny McNally crucially provided discernment of the limits of recreating or simulating vicarious embodied experiences of childhood sexual and physical abuse in virtual reality and informed the decision to position spectators alongside Parragirls in the 3D realm.

Sound was also effectively employed to convey our co-presence with Parragirls. Recordings were made on site and in a nearby studio using binaural, spatialised audio to evocatively situate their voices right beside us. The power of sound to trigger sensory memory was another significant focus during the creation of the film. As Parragirls made running lists of sounds to include, their consistently active and physiological nature was obvious. In order to replicate the present moment, the resonant dynamic acoustics were adopted to conjure the effect of corporeal presence, whether human or otherwise. Adding field recordings taken at Parramatta, such as murmuring voices, shuffling feet, rustling leaves, trees in wind and bats passing by, we found that these roused tactile acoustic traces of memory (see Hall 2010: 84–85).

Finally, as mentioned above, the effect that Parragirls described, of being divorced from their bodies (a post-traumatic effect known as dissociation), became a central feature in the film. This sensation is inherent to our corporeal suspension in the points of light scattered through the infinite darkness of the 3D field, in which we seemingly become weightless or ethereal, passing through walls and soaring above the site at the very end. Ultimately, *Parragirls Past, Present* is an experiment in the reconstruction of embodied trauma in immersive media and how virtual reality can be used to navigate the ethically and emotionally fraught territory of the traumatic experience of others.

New Digital Interfaces and Affordances
for Marginalised Embodied Knowledge

When immersive interfaces are centred on marginalised or stigmatised bodies, a whole new relationship to optical conventions and representational dynamics is required. Technologies of corporeality have radically altered how we see ourselves, and the primary interface for these encounters are screens. It was only twenty years ago that these displays were thought of as static entities, fixed portals through which an external reality or world arrived, either on our television or on movie screens. Since the advent of mobile phones followed by tablets, the sense of the screen as a moving window (Verhoeff 2012) has proliferated in public imagination, whereby today we sense that we can travel with our screens – as Friedberg (2006: 3) envisaged, 'mobile virtuality'.

This mobility has now been combined with immersive extrapolations of stereoscopic virtual reality and other optical schema, which have shifted how we perceive seeing from the fixed frame of the cinema as part of a radical redefinition the 'scopic regimes' of modernity (Jay 1988). And yet the attributes of truly immersive screens mobilise participants in affective ways through strategies of interaction, demanding kinaesthetic and bodily intervention, all of which requires new critical evaluation of the limits of spectatorship, agency and the perceived temporality of real time in museums (Harris 2012). The three examples we have chosen here from a martial arts heritage project convey some of the distinct possibilities of novel embodied relationships with digital interfaces as affordances for difficult heritage.

Novel Interfaces and Avatars for Marginalised Embodied Acts: Hong Kong Martial Arts Living Archive

The Hong Kong Martial Arts Living Archive (HKMALA), instigated in 2012, is an ongoing research collaboration between the International Guoshu Association, City University of Hong Kong, and the Laboratory for Experimental Museology (eM +) at EPFL. This archival project was established to address the decline of Southern Chinese kung fu in mainland China, where a significant portion of traditional martial arts has already vanished due to its oppression since the Chinese Cultural Revolution in 1969 (Chao et al. 2018). Despite the contemporary Chinese Communist Party's burgeoning interest in authorising global narratives of intangible cultural heritage (i.e. UNESCO), the current reconceptualisation of heritage, as Evans and Rowlands argue (2015), predominantly features shifting power relations rather than a real desire to reanimate martial arts communities.

Kung fu practitioners' tacit knowledge is a particularly difficult form of heritage in two regards. First, it must be performed in order to exist. Learning kung fu involves a person-to-person exchange and imitation of movements between an expert and a novice (Chan et al. 2011; Komura et al. 2006). While Hong Kong remains an active centre for elite practitioners, home to some of the most prominent martial artists in the world, the aging of these masters alongside rapid urban development, population growth and cultural transformation endanger

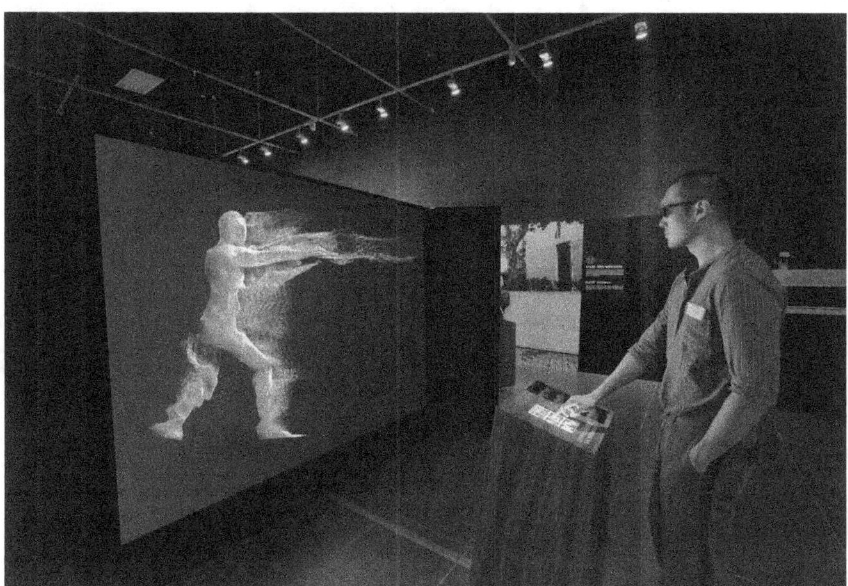

FIGURE 9.3. One side of the six-sided Re-Actor system, showing a motion-captured kung fu performer in 3D. Created by Sarah Kenderdine and Jeffrey Shaw, 2016. Image by Tang Ming Tung. Courtesy of Sarah Kenderdine.

the transmission of these practices to future generations, due to the lack of any method of transmission other than in person. Second, this tacit knowledge is all the more difficult because of the contested politics surrounding contemporary Chinese heritage, which allows for the paradox of its continued oppression in China in tandem with a Western perspective that suspects the revival of Chinese intangible cultural heritage as being a tool of Communist Party propaganda.

In recent years, digital interfaces, including virtual reality high-fidelity 2D motion data and ultra-high-speed and green-screen video, have been harnessed to augment or initiate the computational transmission of embodied traditions in the form of encoded acts. The benefits of these innovations for the transmission of corporeal customs have been recognised by scholars such as Salazar Sutil (2015: 122), who contends that mobile and smart technologies have brought about a 'deep and democratic' change in the 'recording and representation of movement'. The question of how to translate embodied knowledge and encode motion with meaning so it might migrate from expert to novice without a master is central to the HKMALA project (Kenderdine and Shaw 2017). The martial arts reconstruction it has undertaken uniquely combines historical materials with creative visualisations derived from advanced documentation processes for physical movement, including motion capture, motion-over-time analytics, 3D reconstruction, panoramic video and animation. The archive currently contains nineteen styles by thirty-three elite practitioners and is composed of 130 motion-capture datasets of *taolu*, which are prearranged movement sequences used for practising and performing traditional martial arts. Initially created as mnemonic aids for students, *taolu* are considered the primary text for Chinese martial arts, whereby learning consists of memorising these through imitation and repetition. For the first time in history, motion capture has supported the precise recording of these *taolu* in three dimensions, forming the largest motion-data archive of its kind in the world.[2]

Multimodal participation is a core knowledge transmission method harnessed in the HKMALA *Pose Matching* installation, presented in the ArtLab exhibition *Kung Fu Motion* in 2018. It deploys gaming technologies to support a novel pairing of the participant-actor with the screen. Standing in front of a human-scaled projection screen, the actor is tracked using sensors that capture movement and physical position in order to match these with a video sequence of poses presented on the screen, originally performed by a kung fu master. As the participant configures their body to replicate these poses, a corporeal conjunction is created in which the somatic memory of the kung fu master is imprinted on the viewer's body.

Importantly for the museological orientation towards the body, this pose-matching installation elicits the production of tacit artefacts in a generative process that has significant promise for pedagogical as well as archival methodologies. Trninic and Abrahamson (2012: 283), for example, describe the crucial capacity of 'novel motion-sensitive cyber-technologies to both craft and leverage embodied artefacts as a means of fostering learning'. Lindgren and Johnson-Glenberg (2013) have also undertaken research into embodied learning, supporting the case for virtual and mixed reality technologies as a new way of transmitting embodied knowledge to future generations. Furthermore, interaction with the screen acts as a simulacrum for the teacher's body, providing a new vehicle for museums to embark on the transmission of such heritage at risk.

Another original use of computational approaches for embodied transaction is the *Digital Reconstruction of Lam Sai Wing* (2018). So far only exhibited as a video, the larger work is an animated repertoire of moves from the kung fu manual of Lam Sai Wing, a master practitioner of South Chinese traditions in Hong Kong. This virtual reconstruction builds on techniques used in Hollywood movie and game industries for the manufacture of 3D human avatars. HKMALA first applied the method to recreate the performance of Lam Sai Wing's iron wire boxing. In this latest instance, however, another sequence was recorded based on the motion capture of contemporary re-enactments performed by his descendant, Oscar Lam. In yet another uncanny convergence, old photographic portraits of Lam Sai Wing are mapped onto the animated 3D model. The outcome concurrently reanimates the appearance and the embodied acts of Lam Sai Wing through Oscar Lam's body, the fourth-generation carrier of the Lam family hung kuen style.

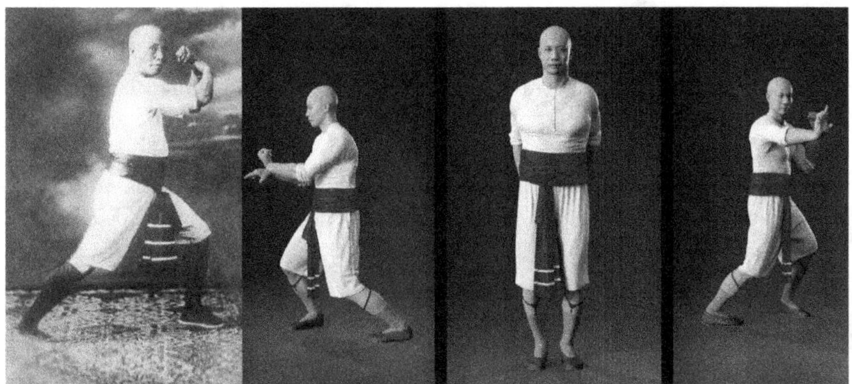

FIGURE 9.4. Digital reconstruction of Lam Sai Wing, 2018. Composite digital image created by Sarah Kenderdine for HKMALA. Image courtesy of Sarah Kenderdine.

In providing both the repertoire and the tools of transmission, *Hong Kong Martial Arts Living Archive* is a prosthesis for the intergenerational continuity of kung fu embodied knowledge in the absence of masters (Kenderdine and Shaw 2016). Future digital strategies arising from this project will help to codify even more complex tacit aspects of its archive for ephemeral registers that only a body can convey (see Spatz 2015).

Conclusion: A Digital Embodied Historiography for Difficult Bodies in Museums

As the public is offered more active roles in the interpretation of heritage in the museum (Giaccardi and Palen 2008), we are reminded that reconstructing heritage is not only about mimesis or authentic high-fidelity replication. The greatest challenge is to open up museums to include difficult bodies.

Although the knowledge embedded in the painted surface of the Walinynga cave does not require the ritual re-enactment of sets of physical movement, such as in kung fu, there is a specific embodied relationship with the place itself. Crawling under the low-hanging rock, away from the vast and searing blue skies of the desert, the body gradually adjusts to this naturally relaxed prone position, which is familiar to sleeping, or camping in the desert, or gazing up at the sky – embodied memories that amplify receptivity. In the *Walinynga (Cave Hill) Experience*, the mutual threat to material and living history resulted in a radical shift in heritage thinking for the Anangu community. The work signals the possibility of virtual place-making with bodies as the locus of a vital future in which museums could host cross-cultural encounters (Witcomb 2015).

Meanwhile, as subjects of systemic national forgetting, Parragirls have faced enormous challenges in terms of the preservation of their heritage. This is because difficult heritage in Australia, as in many other postcolonial societies, is a subject that is either carefully contained or avoided through erasure and denial. The limitations, moreover, of using conventional heritage approaches for a museology of Parramatta Girls Home overlooks the fact that abuse is memorialised in survivors' bodies. *Parragirls Past, Present* demonstrates that it is, however, the people who experienced injustice that are able to construct a bridge to the past through the innovative use of immersive media that makes tacit experiences of trauma both visceral and meaningful to others.

For the Aṇangu in the *Walinynga (Cave Hill) Experience* and for Parragirls in their film, the question of how to structure the reincorporation of their embodied heritage for a museological context was not easy. It entailed reimagining and reinventing the aesthetics and politics implicated in allowing others to immerse their bodies in a sensitive and long-guarded cultural heritage experience. These two works, however, each resulted in a radical reorientation of the spectator's interaction with the digital interface and with the spectacle of simulated tacit experiences.

Similarly, the sophisticated repertoire of the *Hong Kong Martial Arts Living Archive* has required not only suitable memory banks but also new computational approaches and interfaces for their embodied transmission. Supporting the future living history of the archive has resulted in new interactive platforms, which in turn offer the museological domain promising new paradigms for future embodied memory pedagogy and historiography. The archive was also founded with a larger vision in mind: to make feasible museological representations that overcome both the Chinese and the global perception of traditional performed cultural practices as historical (and thus redundant) rather than as alive in the present (Shaw, Kenderdine and Chao 2017).

Since theorist Sharon Macdonald first harkened a 'turn to difficult heritage' (2008; 2016: 14), finding new ways to represent experiences held in the body has become even more crucial for museums. Certain aspects of bodies, moreover, remain marginalised precisely because tacit experiences are rooted in senses and emotions that lack suitable forms and do not fit existing museological paradigms. This challenge is not insurmountable, however. With the engagement of communities of marginalised memory in generating new approaches to digital practice and technological forms of embodied historiography, a whole new era of museology that embraces difficult heritage is on the horizon.

Acknowledgements

Parragirls Past, Present is an outcome of an Australian Research Council Discovery Early Career Researcher Award, number DE160100142.

Lily Hibberd is a multidisciplinary artist, researcher and writer whose practice spans performance, moving image, installation, and archival research. Her work frequently interrogates the intersection of historical memory, science, and technology and has been presented in more than fifty international exhibitions and festivals, including the 22nd Biennale of Sydney (NIRIN), the Perth International Arts Festival, and the Edinburgh International Science Festival. Hibberd has a PhD from Monash University, and a frequent author and co-author of academic and artistic publications. She is founding editor of un Magazine, co-founder of Parragirls Memory Project, and currently a researcher at Université Paris Cité, lecturer at Parsons Paris, and Adjunct Lecturer at UNSW Sydney.

Sarah Kenderdine is Professor of Digital Museology at the École polytechnique fédérale de Lausanne (EPFL), Switzerland. She leads the Laboratory for Experimental Museology (eM+), exploring the convergence of immersive visualization, digital aesthetics, and cultural big data. Sarah directed EPFL Pavilions from 2017 to 2024, and now leads international touring exhibitions as curator-at-large. She is Corresponding Fellow of the British Academy, Visiting Professor at Hong Kong Baptist University, and Adjunct Professor at UNSW Sydney. Sarah has produced more than one hundred exhibitions for museums worldwide and numerous scholarly publications.

Notes

1. *Travelling Kungkarangkalpa*, 2017, was produced and directed by Sarah Kenderdine, codirected by Peter Morse, and created with Chris Henderson, Cédric Maridet, Paul Bourke and Brad May. The Cave Hill Project is a joint initiative of APY, the Cave Hill Custodians, National Museum of Australia, and the Australian National University.
2. The project has thus far resulted in eight international exhibitions, including *Kung Fu Motion* at EPFL's ArtLab (2018) and Melbourne Immigration Museum (2017), and *300 Years of Hakka Kung Fu* (2016) at the Heritage Museum and CityU Galleries in Hong Kong, China (see Shaw, Kenderdine and Chao 2017; Kenderdine and Shaw 2017, 2018).

References

Alivizatou, Marilena. 2006. 'Museums and Intangible Heritage: The Dynamics of an "Unconventional Relationship"', *Papers from the Institute of Archaeology* 17: 47–57.

Australian Government. 2014. *Report of Case Study No 7. Child Sexual Abuse at the Parramatta Training School for Girls and the Institution for Girls in Hay*. Royal Commission into Institutional Responses to Child Sexual Abuse. Retrieved 18 December 2019 from www.childabu seroyalcommission.gov.au/case-studies/case-study-07-parramatta-training-school-girls.

Aykan, Bahar. 2014. 'Whose Tradition, Whose Identity? The Politics of Constructing "Nevruz" as Intangible Heritage in Turkey'. *European Journal of Turkish Studies* 19. Retrieved 18 August 2020 from https://journals.openedition.org/ejts/5000.

Bal, Mieke. 2001. 'Memory Acts: Performing Subjectivity', *boijmans bulletin* 1(002): 8–18.

Bal, Mieke, Jonathan Crewe and Leo Spitzer (eds). 1998. *Acts of Memory: Cultural Recall in the Present*. Hanover, NH: University Press of New England.

Bennett, Tony. 2004. *Pasts beyond Memories: Evolution, Museums, Colonialism*. New York: Routledge.

——— . 2006. 'Civic Seeing: Museums and the Organisation of Vision', in Sharon Macdonald (ed.), *Companion to Museum Studies*. Oxford: Blackwell, pp. 263–81.

——— . 2018. *Museums, Power, Knowledge: Selected Essays*. New York: Routledge.

Branch, Boyd, and Erika Hughes. 2014. 'Embodied Historiography: Rupture as the Performance of History'. *Performance Research* 19(6): 108–15.

Broinowski, Richard. 2003. *Fact or Fission: The Truth about Australia's Nuclear Ambitions*. Melbourne: Scribe Publications.

Butler, Judith. 1999. *Gender Trouble: Feminism and the Subversion of Identity*. London: Routledge.

Cameron, Fiona, and Sarah Kenderdine (eds). 2007. *Theorizing Digital Cultural Heritage: A Critical Discourse*. Cambridge, MA: MIT Press.

Chan, Jacky C. P., Howard Leung, Jeff Tang and Taku Komura. 2011. 'A Virtual Reality Dance Training System Using Motion Capture Technology', *IEEE Transactions on Learning Technologies* 4(2): 187–95.

Chao, Hing, Matt Delbridge, Sarah Kenderdine, Lydia Nicholson and Jeffrey Shaw. 2018. 'Kapturing Kung Fu: Future Proofing the Hong Kong Martial Arts Living Archive', in Sarah Whatley, Rosamaria Cisneros and Amalia Sabiescu (eds), *Digital Echoes*. Basingstoke: Palgrave Macmillan, pp. 249–64.

Collins, John F. 2011. 'Culture, Content, and the Enclosure of Human Being: UNESCO'S "Intangible" Heritage in the New Millennium', *Radical History Review* 109: 121–35.

Crary, Jonathan. 1990. *Techniques of the Observer: On Vision and Modernity in the Nineteenth Century*. Cambridge, MA: MIT Press.

Deleuze, Gilles, and Felix Guattari 1987. *A Thousand Plateaus*, trans. Brian Massumi. Minneapolis: University of Minnesota Press.

Djuric, Bonney, Lily Hibberd and Linda Steele. 2018. 'Transforming the Parramatta Female Factory Institutional Precinct into a Site of Conscience', The Conversation, 5 January 2018. Retrieved 20 December 2019 from https://theconversation.com/transforming-the-parra matta-female-factory-institutional-precinctinto-a-site-of-conscience-88875.

Eccles, Jeremy. 2018. 'Songlines: Tracking the Seven Sisters', *Aboriginal Art Directory*, 6 February. Retrieved 24 December 2019 from https://news.aboriginalartdirectory.com/2018/02/songlines-tracking-the-seven-sisters.php.

Evans, Harriet, and Michael Rowlands. 2015. 'Reconceptualizing Heritage in China: Museums, Development and the Shifting Dynamics of Power', in Paul Basu and Wayne Modest (eds), *Museums, Heritage and International Development*. London: Routledge, pp. 272–95.

Falk, John, and Lynne Dierking. 2008. 'Enhancing Visitor Interaction and Learning with Mobile Technologies', in Loïc Tallon and Kevin Walker (eds), *Digital Technologies and the Museum Experience: Handheld Guides and Other Media*. Lanham, MD: AltaMira Press, pp. 19–33

Friedberg, Anne. 2006. *The Virtual Window: From Alberti to Microsoft*. Cambridge, MA: MIT Press.

Giaccardi, Elisa, and Leysia Palen. 2008. 'The Social Production of Heritage through Cross-Media Interaction: Making Place for Place-Making', *International Journal of Heritage Studies* 14(3): 281–97.

Giblin, John. 2015. 'Critical Approaches to Post-colonial (Post-conflict) Heritage', in Emma Waterton and Steve Watson (eds), *The Palgrave Handbook of Contemporary Heritage Research*. London: Palgrave Macmillan, pp. 312–28.

Gunn, Wendy, Ton Otto and Rachel Charlotte Smith. 2013. *Design Anthropology: Theory and Practice*. London: Bloomsbury.

Hall. Mirko. 2010. 'Dialectical Sonority: Walter Benjamin's Acoustics of Profane Illumination', *Telos* 152: 83–102.

Harris, Jennifer. 2012. 'Turning to the Visitor's body: Affective Exhibition and the Limits of Representation'. *ICOFOM Study Series* 41: 121–33.

Heeter, Carrie. 1992 'Being There: The Subjective Experience of Presence', *Presence* 2: 262–71.

Hibberd, Lily. 2014. 'Making Future Memory', in Paul Ashton and Jacqueline Z. Wilson (eds), *Silent System: Forgotten Australians and the Institutionalisation of Women and Children*. Kew: Australian Scholarly Publishing, pp. 103–15.

Hibberd, Lily, with Bonney Djuric. 2019. *Parragirls Art and Memory: Remaking Parramatta Girls Home*. Sydney: NewSouth Press.

Hooper-Greenhill, Eilean. 1994. 'Learning from Learning Theory in Museums', in Eilean Hooper-Greenhill (ed.), *The Educational Role of the Museum*, 2nd edn. New York: Routledge, pp. 137–46.

Howes, David. 2014. 'Introduction to Sensory Museology', *Senses and Society* 9(3): 259–67.

HREOC (Human Rights and Equal Opportunity Commission). 1997. *Final Report: 'Bringing Them Home: National Inquiry into the Separation of Aboriginal and Torres Strait Islander Children from Their Families'*, April 1997. Retrieved 20 January 2020 from humanrights .gov.au/sites/default/files/content/pdf/social_justice/bringing_them_home_report.pdf.

Jacobs, Marc. 2016. 'The Spirit of the Convention: Interlocking Principles and Ethics for Safeguarding Intangible Cultural Heritage', *International Journal of Intangible Heritage* 11: 71–87.

Jay, Martin. 1988. 'Scopic Regimes of Modernity', in Hal Foster (ed.), *Vision and Visuality*. Seattle: Bay Press, pp. 3–23.

Johnson, Katherine. 2015. 'Rethinking (Re)doing: Historical Re-enactment and/as Historiography', *Rethinking History* 19(2): 193–206.

Kenderdine, Sarah. 2016. 'Embodiment, Entanglement and Immersion in Digital Cultural Heritage', in Susan Schreibman, Ray Siemens and John Unsworth (eds), *A New Companion to Digital Humanities*. Oxford: Blackwell, pp. 22–41.

———. 2017. 'Travelling Kungkarangkalpa', in Margo Neale (ed.), *Songlines: Tracking the Seven Sisters*. National Museum of Australia Press, pp. 82–85.

———. 2018. 'Hemispheres: Transdisciplinary Architectures and Museum-University Collaboration', in Hannah Lewi, Wally Smith, Dirk vom Lehn and Steven Cooke (eds), *International Handbook of New Digital Practices in Galleries, Libraries, Archives, Museums and Heritage Sites*, Abingdon: Routledge, pp. 305–18.

Kenderdine, Sarah, and Jeffrey Shaw. 2016. 'A Digital Legacy for Living Culture', in Hing Chao, Sarah Kenderdine and Jeffrey Shaw (eds), *300 Years of Hakka Kung Fu: Digital Vision of Its Legacy and Future*. Hong Kong: International Guoshu Association, pp. 165–89.

———. 2017. 'Archives in Motion: Motion as Meaning', in Oliver Grau (ed.), *Museum and Archive on the Move: Changing Cultural Institutions in the Digital Era*. Berlin: de Gruyter, pp. 211–33.

———. 2018. 'The Museological Re-enactment of Lingnan Hung Kuen', in Hing Chao (ed.), *Lingnan Hung Kuen across the Century: Kung Fu Narratives in Cinema and Community*. Hong Kong: City University of Hong Kong Press, pp. 137–59.

Kenderdine, Sarah, Jeffrey Shaw and Tobias Gremmler. 2012. 'Cultural Data Sculpting: Omnidirectional Visualization for Cultural Datasets', in Francis T. Marchese and Ebad Banissi (eds), *Knowledge Visualization Currents: From Text to Art to Culture*. London: Springer, pp. 199–221.

Kirsch, David. 2013. 'Embodied Cognition and the Magical Future of Interaction Design'. *ACM Transactions on Computer-Human Interaction* 20(1): 1–30.

Kirshenblatt-Gimblett, Barbara. 2004. 'Intangible Heritage as Metacultural Production'. *Museum International*, 56(1/2): 52–65.

Komura, Taku, Beta Lam, Rynson Lau and Howard Leung. 2006. 'e-Learning Martial Arts', in W. Liu, Q. Li, and R. Lau (eds), *Lecture Notes in Computer Science* 4181. Heidelberg: Springer: 239–48.

Lambert, Nick. 2012. 'Domes and Creativity: A Historical Exploration', *Digital Creativity* 23(1): 5–29.

Lehrer, Erica, Cynthia Milton and Monica Patterson. 2011. *Curating Difficult Heritage: Violent Pasts in Public Places*. London: Palgrave Macmillan.

Lennon, John, and Malcolm Foley. 2000. *Dark Tourism. The Attraction of Death and Disaster*. London: Thomson.

Lindgren, Robb, and Mina Johnson-Glenberg. 2013. 'Emboldened by Embodiment: Six Precepts for Research on Embodied Learning and Mixed Reality', *Educational Researcher* 42(8): 445–52.

Logan, William, and Kier Reeves. 2009. 'Introduction', in William Logan and Kier Reeves (eds), *Places of Pain and Shame: Dealing with 'Difficult Heritage'*. New York: Routledge, pp. 1–14.

Luke, Timothy. 2003. *Museums Politics: Power Plays at the Exhibition*. Minneapolis: University of Minnesota Press.

Macdonald, Sharon. 2009. *Difficult Heritage: Negotiating the Nazi Past in Nuremberg and Beyond*. London: Routledge.

———. 2016. 'Is "Difficult Heritage" Still "Difficult"?', *Museum International* 67(1–4): 6–22.

McConville, David. 2007. 'Cosmological Cinema: Pedagogy, Propaganda, and Perturbation in Early Dome Theaters', *Technoetic Arts: A Journal of Speculative Research* 5(2): 69–85.

Munjeri, Dawson. 2004. 'Tangible and Immaterial Heritage: From Difference to Convergence', *Museum International* 56(1/2): 12–20.

National Gallery of Australia. n.d. Songlines website. Retrieved 19 December 2020 from https://songlines.nma.gov.au/.

Nicholls, Christine. J. 2017. 'Songlines: Tracking the Seven Sisters Is a Must-Visit Exhibition for All Australians', *The Conversation*, online 20 December. Retrieved 13 January 2020 from https://theconversation.com/songlines-tracking-the-seven-sisters-is-a-must-visit-exhibition-for-all-australians-89293.

Pitt, Alice, and Deborah Britzman. 2003. 'Speculations on Qualities of Difficult Knowledge in Teaching and Learning: An Experiment in Psychoanalytic Research', *International Journal of Qualitative Studies in Education* 16(6): 755–76.

Salazar Sutil, Nicolás. 2015. *Motion and Representation: The Language of Human Movement*. Cambridge, MA: MIT Press.

Sandell, Richard (ed.). 2002. *Museums, Society, Inequality*. New York: Routledge.

———. 2016. *Museums, Moralities and Human Rights*. New York: Routledge.

Schorch, Philipp. 2009. 'The Reflexive Museum: Opening the Door to Behind the Scenes', *Journal of Museums Aotearoa* 33(1/2): 28–31.

Schroeter, Jens. 2014. *3D: History, Theory, and Aesthetics of the Transplane Image*. New York: Bloomsbury Academic.

Shaw, Jeffrey, Sarah Kenderdine and Hing Chao. 2017. 'Establishing a Permanent Kung Fu Museum in Hong Kong', in Dickson Chiu, Allan Cho and Patrick Lo (eds), *Chandos Information Professional Series, Inside the World's Major East Asian Collections*. Cambridge, MA: Chandos Publishing, pp. 343–54.

Shelton, Anthony. 2013. 'Critical Museology: A Manifesto', *Museums Worlds Advances in Research* 1(1): 7–23.

Smith, Laurajane. 2006. *Uses of Heritage*. Oxford: Routledge.

——— . 2011. *All Heritage Is Immaterial: Critical Heritage Studies and Museums*. Amsterdam: Reinwardt Academy.

Spatz, Ben. 2015. *What a Body Can Do: Technique as Knowledge, Practice as Research*. New York: Routledge.

Taylor, Diana. 2003. *The Archive and the Repertoire: Performing Cultural Memory in the Americas*. Durham, NC: Duke University Press.

——— . 2016. 'Saving the 'Live? Re-performance and Intangible Cultural Heritage', *Études Anglaises* 69(2): 149–61.

Trezise, Brioni. 2014. *Performing Feeling in Cultures of Memory*. London: Palgrave Macmillan.

Trninic, Dragan and Dor Abrahamson. 2012. 'Embodied Artifacts in Action and Conceptual Performances', *International Conference of the Learning Sciences* 1: 283–290.

Tunbridge, John, and Gregory Ashworth. 1996. *Dissonant Heritage. The Management of the Past as a Resource in Conflict*. Chichester: John Wiley and Sons.

UNESCO. 2003. *Convention for the Safeguarding of the Intangible Heritage*. 2016 edition. Retrieved 13 December 2019 from https://ich.unesco.org/en/convention.

Vergo, Peter. 1989. *The New Museology*. London: Reaktion Books.

Verhoeff, Nanna. 2012. *Mobile Screens: The Visual Regime of Navigation*. Amsterdam: Amsterdam University Press.

Witcomb, Andrea. 2015. 'Toward a Pedagogy of Feeling: Understanding How Museums Create a Space for Cross-Cultural Encounters', in Kylie Message and Andrea Witcomb (eds), *The International Handbook of Museum Studies*, pp. 1:321–23.

Zavala, Jimmy, Alda Migoni, Michelle Caswell, Noah Geracia and Marika Cifor. 2017. 'A Process Where We're All at the Table: Community Archives Challenging Dominant Modes of Archival Practice'. *Archives and Manuscripts* 45(3): 202–15.

A Museum of Deepfakes?

Potentials and Pitfalls for Deep Learning Technologies

Jenny Kidd and Arran J. Rees

Setting the Scene: Situating the Dalí Deepfake

In May 2019 the Dalí Museum in St Petersburg, Florida, launched *Dalí Lives*, a video installation featuring an interactive deepfake recreation of the artist, which had been created with Goodby Silverstein and Partners. *Dalí Lives* was built using more than 6,000 frames of video from archival footage in the museum's collection, and it features 125 videos (45 minutes of footage) that can play in 190,512 possible combinations depending on user responses (Sabina Aouf, 2019). In the videos, captured in figure 10.1, Salvador Dalí welcomes visitors to the museum using a combination of actual quotes and newly scripted text, and ends interactions by taking a selfie with the visitor, which he first shows them, then offers to text to their phone, presumably in the hope that they will spread the word via their social networks. The creators have made efforts to contextualise this Dalí seamlessly in our present-day reality, with scenes featuring him reading from that day's version of the *New York Times* or commenting on the weather outside (Lee 2019).

Deepfakes are 'artificially generated synthetic media' (Westling 2019) wherein faces have been digitally altered or swapped with the assistance of deep learning techniques (Maras and Alexandrou 2019). Readers may well be familiar with high-profile controversial cases of deepfakery, such as the 2018 Buzzfeed and MonkeyPaw Productions deepfake of Barack Obama voiced by Jordan Peele, or the 2019 deepfake of Facebook CEO Mark Zuckerberg by artists Bill Posters and Daniel Howe, which was released to provoke challenging questions about the company's data policy and digital influence (see Rea 2019a).[1]

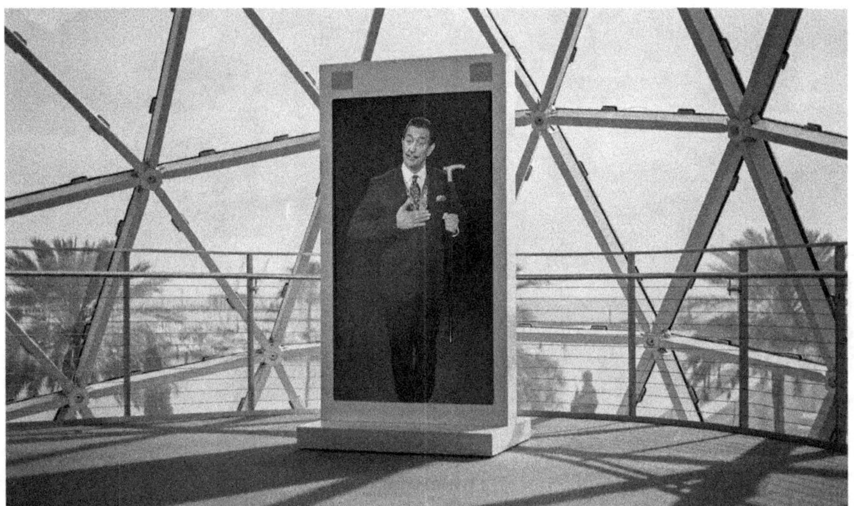

FIGURE 10.1. *Dalí Lives* © Salvador Dalí Museum, Inc. St. Petersburg, FL, 2019. Worldwide rights © Savador Dalí. Fundació Gala – Salvador Dalí, Figueres, 2019. The Fundació Gala – Salvador Dalí reserves photographic rights of Dalí's person.

Grounded in often extensive source data – photos or video footage for example – deepfakes 'learn' when one algorithm creating a 'fake' representation comes into contact with another trying to identify that fake. This forces the initial algorithm to improve, which in turn refines the detection such that 'each algorithm is constantly training against the other' in what is termed a generative adversarial network or GAN (Chesney and Citron, 2019: 2). Unlike previous attempts to use digital technology to re-create or present the human image (computer-generated imagery and the like), deepfakes represent a new level of procedural dynamism where, in time, deep learning 'bootstraps itself into inhuman levels of perfection' (Fletcher 2019: 463). According to Fletcher (2019: 456), deepfakes constitute 'advanced audiovisual counterfeits orders of magnitude more realistic than anything previously seen'.

In *Dalí Lives* we get an example of what Henry Ajder calls 'synthetic resurrection' or 'digital afterlife' (2019).[2] As the title of the installation suggests, it is an attempt to bring Dalí 'back to life' so that visitors can interact meaningfully and memorably with him. In doing so, it is hoped, they will better relate to the artist and the art, engaging more dynamically, emotionally and extensively with them (see figure 10.2). As the museum's executive director, Hank Hine, said in a video created to celebrate the launch of the installation:

> People want access to art, they want a way in . . . What [the installation] adds is a sense of emotion. If visitors can empathise with this man as a human being, then they can relate to the work much more directly and much more passionately. (Dalí Museum 2019: n.p.)

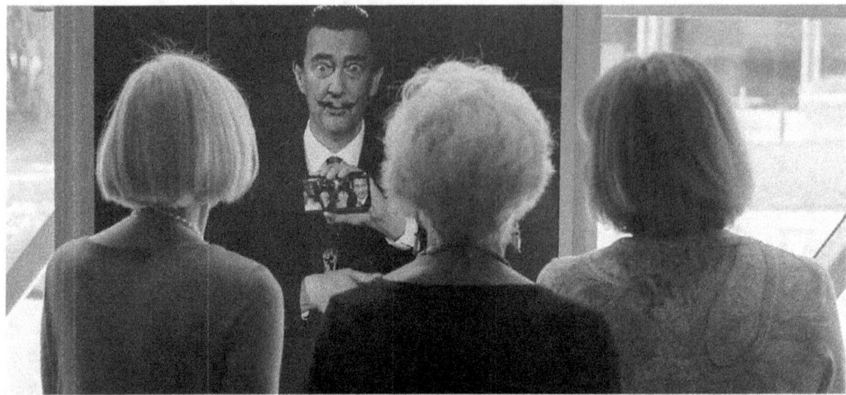

FIGURE 10.2. *Dalí Lives* © Salvador Dalí Museum, Inc. St. Petersburg, FL, 2019. Worldwide rights © Savador Dalí. Fundació Gala – Salvador Dalí, Figueres, 2019. The Fundació Gala – Salvador Dalí reserves photographic rights of Dalí's person.

Dami Lee concluded in a piece about the installation for *The Verge* that 'it's surreal, all right', itself perhaps a fitting tribute to the painter who once said in an interview that 'I believe in general in death, but in the death of Dali [*sic*], absolutely not' (quoted in Lee 2019: n.p.).

Whether the ambitions of the installation are being realised remains an open question. We know little about responses to these encounters with Dalí,[3] but many people are excited by the possibilities here. In an online article, museum technology company Cuseum asked excitedly, 'How much more likely would you be to visit a museum if you could have a conversation with a legendary artist? Or be greeted by a long-gone historical figure upon entering the gallery?' (Cuseum 2019: n.p.). They go further, proposing that such techniques will 'make the museum experience more interactive, relevant, and engaging for audiences, especially those who crave something new' (Cuseum 2019: n.p.), and speculate that deepfakes could not only transform the entire museum experience for visitors but enhance all-important fundraising activity as well. It is easy to imagine that a personalised message from or interaction with one's favourite artist might be persuasive in this regard.

That deepfakes represent something 'new' is without question – the technology only emerged in late 2017 – but it is worth situating the *Dalí Lives* experience within a broader suite of immersive and performative encounters now being produced with and by cultural institutions in the hope of offering more dynamic ways of encountering and interacting with the past (Drotner et al. 2018; Kidd 2018; Kidd and Nieto McAvoy 2019; Lewi et al. 2019). Museums and galleries increasingly find themselves competing for the attention of visitors within a wider 'experience economy' (Pine and Gilmore 1998: n.p.), and the hope is that these forms of interaction might help to ensure visibility in what has become a crowded and complex market for cultural experiences.

Such approaches raise searching questions for those who are interested in difficult heritage, however. If there is something about the use of a deepfake in historical contexts that makes us uneasy, it is perhaps best captured in the following questions: Just what kind of representation of the past is a deepfake, and can it be trusted? What kinds of messaging or narratives might a deepfake be used to amplify, or obfuscate? And just because we *can* vividly re-present or create opportunities to 'meet' a person from the past, does it follow that we *should*? Ethical conundrums associated with 'live' interpretations of the past are not new of course, having been contemplated by those practicing theatre in education and museum theatre for a number of decades.[4] However, they will no doubt also become a more pressing concern within the context of digital cultural heritage given the continued development and improvement of these technologies.

Taking inspiration from John Fletcher's 2019 overview of the impact of deepfakes on the fields of theatre and performance, we wish in this chapter to make some preliminary suggestions for how museum scholars and practitioners might 'respond to the ongoing fallout' from these technological developments (Fletcher 2019: 457). We do not wish to propose a framework for thinking about deepfakes in museums – it is no doubt too soon to predict with any certainty what their impacts might be – but rather to shine a light on some of the broader debates and challenges they bring sharply into focus, in and beyond the specific context of difficult heritages. This chapter seeks to encourage museum professionals working in this space to actively participate in – and seek to lead – work towards a more ethical and critical engagement with deep learning approaches across society, and we contend that they have a valuable role to play in educating people about the manifold positive and negative implications of such technologies.

Firstly, we introduce the deepfake as form and take a look at debates about legitimacy that circulate around its use. Secondly, we connect this with ongoing discussions about fakery, copying and authenticity within museum contexts. Finally, we discuss the deepfake as an object, drawing out the layers of complexity that position it as a difficult heritage in itself, not least when it comes to the question of how it might be 'collected'.

Deepfakes and Notions of Legitimacy

The Dalí Museum is not the only example of experimentation at the intersection of deepfakery and the cultural sector. In an exhibition at Somerset House in London in 2019, artist Alexandra Daisy Ginsberg presented a soundtrack of a natural dawn chorus that segued seamlessly into synthetic birdsong created using deepfake technology, in a bid to highlight the threat to birdlife in urban areas (Alberge 2019). In another example, artificial intelligence (AI) researchers from Moscow used the *Mona Lisa* and other easily recognisable portraits as ways to demonstrate the latest capacity of deep learning techniques to source from single images rather than from many thousands of (moving or still) ones (Palumbo 2019). These developments are connected to a broader suite of experimentation with AI across the arts and culture. For example, in 2016 a fake Rembrandt was made using algorithms and a 3D printer[5], and in 2018 the *Portrait of Edmond Belamy*[6] created by Paris-based arts collective Obvious sold at Christie's for $432,500, more than 43 times its estimate (Christie's 2018).[7] It was notable that the Obvious creation was signed/credited with the algorithm itself rather than the name of the creator of the algorithm: $\frac{min}{G}\frac{max}{D}E_x[\log (D(x))] + E_z[\log(1 - D (G(z)))]$. These examples used similar technology to the deepfake: exploring the interface between art and computation using generative adversarial networks.

Beyond arts and cultural contexts, however, there is great concern about the 'problem' of deepfakes. Discussions about deepfake pornography and ransomfakes, for example, have made international news (Ajder 2019), and in 2019 the free deepfake face-swapping app Zao was launched to great controversy (France-Presse 2019). In legal contexts, debates are oriented around likely impacts of the technology on jurors' capacity to trust video evidence in court (Maras and Alexandrou 2019), or indeed, with audio fakery abounding also, their capacity to trust any kind of testimony at all (Rini 2019). In relation to news, discussion about deepfakes segues quickly into one about the future of journalism in a climate where 'fake news' and disinformation are increasing (Ekström, Lewis and Westlund 2020). According to Sean Dack (2019: n.p.), deepfakes 'have the potential to reshape information warfare and pose a serious threat to open societies as unsavoury actors could use [them] to cause havoc and improve their geopolitical positions'. There are thus widespread concerns that in fundamental ways deepfakery will damage our public discourse, our trust and our political and legal processes. A *Forbes* report in October 2019 noted that there were at that time something like fifteen thousand deepfake videos circulating on social media sites (Brandon 2019), and with the number continuously growing these issues are unlikely to simply run their course.

It is the increasingly realistic representations on offer – and the speed at which the technology is improving – that have sparked such intense scrutiny of and apprehension about deepfakes. Concerns include the potentials presented by these formats for brand sabotage, possible impacts on security (including cybersecurity), copyright and privacy, and negative consequences where they are used for political influence and to undermine our trust. In these latter contexts, concerns about deepfakes centre less on whether they will somehow trick us into believing that they are real and more on what happens if and when 'constant contact with misinformation' through these forms impacts our ability to read, trust and/or critique *all* content (Westerlund 2019: 43). As Regina Rini (2019: 23) notes:

Once information channels are thoroughly saturated with obvious garbage, people fall into a sort of epistemic learned helplessness, where they give up trying to critically assess information and simply believe whatever conforms to their worldview.

As such, deepfakes are deemed by many to be trouble, an almost wholly 'threatening' and 'damaging' development (Westerlund 2019). As a result of such assessments, many critics conclude that citizens and consumers need to be protected from them and that their effects must in time be 'countered' (Chesney and Citron 2019).

Against that backdrop of concern and critique, however, there is a repeated undercurrent of defence and legitimisation of presumed 'positive' uses of deepfake technology in some industries. Of particular note are uses in e-commerce, healthcare, entertainment, the arts, culture and historical education (Westerlund 2019). This latter proposition is especially interesting given the concerns of this chapter, and of this volume. The following quotation from Jeffrey Westling details this legitimation thesis:

> This automated technology for making simulated-reality videos can serve a wide variety of *legitimate* purposes, such as art, education, and even missing persons investigations. In education, for example, teachers can show their students videos of historic figures talking directly to the camera . . . a realistic image depicting the subject of the lessons can make history come to life, allowing them to engage and connect with the lessons of the day. (Westling 2019: 3, emphasis in original)

Chesney and Citron are in agreement about historical recreation as a 'worthy' application of the technology: 'Deepfakes have a number of worthy applications. Modified audio or video of a historical figure, for example, could be created for the purpose of educating children' (Chesney and Citron 2019: 2). Clifford Anderson (2019: n.p.) is similarly excited by the possibilities: 'Deepfakes can serve legitimate ends by bridging cultural divides and forging emotional connections'. Such statements about legitimacy belie concerns about deliberate deception ('lies') in and through the use of deepfake technologies more generally, and suggest that these 'valid' approaches have rather different motivations. This is reminiscent of distinctions that have been made in relation to the use of copies in museums, such as by Marcus Boon, who talks about 'good and bad' copies (2010: 108), and Salomé de Carvalho, who makes the distinction between what he calls innocent and deceptive copies, concluding that they are 'miles apart' (de Carvalho, 2013: 132). Again, it is the notion of 'deception' that is at the heart of these category assessments, a sense that deepfakes by default are predisposed to deliberately mislead or conceal the truth.

Whether the use of deepfakes within historical education or culture is in some way inherently valid is a debate that is yet to be had within museum and heritage scholarship however, and is a pressing concern given the excitement being evidenced within the sector at these developments. The question needs to be asked: Can the use of deepfake technologies be defended wholesale and without reservation as 'legitimate' within these contexts? As much as motivations for their use within museums and heritage sites might not be deemed pernicious, they are clearly not neutral and should be examined. Deepfakes will not be introduced in these contexts within a societal or political vacuum where they become disassociated from broader concerns about their uses as outlined above. Given the fact that this is an emerging form, both for the museums sector and beyond, debates about legitimacy cannot yet be considered resolved, if indeed they ever will be. As Anderson (2019: n.p.) reminds us, these are ambivalent technologies where the 'boundaries between such valid uses and virtual creepiness may be difficult to discern'.

Museums and (Deep) Fakery

In museum contexts, as we have begun to see above, there are a number of potentials for deepfakes, if we are to buy into the legitimation thesis. The Cuseum piece (2019: n.p.) sums up the possibilities as follows: 'In the realm of arts and culture, deepfakes are being used to produce art, engage audiences, and provide personalized experiences to visitors in a way that has never been done before'. Noting that the experimentation that has so far taken place by technologists has simply 'leveraged famous cultural imagery' for experimental purposes, they wonder what the possibilities might be 'when the next wave of fully intentional culture-centric projects start[s] to take form' (Cuseum 2019: n.p.). These quotes allude to a number of claims made regularly for digital heritage work in relation to audience development, e.g. that the use of emerging technologies will in and of itself somehow diversify the visitor profile of an institution and increase engagement, providing more intense and intimate experiences with culture in the process. These claims have yet to be tested, however, in relation to AI and deep learning technologies, and research on these themes would be welcome.

Undoubtedly, there are other debates in the field that we can connect with concerns about deepfakes. Fletcher (2019: 469), for example, notes that deepfakes 'breathe new relevance' into discussions about 'the power of liveness, the significance of presence, the precession of simulacra, [and] the nature of authenticity'. These are of course pertinent and ongoing concerns in relation to museum display and interpretation, not least in the digital environment, and we can begin to think through some of the implications of deep learning technologies in relation to them. Deepfakes are forms of re-creation that connect with broader debates about authenticity and imitation within museum and heritage contexts (see, for example, Jones 1990; Parry 2013; Kidd 2014; Chesney and Citron 2019). This section revisits some of those concerns.

In *In Praise of Copying*, Marcus Boon (2010: 7) posits that as a society we have both a fear and fascination with copying, and that 'it is a part of how the universe functions and manifests'. He goes on: 'Copying is pervasive in contemporary culture, yet at the same time subject to laws, restrictions, and attitudes that suggest that it is wrong, and shouldn't be happening' (Boon 2010: 4). The clearest of these frameworks is copyright and intellectual property law. Yet viewing concerns about copying solely in relation to those frameworks is to see only part of the picture.

We might note that the Dalí of *Dalí Lives* (to return to the example with which we started) is not a 'computer generated duplicate of an exact composition' (Kenderdine and Yip 2018: 279) but a bricolage compiled (neatly and comprehensively) from available audio-visual inputs. Westerlund (2019: 39) notes that 'a GAN can look at thousands of photos of a person, and produce a new portrait that approximates those photos without being an exact copy of any one of them'. Deepfakes are not exact copies then, but 'new representations generated by AI' (Westerlund 2019: 44). In light of that observation, can a case be made for their authenticity?

Whereas in the past people have worked with what might be termed an 'objectivist' sense of authenticity as something intrinsic to things or places, we have in recent decades seen a shift towards a more constructivist understanding where 'authenticity . . . is regarded as an emergent, performed, socially negotiated interpretation and judgment, which is first and foremost part of the "political economy of taste"' (van Neunen 2019: 380). According to David Lowenthal (1990: 17) *all* 'presentations of the past raise peculiarly intractable conundrums of authenticity'; indeed, he proposes that 'all "olden times" are potentially fraudulent'. This is because museum and gallery representations are inherently performative and constructed, not least as they often feature objects or artworks that are removed from their original contexts. Lowenthal goes on to note that debates about authenticity have been intensifying because of trends such as the advancement of technology, increased commodification of culture and the broader devaluation of objective truths about the world (1990). Lowenthal makes an important contribution here in extending debates about authenticity and fakery far beyond concerns solely with legality (see also Keats 2013).

Recent museum scholarship has employed a range of theories in order to debate notions of authenticity, reproduction and fakery – Walter Benjamin's treatise on 'aura' for example, Guy Debord's 'society of the spectacle', Jean Baudrillard's 'simulacra' and Umberto Eco's notion of 'hyper-reality' (see Brenna, Christensen and Olav 2018 for an overview). Scholars have noted the prevalence of imitations and models in museums (Humphreys 2002; Brenna, Eriksen and Mo 2017; Brenna et al. 2018; Alberti et al. 2018), and de Carvalho asserts that they are not inert or passive within those contexts (2010). According to Kenderdine and Yip (2018: 286) the 'proliferation of aura' through digital objects is possible but 'contingent on the presence of transportive and immersive exchanges between viewer and object that connect the viewer to the histories and traditions of the object's cultural trajectory'. Here Kenderdine and Yip remind us of the broader conceptions of authenticity that circulate within discourses about intangible heritages in particular. It is not enough for a digital reproduction simply to exist then; an object such as the Dalí of *Dalí Lives* has to be activated so that its auratic qualities can be observed.

In his 2013 chapter on museums and social media titled 'The Trusted Artifice', Ross Parry (2013: 18) is keen to highlight the extensive 'fictive tradition' of museums, while at the same time noting that this is a history these institutions have often resisted acknowledging:

> This is a fictive tradition of using artifice (alongside the original), the illusory (amidst the evidenced) and make-believe (betwixt the authenticated). These are well-established curatorial techniques of imitation (showing and using copies), illustration (conveying ideas without objects), immersion (framing concepts in theatrical and performative ways), and irony (speaking figuratively, or even presenting something knowingly wrong for effect.

Here Parry gives us an insightful lexicon for considering deepfakes in relation to copying and authenticity, so that we might understand an installation such as *Dalí Lives* as at once imitative, illustrative, immersive and ironic, and in keeping with established curatorial techniques rather than departing from them entirely. In this view, an overemphasis on the questions raised by these techniques about fakery and truth risks turning us toward naïve or misleading assessments of and commitment to the 'real' elsewhere in an institution, which Parry notes would be unhelpful.

But neither would it be helpful to ignore the ways in which the immediacy and intensity of an experience such as *Dalí Lives* extend curatorial work and vision in unprecedented directions and connect it forcefully with current real-world concerns. In our hands and in these contexts, such technologies become forms of museological power, effective means for managing, framing, silencing and disciplining. They are not neutral. The introduction of the deepfake in these contexts could present opportunities for museums to host and participate meaningfully in broader discussions about technocracy and the critical importance of digital, data and ethical literacy. This would seem a 'legitimate' use of an ambivalent technology, and a way to make a virtue of that quality. We can begin to see also how the inclusion of deepfakes could contribute to the broader project of opening up museums and their narratives to scrutiny, presenting us with another opportunity to remind visitors, critics and others that our relationship with notions of authenticity and truth is 'neither static nor timeless' and needs 'constant negotiation, examination, re-evaluation, and upkeep' (Rossi 2010: 338).

Deepfakes as Difficult Heritage

Whilst encountering deepfake technology within a museum may open up possibilities to remind people that our negotiation of authenticity and truth is ongoing, collecting deepfakes as artefacts forces the museum to consider internally the ethics, provenance and use of these technologies in relation to established acquisition, due diligence and preservation procedures. In this context, deepfakes become difficult heritage in their own right, as attempts are made to manipulate them into the institutional frameworks that govern how museums collect.

The established museum procedures in question here can best be located in the International Council of Museums (ICOM) Code of Ethics (2017). As an internationally recognised code, it sets out the foundations that should underpin all other codes (ICOM 2011). In its section on acquiring collections, the code emphasises trust, rightful ownership and provenance. As we have begun to demonstrate above, these all provide their own challenges to the deepfake as museum artefact.

Museums have an established history with collecting copies – they were an important element of many nineteenth-century museum collections, including that of the Victoria and Albert Museum (Aguerre and Cormier 2018: 22). In fact, the Cast Court galleries at the V&A still display some hugely important copies and provide insights into contemporary copying techniques like 3D modelling. However, as we have highlighted, the deepfake is more than a copy – it is a new representation generated by AI, a series of algorithms in conversation with each other, materially ambiguous, and ambivalent at its core.

Although there is a growing confidence in this area, museums have been slow to grapple with the difficulties of collecting digitally. One of the key claims in the digital collecting discourse is that curators cannot collect what they do not materially understand (Park and Samms 2019), or they simply apply the old collecting methods to new materials (Graham and Cook 2010). Haidy Geismar, drawing on Māori approaches to materiality, stresses that the digital object should be understood as existing in a material continuum (Geismar 2018; see also Galani and Kidd 2020). Even if we manage to articulate the materiality of deepfakes in a material continuum, they still raise a number of difficult questions when we position them as artefacts. What actually constitutes the collectable 'thing'? How does that sit within the structures of a museum collection? How does one begin to think about providing access to or caring for such an artefact?

Whilst the digital nature of deepfake technology challenges museums' material traditions, the idea of collecting deepfakes also directly conflicts with some of the foundational notions of trust and ownership proclaimed in the ICOM Code of Ethics. We can begin to understand this by examining the challenges the algorithm presents to collecting. Clifford Lynch highlights how there has been little to no consideration of how traditional stewardship organisations (museums, archives, libraries) document what he calls the 'age of algorithms' (Lynch 2017:

n.p.). Lynch suggests that in principle there are two ways in which an algorithm might be documented. The simplest way would be to capture and preserve the inputs and outputs of an algorithm – for example, the search terms and the results. However, if we are interested in a more comprehensive documentation of how an algorithm works, then a more active intervention would be needed whereby the decision-making process is understood and can be predicted. For example, given a hypothetical search query, what would the outputs be, and what are the factors that might affect them? Lynch follows up by noting that doing this, in most cases, would be fundamentally impossible due to the opacity of proprietary codes and the fact that they are constantly changing (Lynch 2017). There are direct challenges to museum collecting processes here then. Deepfakes, created through multiple opaque algorithms, are more or less impossible to interrogate – to open up and explore transparently – in a way that would satisfy museum provenance research requirements and enable the transfer of title underlined as a requirement in museum acquisition.

Conclusion

There are a number of narratives that play out in the public imagination in relation to where we are headed with artificial intelligence. Some err on the apocalyptic, and others might be understood as more ambivalent. The stories we tell ourselves are informed by (amongst other things) our backgrounds, our socio-economic circumstances, our politics and our professional identities.

This chapter has reviewed an emerging new museum practice – the creation and preservation of deepfakes – in order to shine light on a range of debates about copying, mimicry, authenticity and collecting in the digital work of cultural institutions. It has proposed that deepfakes are not a unique threat in relation to these themes and in themselves are neither a right nor a wrong (Rees 2019; Fletcher 2019), 'legitimate' or otherwise. But neither are they neutral. As we have argued, they are opaque creations that present deep challenges to traditional museological functions, including acquisition.

Any discussion about deepfakes connects to a broader suite of debates about data science and its uses in cultural heritage contexts (Murphy and Villaespesa 2020), whether that be for imaging, geomapping, crowdsourcing or data analytics purposes (among others). They highlight the need for an understanding of data biases, data security, surveillance realism, code transparency and the suite of challenges to ethical automation going forwards. The specific contexts and conditions for potential benefits from the use and/or acquisition of these technologies should be weighed carefully against the possibility of any negative consequences.

We wish to conclude with some questions that are pertinent in thinking about how this particular practice will develop in the next decade. These include:

Which technology partners should we be working with in these endeavours, and what ethical questions are raised in and through such partnerships? How can we understand and connect with broader political and societal debates that emerge in this space, and public opinion on those issues? What kind of changes to digital and data policies – and ethical codes – will be needed to frame these activities going forwards? And are our current policies agile enough to cover the various processes that might come under the umbrella of deep learning in time (including working with data that is donated consciously or unconsciously by visitors)? We need to engage with these questions in a pragmatic way.

We should be willing – and eager – to practice our reflexivity in response to these emerging practices. In doing so, we can position digital heritage researchers and practitioners at the heart of searching, ethical and critical data scientific approaches. Deepfakes within museum contexts might be difficult, playful and surprising, and they may arouse curiosity, but they do not exist in a vacuum. Such practices are indelibly and already linked to debates about democratic processes, trust, truth and transparency. We should be mindful of that responsibility.

Jenny Kidd is a reader in the School of Journalism, Media and Culture at Cardiff University. Formerly a web editor and developer, she is a keen advocate of immersive and participatory media practices, working with a range of institutions to explore and understand their possibilities. Her research is informed by close interaction with the cultural sector. Her books include *Critical Encounters with Immersive Storytelling* (Routledge, 2019) and *Museums in the New Mediascape: Transmedia, Participation, Ethics* (Routledge, 2014).

Arran J. Rees is the Museum Data Manager for the Museum Data Service. With over a decade's experience working in and researching about museums and collections practices, his interests converge around collections management, contemporary digital culture, and data practices.

Notes

1. Both of these examples can be found and viewed easily through an online search.
2. Much like the re-creation of Carrie Fisher as Princess Leia following Fisher's death.
3. Although nearly a year after the launch of the installation there are still many posts appearing daily on social networks attesting to visitors' excitement about interacting with the piece.
4. See Jackson and Vine (2013) and Prentki and Preston (2008) on theatre in education, and various chapters in Jackson and Kidd (2011) on museum theatre and live interpretation.

5. Created by Dutch museums Mauritshuis and Rembranthuis, with Microsoft, ING and the Delft University of Technology. See Reynolds (2016) for more information.
6. *Portrait of Edmond Belamy* is a single artwork created using AI and sourced from a set of fifteen thousand portraits painted between the fourteenth and twentieth centuries.
7. This was followed in 2019 by the sale of Mario Klingemann's *Memories of Passersby I* at Sotheby's (see Rea 2019b).

References

'3 Things you Need to Know about AI-Powered "Deep Fakes" in Art and Culture'. 2019. Cuseum website, 17 December. Retrieved 28 January 2020 from https://cuseum.com/blog/2019/12/17/3-things-you-need-to-know-about-ai-powered-deep-fakes-in-art-amp-culture?utm_source=Social&utm_medium=Twitter&utm_campaign=MT

Aguerre, Anaïs, and Brendan Cormier. 2018. 'Introduction', in Brendan Cormier (ed.), *Copy Culture: Sharing in the Age of Digital Reproduction*. London: V&A Publishing, pp. 19–26.

Ajder, Henry. 2019. 'The Ethics of Deepfakes Aren't Always Black and White', TNW website, 16 June. Retrieved 15 January 2020 from https://thenextweb.com/podium/2019/06/16/the-ethics-of-deepfakes-arent-always-black-and-white/.

Alberge, Dalya. 2019. 'Artist Creates Deepfake Birdsong to Highlight Threat to Dawn Chorus', *The Guardian*, 20 October. Retrieved 3 February 2020 from https://www.theguardian.com/environment/2019/oct/20/artist-creates-deepfake-birdsong-highlight-threat-dawn-chorus.

Alberti, Samuel J. M. M., Alice Blackwell, Peter Davidson, Martin Goldberg and Geoffrey N. Swinney. 2018. 'The Art and Science of Replication: Copies and Copying in the Multi-disciplinary Museum', in Brita Brenna, Hans Dam Christensen and Olav Hamran (eds), *Museums as Culture of Copies: The Crafting of Artefacts and Authenticity*. New York: Routledge, pp. 13–26.

Anderson, Clifford. 2019. 'A New Hermeneutic of Suspicion? The Challenge of Deepfakes to Theological Epistemology', *Cursor_ Zeitschrift Für Explorative Theologie*. Retrieved 15 January 2020 from https://cursor.pubpub.org/pub/andersondeepfakes.

'Behind the Scenes: Dali Lives'. 2019. Dalí Museum website, 11 May. Retrieved 15 January 2020 from https://thedali.org/exhibit/dali-lives/.

Boon, Marcus. 2010. *In Praise of Copying*. Cambridge, MA: Harvard University Press.

Brandon, John. 2019. 'There Are Now 15,000 Deepfake Videos on Social Media. Yes, You Should Worry', *Forbes*, 8 October. Retrieved 15 January 2020 from https://www.forbes.com/sites/johnbbrandon/2019/10/08/there-are-now-15000-deepfake-videos-on-social-media-yes-you-should-worry/#7456f1b93750.

Brenna, Brita, Hans Dam Christensen and Olav Hamran. 2018. *Museums as Culture of Copies: The Crafting of Artefacts and Authenticity*. New York: Routledge.

Brenna, Brita, Anne Eriksen and Gro Bjørnerud Mo. 2017. 'Theorizing Copies', *Culture Unbound* 9(1): 1–5. Published by Linköping University Electronic Press.

Chesney, Robert, and Danielle Citron. 2019. 'Deepfakes and the New Disinformation War: The Coming Age of Post-truth Geopolitics', *Foreign Affairs*, January/February. Retrieved 15 January 2020 from https://www.foreignaffairs.com/articles/world/2018-12-11/deepfakes-and-new-disinformation-war?cid=otr-authors-january_february_2019-121118.

Dack, Sean. 2019. 'Deep Fakes, Fake News, and What Comes Next', The Henry M. Jackson School of International Studies, University of Washington, 20 March. Retrieved 15 January 2020 from https://jsis.washington.edu/news/deep-fakes-fake-news-and-what-comes-next/.

de Carvalho, Salomé. 2013. 'The Concept of "Original" in Conservation Theory Fake? The Art of Deception Revisited' in *estudos de conservação e restauro* 2: pp. 124–35. DOI: 10.7559/ecr.2.3160.

Drotner, Kirsten, Vince Dziekan, Ross Parry and Kim Christian Schrøder. 2018. *The Routledge Handbook of Museums, Media and Communication*. New York: Routledge.

Ekström, Mats, Seth C. Lewis, and Oscar Westlund. 2020. 'Epistemologies of Digital Journalism and the Study of Misinformation', *New Media and Society* 22(2): 205–12.

Fletcher, John. 2019. 'Deepfakes, Artificial Intelligence, and Some Kind of Dystopia: The New Faces of Online Post-Fact Performance', *Theatre Journal* 70(4): 455–71.

France-Presse, Agence. 2019. 'Chinese Deepfake App Zao Sparks Privacy Row after Going Viral', *The Guardian*, 2 September. Retrieved 15 January 2020 from https://www.theguardian.com/technology/2019/sep/02/chinese-face-swap-app-zao-triggers-privacy-fears-viral.

Galani, Areti, and Jenny Kidd. 2020. 'Hybrid Material Encounters – Expanding the Continuum of Museum Materialities in the Wake of a Pandemic', *Museum and Society* 18(3): 298–301.

Graham, Beryl, and Sarah Cook. 2010. *Rethinking Curating: Art after New Media*. Cambridge, MA: MIT Press.

Geismar, Haidy. 2018. *Museum Object Lessons for the Digital Age*. London: UCL Press.

Humphreys, Elen S. 2002. 'How to Spot a Fake', *Materials Today* 5(11): 32–37.

ICOM (International Council of Museums). 2011. *Checklist of Ethics of Cultural Property Ownership*. Paris: ICOM Ethics Committee.

———. 2017. *ICOM Code of Ethics for Museums*. Paris: ICOM.

'Is Artificial Intelligence Set to Become Art's Next Medium?' 2018. Christie's website, 12 December. Retrieved 4 February 2020 from https://www.christies.com/features/A-collaboration-between-two-artists-one-human-one-a-machine-9332-1.aspx

Jackson, Anthony, and Jenny Kidd. 2011. *Performing Heritage: Research, Practice and Innovation in Museum Theatre and Live Interpretation*. Manchester: Manchester University Press.

Jackson, Anthony, and Chris Vine. 2013. *Learning through Theatre*. New York: Routledge.

Jones, Mark. 1990. 'Why Fakes?' in Mark Jones, David Lowenthal and Nicholas Barker (eds), *Fake? The Art of Deception*. Exhibition catalogue, British Museum, pp. 11–15.

Keats, Jonathon. 2013. *Forged: Why Fakes Are the Great Art of Our Age*. New York: Oxford University Press.

Kenderdine, Sarah, and Andrew Yip. 2018. 'The Proliferation of Aura: Facsimiles, Authenticity and Digital Objects', in Kirsten Drotner, Vince Dziekan, Ross Parry and Kim Christian Schrøder, *The Routledge Handbook of Museums, Media and Communication*. New York: Routledge, pp. 274–89.

Kidd, Jenny. 2014. *Museums in the New Mediascape*. New York: Routledge.

———. 2018. 'Immersive' Heritage Encounters', *Museum Review* 3(1): 1–16.

Kidd, Jenny, and Eva Nieto McAvoy. 2019. *Immersive Experiences in Museums, Galleries and Heritage Sites: A Review of Research Findings and Issues*, PEC discussion paper, Creative Industries Policies and Evidence Centre, November. Retrieved 15 July 2021 from https://www.pec.ac.uk/assets/publications/PEC-Discussion-Paper-Immersive-experiences-Cardiff-University-November-2019.pdf.

Lee, Dami. 2019. 'Deepfake Salvador Dalí Takes Selfies with Museum Visitors', The Verge, 10 May. Retrieved 15 January 2020 from https://www.theverge.com/2019/5/10/18540953/salvador-dali-lives-deepfake-museum.

Lewi, Hannah, Wally Smith, Dirk vom Lehn and Steven Cooke (eds). 2019. *The Routledge International Handbook of New Digital Practices in Galleries, Libraries, Archives, Museums and Heritage Sites*. New York: Routledge.

Lowenthal, David. 1990. 'Forging the Past', in Mark Jones, David Lowenthal and Nicholas Barker, *Fake? The Art of Deception*. Exhibition Catalogue. British Museum, pp. 16–22.

Lynch, Clifford. 2017. 'Stewardship in the "Age of Algorithms"', *First Monday* 22(12). Retrieved 24 August 2020 from https://firstmonday.org/ojs/index.php/fm/article/view/8097.

Maras, Marie-Helen, and Alex Alexandrou. 2019. 'Determining Authenticity of Video Evidence in the Age of Artificial Intelligence and in the Wake of Deepfake Videos', *International Journal of Evidence and Proof* 23(3): 255–62.

Murphy, Oonagh, and Elena Villaespesa. 2020. *The Museums and AI Network Toolkit*. London: Goldsmiths University of London.

Palumbo, Jacqui. 2019. 'AI Researchers Created an Uncanny Video of the Mona Lisa Talking', Artsy, 5 June. Retrieved 3 February 2020 from https://www.artsy.net/article/artsy-editorial-ai-researchers-created-uncanny-video-mona-lisa-talking.

Park, Juhee, and Anouska Samms. 2019. 'The Materiality of the Immaterial: Collecting Digital Objects at the Victoria and Albert Museum', MW19: Museums and the Web, Boston, 2–6 April. Retrieved 11 May 2020 from https://mw19.mwconf.org/paper/the-materiality-of-the-immaterial-collecting-digital-objects-at-the-victoria-and-albert-museum/.

Parry, Ross. 2013. 'The Trusted Artifice: Reconnecting with the Museum's Fictive Tradition Online', in Kirsten Drotner and Kim Christian Schrøder (eds), *Museum Communication and Social Media: The Connected Museum*. New York: Routledge, pp. 17–32.

Pine, B. Joseph, and H. James Gilmore. 1998. 'Welcome to the Experience Economy', *Harvard Business Review*, July–August. Retrieved 9 August 2020 from https://hbr.org/1998/07/welcome-to-the-experience-economy.

Prentki, Tim, and Preston, Sheila. 2008. *The Applied Theatre Reader*. New York: Routledge.

Rea, Naomi. 2019a. 'Artists Create a Sinister "Deepfake" of Mark Zuckerberg to Teach Facebook (and the Rest of Us) a Lesson about Digital Propaganda'. Artnet, 12 June. Retrieved 15 January 2020 from https://news.artnet.com/art-world/mark-zuckerberg-deepfake-artist-1571788.

———. 2019b. 'Sotheby's Is Entering the AI Art Fray, Selling a Surreal Artwork by One of the Movement's Pioneers This Spring', Artnet, 8 February. Retrieved 4 February 2020 from at https://news.artnet.com/art-world/sothebys-artificial-intelligence-1460332.

Rees, Geraint. 2019. 'Opinion: How the Technology behind Deepfakes Can Benefit All of Society'. UCL News, 29 November. Retrieved 15 January 2020 from https://www.ucl.ac.uk/news/2019/nov/opinion-how-technology-behind-deepfakes-can-benefit-all-society.

Reynolds, Emily. 2016. 'This Fake Rembrandt Was Created by an Algorithm'. Wired, 4 July. Retrieved 11 May 2020 from https://www.wired.co.uk/article/new-rembrandt-painting-computer-3d-printed.

Rini, Regina. 2019. 'Deepfakes and the Epistemic Backstop', working draft. Retrieved 15 January 2020 from https://philpapers.org/archive/RINDAT.pdf.

Rossi, Michael. 2010. 'Fabricating Authenticity: Modeling a Whale at the American Museum of Natural History, 1906–1974', *Isis* 101(2): 338–61.

Sabina Aouf, Rima. 2019. 'Museum Creates Deepfake Salvador Dalí to Greet Visitors'. Dezeen, 24 May. Retrieved 11 May 2020 from https://www.dezeen.com/2019/05/24/salvador-dali-deepfake-dali-musuem-florida/.

van Neunen, Tom. 2019. 'Algorithmic Authenticity: Sociotechnical Authentication Processes on Online Travel Platforms', *Tourist Studies* 19(3): 378–403.

Westerlund, Mika. 2019. 'The Emergence of Deepfake Technology: A Review', *Technology Innovation Management Review* 9(11): 39–52.

Westling, Jeffrey. 2019. 'Are Deep Fakes a Shallow Concern? A Critical Analysis of the Likely Societal Reaction to Deep Fakes', TPRC47: The 47th Research Conference on Communication, Information and Internet Policy 2019, SSRN, 24 July. Retrieved 24 August 2020 from https://ssrn.com/abstract=3426174.

Afterword

Alexandra Bounia, Theopisti Stylianou-Lambert
and Antigone Heraclidou

The COVID-19 pandemic led to an acceleration of digital transformation in public service institutions, including museums and heritage organisations (Gabryelczyk 2020; Agostino, Arnaboldi and Diaz Lima 2021). Most institutions were quick to respond to the closing of heritage sites and cultural heritage provisions worldwide by exploring new ways of engaging with their audiences, using websites, social media platforms, and any digital resource available to them. In addition, many national and international agencies have provided incentives – usually in the form of grants or other funding initiatives – to further encourage and support heritage institutions in these efforts to keep their audiences engaged online and offsite, while taking advantage of the opportunities offered by digital technologies.

However, and despite the efforts made by almost all institutions to the extent of their abilities (see NEMO 2021 about financial constraints and the impact of the pandemic on heritage institutions) and the subsequent 'acceleration', it seems that the issues identified by the chapters presented in this volume – all of them written or finalised during the pandemic but reflecting on previous experiences and case studies – remain still very important and relevant. As mentioned in a recent UNESCO report (2021: 23):

> It appears that although the online offer was abundant, questions on difficult subjects or heritage linked to painful episodes (armed conflicts, terrorism) were generally not explored by these means, perhaps in order to contribute to resilience with regard to the current situation, which is very distressing.

COVID-19 has been a challenging experience, itself; it is part of a traumatic heritage on a global level, but it has also become a new focus for reconsidering issues of 'power, (in)justice, (lack of) privilege, comfort and care' (Kist 2020:

345). This problematisation includes two aspects that are relevant to the discussion of this volume: first, how is the difficult heritage of COVID-19 and its repercussions being documented, especially in the context of digital acceleration; and second, how can institutions dealing with difficult heritage respond, or create digital content that will be appropriate for such a time of crisis (see also Kist 2020)?

When it comes to the first question, heritage institutions have had two interesting responses in the face of the pandemic: on the one hand, many institutions turned to their communities and used digital platforms and tools, mostly social media, to engage as wide an audience as possible in order to support them during the hardships of the lockdown. In some cases, as for instance in the case of museums in Singapore, heritage institutions became a 'public health resource', as they were set to support 'well-being' for those suffering the most (Tan and Tan 2021). On the other hand, several institutions highlighted the inclusiveness of their rapid collecting initiatives; in other words, everybody's COVID-19 story was equally important and should be included in the narrative offered in the museum in the present and in the future. For instance, the Museum of London emphasised the need for inclusive collecting of stories that should 'reflect the voices and experiences of a broad range of Londoners' (Museum of London 2020); the Amsterdam Museum in the Netherlands highlighted the 'participatory and dynamic manner' of their collecting processes (Amsterdam Museum 2020); while the Museum of European Cultures in Germany explained that all contributions to the crowdsourcing campaign of the institution would be registered in the collections 'regardless of language' (Staatliche Museen zu Berlin 2020). In some cases, as for instance in the initiative of London's Museum of Home, participation from diverse areas of society was pursued: city dwellers, people from the countryside, key workers, people living alone and parents with little children were among the groups explicitly targeted by the institution (Bounia 2020; Debono 2021). Digital media allowed for these stories to be collected; however, it is still unclear whether these collections will also be used to bring to the surface omitted narratives or will allow for reinterpretation of existing collections and creation of new stories for the institutions after the normalisation of the situation.

Research undertaken regarding the provisions in museums in the United Kingdom and the United States (Samaroudi, Rodriguez Echavarria and Perry 2020; King et al. 2021) also identifies an effort in engaging nontraditional audiences. However, the need for more support of vulnerable groups was also identified, along with the need for more imaginative and extensive use of emerging technologies, such as virtual tours (Samaroudi et al. 2020). Regarding vulnerable groups, as other pieces of research have also identified (see, for instance, Tan and Tan 2020), access to digital devices, connections, digital competencies and literacy required is not equally available to all, due to multiple reasons, ranging from financial means to disability and age. Therefore, institutions need to take into consideration issues of inclusion and participation when they make decisions about the use of digital media.

On the other hand, the idea of embodiment, or presence in the space of the museum, became very prominent under the circumstances of the pandemic. As museums were physically inaccessible for a long time (and for different periods in different parts of the world), the idea of online visitors being present in the galleries or the sites has been very important for many professionals and organisations (King et al. 2021). However, the possibilities of digital technologies to offer embodied experiences, and as a result, encourage active participation, task accomplishment and practical actions, remain to be pursued (Rahaman 2018; King et al. 2021; see also Lopez Rodriguez 2020 for an epistemological approach). Despite the fact that many institutions took advantage of VR, AR and 3D object exploration technologies to create virtual tours for their online visitors or to encourage them to explore their collections in a more 'tactile' manner, the number of cases was rather limited due to financial constraints and lack of time and skills from the staff.

During COVID-19, the immediate response of museums with the necessary resources was to quickly make their cultural products available to remote audiences and remain relevant. Technological tools seemed to offer the needed solutions. However, as already mentioned in the introduction of this book, technology can be a powerful tool, but it is not a panacea. Going beyond 360-degree views of exhibitions, online educational programs and 3D renderings of object and site, what is still missing is experimentation with the possibilities of emerging technologies and how they can effectively contribute to the three main concerns discussed in this volume: (1) revealing missing or underrepresented narratives, (2) eliciting affective and empathetic responses and (3) creating a sense of presence, immersion and embodiment. These issues are still relevant and perhaps more urgent than ever.

To conclude this short afterword, while acknowledging the changes – the 'acceleration' – in the relationship between heritage institutions and technology that COVID-19 has inspired, the reality seems to be that not many institutions were ready to adopt new approaches or use technology in innovative and inspiring ways that would allow for omitted narratives to come to the surface, give space for reinterpretation of collections and creation of new stories, provide a multiplicity of stories and approaches and elicit emotional and empathetic responses to past and present experiences. For the opportunities of emerging technologies to be further and fully explored we need time, development of new skills for heritage personnel, funding and an open and transparent approach towards the past and the present. The latter could, in fact, prove to be the most challenging of all, as entrenched mentalities and biases are very difficult to overcome even in the most progressive societies.

In that sense, COVID-19 has given heritage institutions a good opportunity to rethink their ethical stance and bring to the fore issues such as: giving voice to the victims, inclusion, multiperspectivity, extension of curatorial practice and heritage institutions as ethical spaces for care. These are fundamental elements that emerging technologies can and should support now and in the future if they aim to talk about difficult heritage in an honest and meaningful way.

Alexandra Bounia is professor of museology at the University of the Aegean (Greece). Her research interests focus on the history, theory and management of collections, museum ethics, museum and cultural heritage sustainability, the role of museums in dealing with difficult and political issues, as well as digital heritage and museums. She has published in Greek and international journals and participates in national and international research projects. Among her most recent publications are: *The Political Museum: Power, Conflict and Identity in Cyprus* (co-authored with Theopisti Stylianou-Lambert) (2016, Routledge); *Emerging Technologies and Cultural Heritage* (co-edited with Despina Catapoti) (2021, Alexandria Publications, Athens, in Greek). In 2025 the edited volume entitled *The Ethics of Collecting Trauma: the role of museums in collecting and displaying contemporary crises* was published by Routledge (co-edited with Andrea Witcomb). She has served as the Chair of ICOM Greece (2016-2018), and the Secretary of the Board for ICOM-COMCOL (ICOM Committee on Contemporary Collecting) (2019-2022).

Theopisti Stylianou-Lambert is Professor in the Department of Multimedia and Graphic Arts at the Cyprus University of Technology and the co-leader of the *ITICA/Museum Lab* research group at CYENS Centre of Excellence. Her research and artistic practice focus on museums, photography and emerging technologies. She co-authored *The Political Museum* (Routledge, 2016) and co-edited *Museums and Technologies of Presence* (Routledge, 2023), *Museums and Visitor Photography* (MuseumsEtc, 2016), *Museums and Photography: Displaying Death* (Routledge, 2017), and *Photography and Cyprus: Time, Place, Identity* (Routledge, 2014). Her artistic work has been showcased in numerous exhibitions internationally. She earned her PhD in museum studies from the University of Leicester (UK) and her MA in visual arts/museum education from the University of Texas at Austin (USA). Theopisti is also the recipient of several scholarships and awards, including a Smithsonian Fellowship in Museum Practice (USA), a Fulbright Fellowship (USA) and an Arts and Humanities Research Council Award (UK).

Antigone Heraclidou is a Postdoc Fellow at the Centre for Geopolitics, Peace and Security at the UiT The Arctic University of Norway. She holds an MSc in international history from the London School of Economics and a PhD in modern history from the Institute of Commonwealth Studies, University of London. She is the author of *Imperial Control in Cyprus: Education and Political Manipulation in the British Empire* (2017), and co-editor of *Cyprus: From Colonialism to the Present: Visions and Realities; Essays in honour of Professor Robert Holland* (2018), and "Political Actors in the Mediterranean, 1918–1964: Cyprus and Malta Compared," special issue of the *Journal of Mediterranean Studies*, 23(1) (2014). She has also published her work in international journals and was the co-organizer of three international academic conferences in London. She has taught history modules at the University of Cyprus, the Open University of Cyprus and the European University of Cyprus. She worked closely with several museums in Nicosia. Her research interests include Cyprus's colonial history, decolonisation and cultural heritage.

References

'#CollectingCorona: Sammelaufruf des Museums Europäischer Kulturen'. 2020. Staatliche Museen zu Berlin website. Retrieved 1 July 2020 from https://www.smb.museum/nachrichten/detail/collectingcorona-sammelaufruf-des-museums-europaeischer-kulturen/.

Agostino, Deborah, Michela Arnaboldi and Melisa Diaz Lima. 2021. 'New Development: COVID-19 as an Accelerator of Digital Transformation in Public Service Delivery', *Public Money and Management* 41(1): 69–72.

Bounia, Alexandra. 2020. 'Contemporary Collecting and COVID-19'. *COMCOL Newsletter* 52: 8–13.

'Corona in de Stad'. 2020. Amsterdam Museum website. Retrieved 1 July 2020 from https://www.amsterdammuseum.nl/tentoonstellingen/corona-de-stad.

Debono, Sandro. 2021. 'Collecting Pandemic Phenomena: Reflections on Rapid Response Collecting and the Art Museum'. *Collections: A Journal for Museum and Archives Professionals* 15(2–3): 1–7.

Gabryelczyk, Renata. 2020. 'Has COVID-19 Accelerated Digital Transformation? Initial Lessons Learnt for Public Administrations'. *Information Systems Management* 37(4): 303–9.

King, Ellie, M. Paul Smith, Paul F. Wilson and Mark Williams. 2021. 'Digital Responses of UK Museum Exhibitions to the COVID-19 Crisis March–June 2020', *Curator: The Museum Journal* 64(2): 1–18.

Kist, Cassandra. 2020. 'Museums, Challenging Heritage and Social Media during COVID-19', *Museum and Society* 18(3): 345–48.

Lopez Rodriguez, Luis Javier. 2020. 'Museums of Scarcity and Art Deserts', *Thesis* 9(2): 205–25.

'Museum for London: Collecting COVID'. 2020. Museum of London website. Retrieved 1 July 2020 from https://www.museumoflondon.org.uk/discover/museum-for-london-collecting-covid.

NEMO. 2021. *Follow-Up Survey on the Impact of COVID-19 Pandemic on Museums in Europe: Final Report*. Retrieved 25 April 2021 from: https://www.ne-mo.org/fileadmin/Dateien/public/NEMO_documents/NEMO_COVID19_FollowUpReport_11.1.2021.pdf.

Rahaman, Hafizur. 2018. 'Digital Heritage Interpretation: A Conceptual Framework', *Digital Creativity* 29(2–3): 208–34.

Samaroudi, Myrsini, Karina Rodriguez Echavarria and Lara Perry. 2020. 'Heritage in Lockdown: Digital Provision of Memory Institutions in the UK and US of America during the COVID-19 Pandemic', *Museum Management and Curatorship* 35(4): 337–61.

Tan, Michael Koon Boon, and Chih Ming Tan. 2021. 'Curating Wellness during a Pandemic in Singapore: COVID-19, Museums and Digital Imagination', *Public Health* 192: 68–71.

UNESCO 2021. *Museums around the World in the Face of COVID-19*. Paris: UNESCO.

Index